DYING TO LIVE

P 61
62
65
71
73
76 read PolyCARP Johns student
77 Pole
81
83
88 Answer to a Hindu Priest   Jesus only way to Father
89
99

IAN MURPHY

Dying to Live

From Agnostic to Baptist to Catholic

With a Foreword by Scott Hahn

IGNATIUS PRESS   SAN FRANCISCO

Cover art:
Christ by Arturo Rey on Unsplash
Other photos courtesy of the author

Cover design by Enrique J. Aguilar Pinto

© 2020 by Ignatius Press, San Francisco
Foreword © 2020 by Scott Hahn
All rights reserved
ISBN 978-1-62164-278-7 (PB)
ISBN 978-1-64229-117-9 (eBook)
Library of Congress Control Number 2019947846
Printed in the United States of America ∞

For George E. Murphy and John Szelesta,
my two Catholic grandfathers,
who prayed their family home

CONTENTS

FOREWORD

By Scott Hahn

Most of us converts can speak of a long pursuit by the Hound of Heaven. But only Ian Murphy can begin his story with a helicopter chase. And the plot only gets stranger and more exciting from there.

This is one of those few religious autobiographies that could just as well be an action movie—though the best action is interior and the Best Supporting Actor award goes to the Almighty.

Ian Murphy is a likable rebel, and in these pages we get to trace his development from the child who can't stop asking why to the teen who won't shut up when ordered to do so—and then to the adult who can't stop asking why.

The story turns more than once on questions of authority.

What authority does a school have over a student? What authority does a boss have over his employees? What authority does an Elvis impersonator have over anything?

What authority does a pastor have over his congregation? What authority does a congregation have over its pastor? And does a "denomination" have any real authority at all?

From the age of reason, it seems, Ian Murphy has been seeking authority that speaks the truth—and questioning any authorities that tried to stake a claim on his behavior. His interlocutors here are a surreal cast of dozens, including university bureaucrats, an ACLU lawyer, a Hindu priest, a philosophy prof with deep-seated prejudices—and the aforementioned Presley mimic.

The people most likely to wield power are least likely to speak with genuine authority. Yet this is not a cynical book. Standing patiently in the background are quiet presences: Ian's two Catholic grandfathers and his Uncle Tim. They persist in love, even when Ian mocks their religion. Unlike the sophists who hold power, they stand with confident authority. They pray. They turn the other cheek, and they turn again. They answer questions when asked. They invite. They wait. They wait. They welcome.

Along the way we join them in witnessing an occasional miracle.

I admit I was gratified to notice an occasional reference to some of my books, too.

I suppose it's not too much of a spoiler to say that, by the end of the book, Ian the rebel does find his way to authority he can trust.

The journey there, though, is a wild ride. You're going to love it. I envy you the chance to read it for the first time. So now I'll get out of your way. Here comes the helicopter.

Murphy's Law

My spirits soared when the announcement came through our school-wide loudspeaker. The year's class rankings were finalized, and the principal formally congratulated Mount Pleasant Area High School's 1993 co-valedictorians, Dora and Ian. I thanked God the four-year contest was finally over. Thanking God was now something I could do, because my journey out of agnosticism had ended in dramatic fashion back when I was fourteen years old. Before that part of the story unfolds, however, this testimonial needs to begin like a friendship—by stumbling somewhere into the middle of a person's life.

To prepare our commencement speeches, Dora and I met with one of the teachers in the English department, a wonderful woman who had once let me teach Homer's *Iliad* to her younger classes. She was my favorite teacher from junior year, and at this point in my life, I considered her a friend. I was glad to know that she would be helping us with our speeches. "Congratulations to each of you on your perseverance and hard-won accomplishments," she said to me, Dora, and some other students who would be giving speeches during the graduation ceremony. "You have earned the honor to say farewell to your fellow classmates at commencement. Think about what you want to say to them as you embark on the adventure of living and write a speech proposal."

For me, there wasn't even a question about what I wanted to say. I wanted to talk about Jesus! When it comes to the adventure of living, Jesus is everything, and I couldn't wait for the chance to invite all of my classmates to taste and see for themselves that the Lord is good. Nothing else mattered more than that. With unbridled excitement and an electrifying purpose, I set about writing my speech proposal.

I prayed, "Lord, as long as I draw breath, the stones won't have to cry out on your behalf. I will tell them that you love them." After I finished writing the proposal, and with excitement all over my face, I handed it to the speech advisor a few days later.

"I'm so happy for you, Ian," she said, placing my proposal on her desk to read later. "I know how much giving the valedictory means to you."

Later that day, she caught me between classes in the hallway and asked for a one-on-one meeting. "Do you have study hall today?" she asked.

"Yes, my last period of the day is a study hall," I answered.

"Great, please meet me in my classroom then," she said, handing me a hall pass.

The end of the day came, and as I walked toward her classroom a chill ran down my back. My knees trembled so badly that it became difficult to walk. I felt as though I was in one of those bad dreams in which you're drowning in fear itself, unable to speak or move, trying to run away through tar. "Lord God, protect me from the enemy. I sense him in this place. Give me your wisdom and grace for my friend."

The speech advisor was waiting for me with my proposal in her hands, and for the first time ever, she looked angry with me. Wasting no time, she got straight to the point. "You can't say this," she said.

I responded politely yet firmly, "Yes, I can."

She responded back, "No, you can't. You cannot say 'Jesus' at commencement."

I answered again, "Yes, I can. With all due respect, this is a free country. We have freedom of speech in this country. We have freedom of religion in this country. These constitutional liberties are safeguarded by the Bill of Rights. Veterans died for our freedom! I am free to believe as a Christian. I am free to speak about what I believe. And the audience that day is free to disagree with me. These liberties make our country great!"

She replied, "Thanks for the history lesson. You cannot say 'Jesus' at graduation. It's school policy."

I responded, "I am aware of my constitutional rights. You cannot deny my freedom of religion. And you may not censor my freedom of speech. Mount Pleasant rules do not override the U.S. Constitution."

She argued, "Your beliefs do not represent the beliefs of all of your classmates, Ian."

"But I'm not speaking in a representational capacity at the commencement ceremony. I wasn't elected. I'm not their representative. You yourself said that, as valedictorian of my class, I had earned this right: to say farewell to my classmates, and tell them what I want to say to them, as they all embark on the adventure of life. And this speech proposal is what I want to say to them."

She looked down for a moment, then looked up and answered, "I did say that, didn't I?"

I summarized, "I am allowed my religious convictions, and you are allowed to disagree with me."

After a long silence, she said, "You are not permitted to give this commencement address. I'm not asking you. I'm telling you. This meeting is over."

I answered, "So be it. I will have to escalate this matter to the school administration."

Exasperated, she replied, "You still don't get it, do you? I am speaking *for* the administration right now! I already met with the final authority in this matter, and he was the one who told me to meet with you and make crystal clear that you are not permitted to give this speech! And I know you, Ian. Your convictions are strong enough that you would hand in some fluff speech to get past me and the administration, and then walk up to that podium at commencement and give the talk you want. So I want to make myself perfectly understood. I will be waiting at the power chord of the sound system at graduation ready to pull the plug and silence you. If you say 'Jesus' at commencement, I will pull that plug. I will silence you myself. Do I make myself clear?"

"Yes, perfectly clear. It isn't right. But it is clear."

When the Lord described how his name will bring a sword that divides even families, he wasn't kidding. This teacher was family. And my stomach felt as though a sword had just run it through.

When I got home, I went straight to my bedroom and began the process of prayerfully navigating the psychological, emotional, and spiritual storm that had just blown into my life. My inner emotional weatherman was saying, "We've got an unprecedented *in trouble with my teacher* front blowing up here from the south, and it's colliding with this dashed-dreams system, all in a jet stream of spiritual conviction. Yes, folks, it's going be a teenage crisis tonight."

The bigoted censorship that had just blindsided me was, objectively speaking, as immoral as it was illegal. But this wrong action had come from a good woman. I knew that my advisor wasn't being intentionally malicious. The most common defense I hear in any personal conflict is "but I wasn't malicious" or some version of that sentiment, as though a good intention justifies any act. In reality, very few acts of wickedness are performed in a state of blatant, self-aware malice. On the contrary, in most cases the perpetrator believes himself to be promoting the good. Evil typically masquerades as light. I knew that my advisor had missed the mark, but I also knew that she thought she was in the right.

Nothing clarifies, illuminates, and exposes the matters of the heart like Jesus Christ. And as I prayed, a path through the storm began to appear. First I decided to forgive my teacher and leave her in God's merciful hands. Then I thought, "This is exactly where I was when God gave me the miracle that brought me to faith. The Lord knows what he's doing in this situation, too, because *he is Lord*." I looked at my dresser, where my eighth-grade American Legion award for patriotism was displayed. I thought about my two Catholic grandfathers, who were both veterans, and how they risked their lives so that I could live in a free country. Knowing that pride precedes a fall, I knew that whatever I did, it had better be done with humility. It had to be about Jesus, not anything else.

I prayed, "To me, most of reality is invisible. But you see the hidden stuff, Lord. I am duped everyday by my shortsighted look at how things appear. Give me the grace to trust you, and not live according to my own understanding. Give me the grace to live by faith, not by what I see. I need to know that, while Goliath *looks* bigger than David, the giant is no threat to you, the Almighty God. Some 'Ian luck' would be nice right about now too."

Prayer is a real conversation. But beyond that, it's also a process of tuning *out* the wrong radio frequencies, and tuning into the right one. Saying prayers is a great way for me to *start* praying. In other words, the longer I commune with the Almighty, the more deeply and clearly I enter into a state of ongoing receptivity to the Lord's perpetual instruction. It's like finally tuning into a heavenly station that's been broadcasting to you the whole time, while tuning out the distracting noise of earthly cares. Taking my crisis to the Lord was the best thing that I could have done. The longer we talked about it, the more "tuned in" I became. Then God's love cast out the fear, and a pathway lit up through the darkness, as the lights to my grandfather's pool illuminate the sidewalk when headed for a night swim. I knew what to do.

My intention was to sacrifice the experience of actually giving my commencement speech, for the chance to have it printed instead. In particular, I would ask whether our local newspaper, the *Mount Pleasant Journal*, would be willing to print my valedictorian speech so that my community would have it available. If the *Journal* was willing to print it, then at the graduation ceremony, I would say, "If you would like to read my speech, it is printed in the *Mount Pleasant Journal*. Thank you." Then I would simply sit back down.

This plan covered every aspect of what I was concerned about. I would not act ashamed of the name of Jesus. My civil liberties would be honored. And this course of action wouldn't make it a big ruckus about me. It was humble and motivated by the Lord's commission to proclaim the gospel. Yes, I would miss out on the opportunity to give my valedictorian address at graduation, but it was worth it. God gave me his own Son; I could give him my speech. I would decrease, so that he would increase. And this plan helped to act mercifully toward my speech advisor too. All around, it was a good idea.

I related everything to my parents, and they agreed with my approach. With their approval and prayer support, I picked up the phone and called the newspaper. "Hello, this is the *Mount Pleasant Journal*," said a friendly man on the other end of the line.

"Hi, I'll try to be quick for you," I said. "My name is Ian, and I'm co-valedictorian at Mount Pleasant. The high school administration has forbidden me to give my graduation speech because it's about Jesus Christ. And even if they allowed it, one faculty member has already promised to pull the plug on the sound system herself, in order to silence me if I say the name of Jesus. I am not ashamed of Christ, and I believe that I have freedom of religion and freedom of speech in this country. So, I was wondering if you would be willing to print my speech. Then I will just tell everybody at commencement that it's available to read. What do you think?"

"They WHAT?!" the man asked.

"They won't let me give my valedictorian speech because I want to talk about Jesus," I repeated.

"They can't do that, this is America! What the hell!" he exclaimed.

"I know, I tried to explain it," I said.

"Listen, when we get something this big, we're obligated to send it up the chain. Please hold."

I wasn't on hold for long. After only a few seconds of elevator music, a robust individual with a hint of a New York accent came on the line.

"All right kid, what's your story?" he asked.

"My high school won't let me give my valedictorian speech at commencement because I talk about Jesus," I said.

"They WHAT?!"

At that point, he tried to muffle the phone, and yelled, "Weeeee've gotta a hot one!"

"Where do you live?" he asked.

"I live out in the middle of the forest past the dairy farms of Acme, Pennsylvania," I explained. "Down a mile-long dirt road. It's *not* easy to find."

"Are you home now, and will you be there through the evening?" he asked.

"Yes sir," I answered.

He spoke with urgency in his voice, "Just give me your address, I'll be there. I can't make you keep this between us, but if you give me first dibs on this story, I promise that I will take the best care of you. This topic is very important to me."

"I appreciate this so much. Sure, I won't call any other press," I said. "I'll wait for you." Then I gave him my address and my best attempt at directions through the woods.

"They can't do this," he said before hanging up. "We have freedom of speech and freedom of religion here in this country, last time I checked anyway. Freedom of press, too—I'm on my way."

I looked at Dad and Mom. "I don't know why they want to come here," I said. "All I'm looking for is permission to print my speech. It's not even written yet; all I have is the proposal."

"He sounded sincerely interested in supporting you," said Dad. "I think they may be able to help."

Mom agreed, "We've all covered this in prayer, so let's see what the Lord is up to." Then we all waited.

The news van arrived in fifteen minutes, and to this day, I'm puzzled by how he found us so fast. The man looked exactly as I pictured him. Boisterous and fun, he was obviously feeling jazzed about scoring a possible front-page headline. At the same time, he was genuinely in my corner with patriotic convictions of his own. He thanked me profusely for the exclusivity, and he reiterated his promise to take good care of me. He interviewed me for over an hour, taping everything on his recording equipment, personally intrigued by everything that had happened so far. I put on my favorite black dress shirt for a picture, posing at the desk where I had written the speech proposal.

The animated interviewer asked, "If you're not free to say what you want, then what kind of commencement speech do they want from you?"

"I think they want me to write some generic fluff speech that doesn't actually say anything at all, like some of the graduation speeches I've heard before. I would bore them to tears. It's funny how we're free to say nothing. In fact, it's like we're free to say anything we want, as long as it's not Jesus."

"Ian, you are in the right here. And I will do whatever I can to help protect your liberties," he said.

"All I want is permission to have my speech printed in the local paper. That is all I am looking for here," I explained.

"I understand," he said, "but unfortunately I cannot guarantee that. I wish I could. But what I *can* promise you is that I will do everything in my power to make that happen. Which reminds me, do I have your permission to release this story to the AP wire?"

"What's that?" I asked.

"The Associated Press—it's a news network from which other media can pull stories they would like to report. I would need your permission," he explained.

"Will it help get my speech printed?" I asked.

"It can only help," he assured me.

"Okay, then yes, you have my permission," I replied.

"Could you say that a little bit louder?" he requested.

"You have my express consent to release everything we've talked about today to the Associated Press," I said loudly.

The reporter lit up like a child who had just unwrapped his favorite Christmas present. "Thank you! And good luck. We'll be in touch," he said.

Scratching my head, I quickly shifted my attention to packing for our family's road trip the next day. We were driving to Michigan for Uncle Tim's wedding. I still had to go to school in the morning because I had an Advanced Placement calculus exam, which I couldn't miss. My family planned to pick me up at noon.

I woke up at 6:00 A.M. on Friday, May 21, 1993, to an odd phone call. An excited and fiery man said that it was an honor to talk to me, and that he and the other protestors were all ready to go. They just wanted my permission.

Bleary-eyed and not fully awake yet, I asked him, "Wait a minute, what is it you want to do exactly?"

"We heard about your story from the press office last night, and we stayed up all night making the picketing signs! My political organization is all ready to picket your high school for you, and try to get your principal fired!" he exclaimed. "We want to be the first thing he sees when he shows up to work today."

"No, please don't," I said. "I have a big calc test today."

"But we worked all night on these picketing signs," said the man, sounding a bit deflated. "We believe in you!"

"I am grateful for your support," I said. "You went through a lot on behalf of somebody you don't even know, working through the night. That means the world to me, it really does. Honestly sir, I appreciate you, and I want you to pass my personal and heartfelt appreciation to everybody else there with you."

"Thank *you*, Ian, I will do that," he said choked up, as though the governor himself had paid him a personal compliment.

Then I added, "Now I know that I am truly not alone in this endeavor, thanks to your support. God bless you all. But please don't picket my school with signs trying to get my principal fired. God *will* take care of this. Thanks again."

"We'll do whatever you think is best. You're the free speech kid! We're here for you. If you change your mind, we'll be here ready," he said.

I suspect that he and the other members of his political organization waited all day in case I called back. I went back to sleep.

When I arrived at school, a group of people was marching around the school with signs.

"That's weird," I thought. "I think I had better take this exam and bolt."

I went to my locker, where one of my classmates complimented me for how awesome I sounded on the country music station that morning.

"I wasn't on the country music station," I said.

"Yes you were! We heard you!" he said.

"I promise, I wasn't on the radio," I said.

"Listen to you! No, that was you! Good job," he said.

Another person then thanked me for the fine job I did talking on the oldies station that morning.

A third classmate approached me and said, "You were on classic rock, man! All right! Then they played some Zeppelin."

"I'm sure I would remember opening for Led Zeppelin," I said, utterly confused. "This doesn't make any sense."

That's when my girlfriend Marie walked up to me holding the tristate *Tribune Review* newspaper. On the front page was a gigantic color picture of me beneath the headline "Commencement Speech about Religion Rejected." At that point it started to occur to me what was happening. Then I think I said a swear word.

Because of the AP, my interview the day before not only made the front page in a paper whose reach extended into three states, but was picked up by popular radio stations that played it over the airwaves all through the morning. In the middle of my calculus exam, I was summoned to the school office. Thankfully my math teacher communicated to the administration that I would be there after I had finished the exam.

At the office was my father with one of the school principals. There was a third individual waiting for me as well. He was an unnamed school administrator who appeared furious. The administrator began yelling, "How could you do this to me? How could you?!"

Afraid to make eye contact with the enraged official, I looked instead to the caring and protective principal. I relayed to him how the speech advisor had not only explained that she was speaking on behalf of the administration in censoring my proposed commencement address, but also promised to pull the plug on me herself.

"I understand," he said. Then he looked at my dad and said, "I think you should go ahead and get him away from here."

My dad replied, "Yeah, me too, thank you." They nodded to one another in agreement, having one of those whole conversations that people can have with a single look. Then my father escorted me to the car, past a growing throng of protestors and media outside.

The long drive to Michigan gave us hours to unpack everything that was happening. Dad and Mom were both proud of me, as was my whole family. My dad explained how the phone had been ringing off the hook all morning. The line was flooded. He described how, as soon as he would hang up, somebody else was already on the line with him. Realizing that they could not possibly talk to everybody, they began taking names and numbers as quickly as possible. Most people simply wanted to voice their support, but my parents listed everybody who desired a return call.

We hashed it all out so much during that drive that my sister, Sarah, lamented. "I took a four-hour car nap, and when I woke up, Dad was still going off about Ian's fame," she said. "Don't get me wrong, I couldn't be more proud of my big brother than I am right now. I'm simply adjusting to the fact that this is all I am going to hear about for a very long time." We both had a good laugh about that.

Meanwhile back at home, my sister's boyfriend was handling all the incoming calls during our absence. He touched base with us and explained that reporters were now at the house looking for me, pleading with him to disclose our destination.

"And these calls have not stopped all day," he explained, exhausted. "The phone line is still flooded. And reporters keep showing up. I have pages of callbacks here, but this one's particularly important. Channel Four News wants a televised interview so much that they dispatched a helicopter, willing to fly the entire way to Michigan! Do you realize that you are literally being sought after by a helicopter news crew? They are begging me to tell them where you're staying!"

"No, don't tell them," I said. "Do not give them the address. Tim's wedding is tomorrow, it's his day."

"I know; I didn't tell them the address. They only know that it's Michigan, so you should be fine," he said.

As we proceeded on our trip, I kept searching the sky outside the car for helicopters.

Unsuccessful in their pursuit, Channel Four sent a camera crew to the house to film my senior class picture hanging on our wall, so I still opened the television news that evening. The media team changed their normal opening audio to "Pomp and Circumstance". While playing the well-known graduation processional, the local television news began their evening program with a slow zoom-in of my photo. And of course it was one of the worst pictures of me ever. To help keep me humble, God had arranged that the picture was taken on a bad hair day. I sported this large tuft of hair rising up from my cranium on one side but not the other, which shaped the contour of my overall head to look like the green clay animation character known as Gumby.

Not long after our arrival near Hillsdale College in Michigan, Uncle Tim approached me privately, wearing a proud but mischievous smile. "Looks like God is doing amazing things in your life, Ian, and I would like this wee book to be a part of it," said Uncle Tim, handing me a copy of *Rome Sweet Home* by Scott and Kimberly Hahn. My uncle had recently become Catholic, which, according to my anti-Catholic father, placed Uncle Tim in league with the Anti-Christ.

The cover of the Hahn's book looked to me like one of those Whore-of-Babylon pictures from my father's Jack Chick tracts. "This looks Catholic!" I complained.

"It is Catholic," said Tim.

With arrogant bluster, I challenged my uncle. "I am going to tear this book to shreds!" I promised.

With love all over his face, Uncle Tim replied, "I would enjoy hearing whatever you think about it. Please read it, and no matter what you think, I would love to listen to anything you have to say. Let me know when you're done, and we'll talk about it, okay?"

As a kind word turns away wrath, Tim totally disarmed me. You could almost hear my figurative battle gear clanging onto the floor. I didn't admit it to him at the time, but I was taken aback that the Catholic in the room was the one who was acting like Jesus. I sure wasn't.

"Yeah, okay," I said, begrudgingly taking the book, and then quickly changing the subject to the topic of pre-wedding jitters.

At Tim and Steph's wedding Mass the following day, they distributed the Eucharist. Standing next to my father, I looked at him and noticed that he felt deeply distressed. "Don't worry Dad, you don't stand alone. I won't take part in this," I whispered adamantly, aware that I was hiding a copy of *Rome Sweet Home* back in my room.

Squeezing my shoulder, my dad whispered back, "Thank you, son, *thank you*. I know that you would never betray me."

The Hahns' book haunted me from that moment onward, as if Edgar Allen Poe's "telltale heart" were beating inside my suitcase. Not only would I *not* be able to tear the Hahns' book to shreds, I would eventually be persuaded by it. And Dr. Hahn would one day mention me in one of his other books. If someone had said all of this to me back in 1993, I would have laughed and laughed.

Aside from the feeling that the river Tiber was cutting through my family, Uncle Tim's wedding was among the most joyful we have ever celebrated. But the happy diversion reached its end, and eventually we had to drive back into a three-ring media circus. If you have ever seen footage of the paparazzi thronging some Hollywood actor, it was just like that. A frenzy of flashing bulbs, reporters, television cameras, and microphones in my face became a common phenomenon at school, at my house, and even on the streets. As I would soon find out, not even the men's locker room in the high school gymnasium was a safe hideout.

Through the Associated Press, media companies from across the country picked up my story. People mailed me copies of newspapers from a number of different states including Texas, New Hampshire, Colorado, Maine, California, and New York. I was a guest on television and radio news programs. Through the Gideons International, over a thousand Bibles were donated or funded in my honor. Letters and postcards flooded in from around the country, mailed to the school and addressed to my attention. Some pieces of mail contained cash, so I made sure to open every single letter. From veterans' organizations to churches, I was praised for being "the free speech kid". And girls liked me! Glory, fame, cash, fan mail, and women? Seriously, running that much positive attention through my eighteen-year-old male ego felt like running five hundred volts through a fifty-volt wire. Those were heady days. I confess, they felt good.

The attention was not all positive, however. Pittsburgh's KDKA Radio invited me to appear as a guest on one of their evening programs, along with the president of the Pittsburgh chapter of the

American Civil Liberties Union (ACLU). Despite their name, the ACLU was actively fighting against my speech. I accepted the station's invitation, and at eighteen years old, I found myself in a head-to-head debate against a high-ranking political activist, on live radio.

"Ian, let me ask you this," said the facilitator, "suppose another classmate of yours, scheduled to speak at commencement, was a Muslim who wanted to talk about Islam in his graduation speech. What would you say then?"

"That I would die for his right to do so!" I answered firmly. "In this great nation, he would be free to practice his religion, and free to speak about it. And the audience would be free to agree or disagree with him. And those freedoms make us great! Our liberty came to us at the highest price. We should use it. And we should defend it."

The ACLU chapter president then claimed that my proposed speech violated the Establishment Clause of the Bill of Rights, because this clause prohibits the establishment of a nationwide religion that all citizens would be forced to follow. I made my best effort to explain that my graduation speech was not establishing a national religion. I wasn't forcing anybody to worship or pray as I do. Not only would that kind of oppression be wrong, but I certainly didn't hold the political authority even to attempt such tyranny. I was a high school student. I was just saying what I believe. Whether or not my audience believed it remained entirely up to them.

Then the ACLU chapter president completely changed his argument. In particular, he answered me by claiming that the Bill of Rights *applies to everyone except Christians*. Yes, he said that, with the phone lines open. The debate was over.

All across the country I was called a hero. Even many non-Christians, including atheists and agnostics, rallied behind the free speech kid. "I don't agree with his religion myself, but you've got to respect him!" said one man in a newspaper interview. "He should be allowed to say what he believes." Another man, who did not think I should mention Jesus in my speech, said, "But I admire his convictions and determination."

While many people supported me, plenty of others did not. As commencement drew near, many of my classmates began to express increasing levels of hostility. One of my dearest friends published a letter in the *Mount Pleasant Journal*, claiming that I had confided in her about a plot to use graduation as a chance to get famous. Not only was it completely false, it was the opposite of what had actually happened. Heartbroken, I confronted her about it.

"Yeah," she said angrily, "I lied, and I did it on purpose, and I would do it again! I wanted to be famous, too, and I knew that all I had to do was lie about you. They ate it up like candy. I don't care that I'm a liar, and I don't care what it puts you through. Now I'm in the newspapers too!" Then another friend made similar claims. In her letter to the editor she wrote, "He used his speech as a personal platform. Ian was publicized on every Pittsburgh television station, many radio stations and newspapers." She said that my speech was coming from inappropriate motives and not from the heart. Someone else wrote:

> Amid the glare of television lights, photographers' flashes, a freedom of speech controversy and proud families, the Mount Pleasant Area High School Class of 1993 has taken its place in history. Undoubtedly, many wished Mount Pleasant had never made the news. Others basked in the limelight, showing off for the cameras, offering their opinions pro and con, and enjoying their chance at immortality. Murphy got what he wanted. But he didn't do a good job of it.

Gossip about how I had intentionally planned the whole media blitz spread like wildfire, and in more than one of my classes, I endured the false accusations and jeers of both students and teachers. Whenever I explained that I had only asked that my speech be printed in the local paper, I received a few apologies, but it was never enough to stop all the damage done by the slander.

Word also spread of a public protest that my class was going to hold against me at graduation, but I didn't know what they were planning exactly. That initial boisterous reporter from the *Tribune Review*, moved by what had resulted from his article, published a follow-up article about the planned classmate protest, in hopes that the public attention might discourage participation in anything physically violent. I am grateful for his efforts, both to defend my freedom and to protect me from harm. He certainly kept his word to take care of me. But unfortunately, his follow-up piece was not the deterrent against violence that he and I both hoped it would be.

One day, a classmate of mine pulled me aside and told me that at some point in time he was going to pull me into a dark room and beat me senseless. He said he wanted me to be afraid until it happened. While he never carried through on the threat, two other guys from my class did. One afternoon, in Mount Pleasant's dark auditorium, they kicked me over and over again. I wore long-sleeved shirts over the bruises on my arms to keep the beating a secret from my parents. I didn't want them to worry about me or to pull me out of the graduation ceremony in fear for my life.

At the awards ceremony in the auditorium that formerly had been the happy place of band concerts, high-school plays, and standing ovations, my class booed me. When I was called onto the stage to accept the Most Likely to Succeed and Best Scholar awards, which my classmates had elected me to receive, the deafening roar hurt my feelings as well as my ears. Backstage I approached Marie for comfort, but she complained that because of me, she would never have the experience of a normal high school graduate. I had thought she would be proud of me for my stand for our Lord. Instead, she explained how she wished that she could just get along with everybody else. I had never been more popular in my life, or more lonely.

In a bittersweet mix of persecution and fame, the mission continued. The American Center for Law and Justice contacted me, promising to defend my case on a pro bono basis. They sent a letter to the school administration on my behalf, explaining their willingness to take the matter before the highest court in the land, if need be, unless they allowed me to give my speech. The American Center for Law and Justice assured me that I was no longer alone in my struggle against the ACLU, whom they had fought against before.

Soon thereafter, I got the good news. After all the attention and the pressure, the school administration announced that I was indeed permitted to give my valedictory speech according to my original proposal, with their full support. And I was assured that my talk would be protected from censorship by any opposing faculty members. As my initial media contact reported in yet another follow-up story, "If Ian Murphy wants to give a June 3 commencement address recommending belief in God and the teachings of the Bible as a way of dealing with social issues, there is nothing administrators could—or would—do to stop him." He quoted the principal, who said, "No one is going to pull the plug."

Graduation night finally arrived. The weather was stormy both before and after the occasion, but it was oddly dry for the duration of the outdoor ceremony. The last student to speak, I approached the podium in the middle of the football field, looking out upon a multitude of television cameras, news reporters, and microphones, as flash photography lit up an overflow audience in the stands. In front of all the media stood a wall of security officers, holding the paparazzi at bay until the end of the event. I felt a few drops of rain as I approached the microphone, but thankfully that was all.

Then the protest from my classmates took place. I turned around to face the class before saying my farewell, and in unison, the major-ity of them slowly raised their graduation programs to hide their faces from me while I spoke. One girl named Tina Curry, who played games with me on the playground back in second grade, stood up clapping for me and encouraging me. With great courage she stood alone against the protest, and through her, God gave me the grace I needed to continue.

I prayed silently for a moment, "Thank God for Tina. As for the rest of them, they know not what they do." Then I resorted to the same prayer which began my unofficial ministry to skeptics four years prior, "Lord, do I care enough about them to tell them about you? Yes, I do. Please speak through me, and advance your kingdom tonight, in Jesus' name, amen." Then I gave my speech about how Jesus and the Bible were my roadmap through all of life's adventures. "I believe I would be lost and helpless in the upcoming adventures if I did not rely on Jesus and the Bible," I said in closing. My school had attempted to silence the name of Jesus. Now, because of that attempt, hundreds of thousands of people were hearing the gospel broadcasted and televised.

One viewer wrote to a newspaper:

Dear Expression, As I watched the news, tears flowed freely when the brilliant young man, Ian Murphy, gave his valedictorian address at Mount Pleasant High School's graduation. Some of us adults would do well to be as sure of the most important thing in our lives as Ian is. With no apologies, no hesitation, he stated that he bases his life on the principles in the Bible and that he will continue to do so. Praise God! If I was spiritually moved that the tears had to be released, imagine how that precious, pure heart of Jesus rejoiced!

As the *Tribune Review* reported the event:

> The Mount Pleasant senior, the son of Mike and Eileen Murphy, was ultimately given the blessing of the school district administration to go ahead with his original speech. The ovation by the audience following the address was one of apparent support. He began under a light rain that held off long enough for the ceremonies to be completed. Murphy said, "I believe that the Bible is a trustworthy guide through the adventures ahead. The Bible says that Jesus died for our sins. It also says that we can be with him someday if we accept that forgiveness and live our lives for God instead of ourselves." In the end, Ian Murphy was given an opportunity to tell his fellow high-school graduates how he feels about the Bible—and let them decide whether to accept it as their solution.

After the speech our class president, Jason, placed the valedictorian medal around my neck and personally congratulated me. I marched out through flash photography and the cheers of supporters, thronged by television cameras and reporters in the school parking lot. Suddenly I was surprised by the acute sting of a hard object hitting me in the cheek. One of the student protestors was now hurling New Testaments at my face. He had procured a box of Gideon Bibles, which had been given in dedication to my cause, and was throwing them at me. It was painful. But as I prayed for him, my heart broke with the sense that he wasn't getting the love that he needed at home. And I have to hand it to him, he was creative. Anyone can pitch a blunt object at another person to inflict injury. But to use Bibles donated in my honor for a modern-day stoning—he had really put some thought into that.

Apart from a couple more bruises, it was a heavenly night. My paternal grandfather, known affectionately as "Grampa", noted how God had protected my message from the weather. And my maternal grandfather, known affectionately as "GingGing", embraced me, and said, "I'm proud of you, son." Even though they were Catholic, their love made my night.

The blitz died down through the summer, so I was surprised when the media was back on the lawn furniture one afternoon.

"I thought this was all over. What's this about?" I asked a familiar reporter who had interviewed me several times before.

She answered, "You know how we usually rehearse, get some shots of us walking and talking together, and get a few takes?"

"Yes, I remember the drill," I answered her.

"We're not going to do any of that this time. Remember to look right at me and not into the television camera in five, four, three, two, one ..."

The red recording light on the TV camera lit up, as the news-woman began, "Ian Murphy, we are here as media envoys on behalf of Senator Arlen Specter. He personally wants you to know that he wishes he could be here himself. He has specifically requested a live reaction from you regarding a very exciting piece of news. He followed your story. And inspired by your uncompromising and courageous stand for freedom of religion and for freedom of speech in this country, Senator Arlen Specter drafted a bill to the United States Congress officially protecting graduation speakers like you from any future attempts at unlawful censorship. That bill passed through both houses of the U.S. Congress, and was just signed by the President of the United States! Ian, how does it feel to know that you just influenced the laws of our country?"

Shocked to discover that I had given new meaning to Murphy's Law, I leaned forward into the microphone and answered, "Good."

"There you have it folks, the free speech kid says that it feels *good*, back to you at the studio!" she said. After they stopped recording, I begged for a retake.

She responded, grinning ear-to-ear, "No way, that was priceless. Absolutely precious. He's gonna love it."

Only several months ago, I ran into a guy who had watched that brief interview back in 1993. He explained, "I remember that! I totally remember that! I was with my ailing dad at the hospital, when that clip aired. We hung on the edge of our seats to hear your reaction to the senator's message. Then you leaned forward and said 'good'. My dad looked at me after the anticlimactic moment and said, 'That's all he had to say? What a putz.' Yeah, I totally remember that."

Although the frenzy had passed, the snowball effect had only begun. My story ended up as a feature in an inspirational youth video published by the Christian and Missionary Alliance Church, the host of my annual summer camp. Some students and faculty from the Pennsylvania Governor's School for International Studies, which I had attended the previous summer, followed the story and contacted me to express their gratitude by phone and in person. My old roommate from the program said, "Wow, you took your Governor's School *newsman* character to a whole new level!"

In the middle of my attempts to score a free flashlight from the army, the recruiter said, "Wait a minute, are you *the* Ian Murphy? The free speech kid? Oh man, what you did is exactly what our armed forces are fighting for!" Somebody mailed me a recording of a cable TV preacher giving a sermon about me. Another time, a stranger approached me in a park and asked, "Are you *the* Ian Murphy? The free speech kid? I was one of the security guards holding back the camera crews at your graduation, dude! I loved your speech. I just loved it." A lawyer also recognized me, and told me that I was his inspiration for going into his field. He thanked me by taking me out for an expensive dinner in Pittsburgh. In addition, a college student once told me that my story was published in her textbook, and that her university law course included an entire section about me. From a Greyhound bus in California to a church in Illinois, to this day I am still occasionally recognized as the free speech kid.

But the most remarkable result of all was when one of my classmates called me up and told me that she was now a Christian because of my graduation speech.

She explained in detail, "I was among the protestors at commencement, Ian. I'm really sorry about that. Please forgive me. I hid my face from you. You used your freedom to care about us. We used ours to cause pain. We were wrong. But for what it's worth, I know that now, and I know Jesus now! I know he's real, and I asked him into my heart. I gave my life to Christ. After your speech, I complained to my mother about all the attention you were getting. I was jealous. My mom challenged me to look into your message for myself, and then make up my own mind about what I believed. And so I did. And you were right, every word.

From the bottom of my heart, thank you for caring enough about me to tell me the good news of Jesus Christ. I'm a Christian now because of it!"

Maybe the whole thing was for her.

2

The Bible Is Not Cereal

The bold stand that I had taken for the name of Jesus at my high-school commencement ceremony might lead people to suppose that I grew up an avid churchgoer. On the contrary, aside from holidays and some occasional events, church was not a regular part of my life for most of my upbringing. In fact, there were periods across my childhood in which the subject of God filled my heart with distressing questions and marked anxiety. The 1993 graduate whose Christian convictions inspired a national law used to be a firm skeptic who doubted there was a God. Growing from one to the other was a good journey, but not a smooth one.

On October 15, 1974, I was born. Mom says that my birth was the easiest of her five deliveries. At first Mom and the doctor and the nurses were scared because I didn't cry. But they confirmed that I was indeed breathing fine. Mom explains that my first cry sounded less like a cry and more like I was repeating the word "bow" over and over again. I wish to prevent any silly notions that I entered into the world preaching, telling people to "bow", or kneel, before the Almighty. When I said "bow" it was just my version of crying. Mom told me that during a family camping trip in the Midwest, I was outside crawling around when a dust storm blew into the area. Mom tells me that she couldn't see where I was—but all she had to do to find me was to follow the sounds of "bow" from within the dust clouds.

My parents, Michael and Eileen, were both Christians of strong faith and sincere friendship with Christ. At the same time, however, we did not go to church. My parents weren't just *nominal* Christians, who professed the faith *in name only*. Oh no—they were the real deal. Each of them truly believed that Jesus was who he said he was, and that he revealed God to the world. They were best friends with the Lord. The joys and the challenges of their respective walks with God were those of a real marriage, as they showed me an authentic personal relationship with the Almighty. But we didn't go to church. It may seem odd that such serious Christians didn't join a church and attend services on a regular basis. To provide clarity to this puzzle, let me explain—my parents were hippies.

The hippie in his natural habitat listens to the Beatles, wears a tie-dyed shirt if he is wearing a shirt, is suspicious of established organizations, and is often found camping in the woods, smoking pot, and talking about freedom. The delicious irony of it all is that my hippie parents raised five conventional professionals. I guess the only way to rebel against liberal parents is to be a conservative kid.

My parents weren't flag-burning revolutionaries, but they did participate in peace communes, and they traveled the country camping. My dad recalls sitting half-asleep in a mud puddle at Woodstock when a police officer on horseback, who was attempting to disband the crowd, asked him to go home. Still under the effects of whatever he had been smoking, my father peeled his eyes open and looked up. He heard the cop's voice, but saw the mouth of the horse moving, and surmised that the horse was talking to him. "The horse told me that the show was over, and that I should go home now. So I listened to the horse and did as it said," Dad explained.

The second oldest of their five kids, I watched as family life grounded my parents. The responsibilities of child-rearing brought an end to the camping circuit and the commune crowd. What remained deeply instilled within them was that characteristic suspicion of institutions, including religious institutions, which is among the most important contributions that hippies bring to the wider society.

More than once, history has witnessed good ideas with benevolent intentions behind them become poisoned by the cold, dehumanized processes of outsized bureaucracy. Take the phrase "human resources", in which "human" becomes a descriptive for what kind of resource the employee is to the company. Stick the corporation's financial resources in the bank, put the computer resources in the tech room, put the office supply resources in the cupboard, and place the human resources in the cubicles. I believe that the hippie voice is still an important check against institutional dehumanization.

Although my parents emphasized that institutionalized religion simply cannot be trusted, they always encouraged their children to join a Christian community if they felt called to do so. At the same time, they taught their children about Jesus. They told us that he was God's Word, showing how much the Creator loves us. They told us about the miracle of Christmas and the defining miracle of Christ's Resurrection at Easter. They taught us that Jesus ascended to heaven and sent us the Holy Spirit. That way, we can walk with the Lord in personal friendship every day. Most importantly, they modeled that friendship and explained that each of us would have to choose the friendship of Jesus for ourselves, because a person's relationship with God must be authentic. I remain grateful for the perspective my parents gave me, and for the desire for authenticity that it cultivated within me from a very young age.

My parents always stressed the importance of the Bible, and they told us that it was the Word of God himself and a trustworthy guide to everything we needed to know about our faith. When I was three years old, I thought that the Bible they were talking about was Quaker oatmeal. I have no idea what successful advertising strategy planted into my little-boy brain a connection between the Word of God and the canister with the wise and friendly face.

Sometime following my fourth birthday, I learned the truth at the grocery store. I didn't sit in the cart this trip. I was a little man on a mission, feverishly walking around because I was a big boy now, helping my mom retrieve items from the lower shelves.

"Can we get some Bibles?" I asked, excited.

With a delighted but at the same time concerned expression Mom answered, "We already have Bibles at home."

"No, I ate them all up," I explained.

"That's deep, man, digesting the Word ... but seriously, we have Bibles at home."

"No, seriously, it's gone."

Mom replied, "Well, they don't sell Bibles at the grocery store anyway."

"Yes they do, the cereal aisle has a whole row of Bibles!"

"Ian, why don't you go get me a Bible and show it to me?" Mom said.

I raced to the cereal aisle with purpose, grabbed a container of old-fashioned rolled oats and returned to present the prize to my mother.

"Look, the Bible!" I exclaimed.

"Ian," she said patiently, "that's not the Bible. That's oatmeal."

I was distraught.

"What's the Bible?" I questioned.

"The Bible is a book, son," Mom explained, seeming worried that poor parenting must somehow rest at the core of this colossal misunderstanding.

"Did the oatmeal man write it?" I asked.

"No."

"I want to read it," I said.

Something washed over me in that moment. I experienced the heavenly Father's intimate care for a little four-year-old. It can only be explained as grace. When Mom told me what the Bible was, I was moved in the core of my tiny being to *read that book*.

At four years of age, my reading was very limited. While my parents had started to teach me how to read while I was still very young, my vocabulary was still quite limited. So I began with the ten-volume set of Arthur Maxwell's *The Bible Story*. Since it had pictures, I would find words I knew and match them to the scene.

As I got older and my reading skills improved, I kept going. We had a *Living Translation* of the Bible with a purple cover, which I remember picking up at some point during my kindergarten years because it was a "real Bible". It felt *grown up* for me to use a real Bible. I would thumb through its pages trying to find sentences that I could read. But through kindergarten, I mostly used the picture Bible.

By the time I reached second grade, my reading abilities had reached the point where I could comfortably read from the children's Bible without relying on the pictures. That summer, I started over at the beginning of volume 1, so that I could properly read the whole thing. I had nearly completed the entire set by the time I was eight years old. Problem was, I couldn't believe it.

The Gospels sounded too good to be true. I wanted to believe them, but at that point, I wondered if I had spent the last four years reading an epic fable. In the second grade I asked myself the scariest questions ever: "What if there is no God? What if I'm just an accident? What is the meaning and purpose of my being here? When I die, is it lights-out—and I won't remember ever existing at all? Do I have a Creator? If I do, then why did God make me?"

These doubts and questions would increasingly haunt me for years to come.

3

Crisis of an Agnostic

In a town in Michigan there lived a Protestant—not just any Protestant, but my godfather and uncle, Tim Murphy. I am convinced
that the Lord's favorite manner in which he reveals himself is
through other people made in his image and likeness. In my own
life, Uncle Tim has been sent to me at the most decisive moments
of my life.

During one of these key moments, Uncle Tim told me about the
debate he had with two Calvinists about "double predestination".
Lengthy theological explanations of doctrine, as important as they can
be, are not the purpose of this book—telling the story of how God
entered into a personal relationship with me is. But for that testimony
to make sense, just a little context is needed here. Briefly, "double-
predestination" is a later development of the thought of John Calvin,
a Christian thinker from the sixteenth century. This particular strand
of Calvinist thought claims that God predestines certain people to
go to heaven, while predestining other people to go to hell. That bit
about people being predestined to hell is highly problematic, especially because it isn't true.

Personally, I don't think that John Calvin believed this. I think that
Calvin admirably wrestled with the mysteries that Christ revealed,
said some really good stuff, and made some mistakes, too, like all of
us. But this God foreordaining hellfire for people—I don't think Calvin himself taught *that*. Rather, double-predestination comes from a
later thread of Calvinist theology. False doctrines often (if not always)
result from faulty assumptions that rest underneath; in this case, the
assumption is that human free will somehow compromises the sovereignty of God. In truth, free will is no threat to God's sovereignty.
Actually, it's an expression of it.

Being all-powerful, God was able to make human beings with free will. God didn't make robots, forced to follow a predestined program, with no say in the matter. God wants real friendship, love freely chosen. In a sense, God limited his divine power in order to allow human freedom. God could use his power to sweep over the world and force his will upon the creation. Instead, he chooses to allow the present state of affairs for a time, letting us choose whether we want to have a relationship with him, or not. Saying that God *doesn't* force his will is very different from saying that he *couldn't*. God is indeed sovereign. And we are indeed free to choose whether we accept his love, or reject it.

The two Calvinists who debated with Uncle Tim were friends of his. They tried to persuade him that human free will doesn't really exist, and that God predestined certain people for hell. They purported that, because such people are allegedly predestined for hell by the Creator, they have no choice in the matter. According to double-predestination, we are all in a sense *preprogrammed*. Personally, I wonder what happens to justice, morality, and accountability under the claim that people have no free will. But I can't get past the notion of people trying to protect the sovereignty of God, in the first place. That would be like trying to protect a lion, when the lion can defend himself just fine. I also can't get past trying to convert people to the idea that you can't convert.

Uncle Tim explained that this particular interpretation of Calvin's thought is incorrect. Technically it's not a Christian teaching, because it's not biblical. As Scripture makes clear, the Lord does not want anybody to perish, but for everyone to come to repentance. Tim turned his friends' attention to the Gospel of Matthew, where Jesus says, "O Jerusalem, Jerusalem, killing the prophets and stoning those who are sent to you! How often would I have gathered your children together as a hen gathers her brood under her wings, and you would not!" (23:37).

Tim said, "You see here in the New Testament how Jesus says that he wanted to gather people like a hen gathers her chicks. Jesus says that, even though it was his will to gather them, they didn't choose him. That statement makes no sense if God had already predetermined their destinies. Jesus is lamenting that God's children were regrettably *unwilling* to be gathered. Now how could Jesus have expressed grief about their unwillingness to follow him, if human beings never had any free will to begin with? How could the Lord lament over their rejection of him, if he had predestined them to do so?"

They responded that Jesus was ignorant about these truths that Calvinism later illuminated.

As Tim was telling me this story, he said that he replied, "So what you're telling me is, if only Jesus was as enlightened as you?" Then he went straight away to find a program for the Rite of Christian Initiation of Adults (RCIA), and he became Catholic. Then my uncle clarified, "It was peaceful, and we're still friends. But I did point out their error, and yes, that exchange was my inspiration for entering RCIA." Uncle Tim thus became the first Catholic convert in my family. Eight others from my family have entered the Catholic Church from various backgrounds. I was the sixth convert, but he was the trailblazer.

Returning to the time of my youth, the years that took me from eight to fourteen were made of a distinctive batch of ingredients: (1) a quasi-removed and critical stance toward modern American Christian culture, (2) a focused interest in Jesus Christ and the Bible, and (3) the ever-intensifying anxiety of agnostic doubts.

As Christians who each possessed a fierce love for the Lord, Dad and Mom maintained at least some degree of connection with Christian community. It was a sort of detached engagement. Occasionally, especially at Christmas and Easter, we would participate in children's activities hosted by one of the local denominations. One time, we went door-to-door singing Christmas carols, which by itself was great. But what I didn't like was how the children's minister presented the evening. "When we're all done with the work, we're gonna come back here and have some real fun, eating some devil's food cake!" she said, giving an extra excited intonation to the word "devil's".

"First the Jesus, then the fun?" complained my older brother, Sean.

I agreed, "Yeah, she made it sound like boring homework comes from God, but cake and fun come from the devil."

Sean and I have continued an ongoing conversation about this topic ever since. Another time, I complained, "Hey, remember that night of caroling, when *first* we had to serve the Lord, only *then* could we have fun eating the devil's cake?"

"I'll never forget it."

I said, "If God is really God, then he's the God of everything, including cake and fun. They made it sound like he's only the God of church stuff. Why don't they talk about fishing and pizza at church? If God created everything, then he created fishing and pizza, too. The devil didn't invent the cake. But I think that the devil likes it whenever the church gives him credit for the good stuff."

Sean agreed. "Yeah, God should get the credit for all good music, including the Beatles, not just church songs."

Later I continued, "Ever notice how much that devil's food cake theology has embedded itself into our society? Look how many desserts are named after Satan and his ways. Cookie fudge fantasies, mousse madness, frozen treat temptations, death-by-chocolate ... with all of this imagery about madness, forbidden temptations, and death, the dessert menu sounds like it's giving me a theological treatise on the fall of humanity in the Garden of Eden. It's unbelievable how much our society associates the goods of creation with the enemy. Have we forgotten that God created the cocoa bean? God created people. And God created chocolate. Therefore, God wants people to be happy."

Years after that I added, "And how come it's 'Christian art' only if there's a Bible verse slapped into the middle of some otherwise beautiful vista of the forest? If God made everything through Christ then doesn't it already glorify him to paint his beautiful trees? To interrupt the scene with painted text in order to 'make it Christian' implies that these might somehow have been evil trees, not part of the Creator's creation. What a relief for me to know that the trees in this painting come from God."

And so went the sarcastic, sometimes uncharitable rant of the Murphy boys. Sean had a distaste for churchy culture that surpassed even my own. Yet he entered the Catholic Church before I did.

No doubt it was my anti-establishment childhood that engendered these critical observations. Nevertheless, dabbling in church functions from time to time definitely had its moments. The activities were occasionally quite fun, and I made a few friends. But I never totally embraced it. There was this overall feel to church socializing that was simply not to my liking, especially wherever it seemed fake. I sometimes felt as though the people would like me only if I said the churchy things that I was *supposed* to say.

In contrast, whenever I spent time with close friends and family, the experience felt real. I knew those people liked me. If I was going to be friends with my Creator, I didn't want it to be fake or forced. It couldn't be as though I were wearing some meeting-mode personality garb that I could put on in public, and then take back off when I got home. If God was real, then he's God of everything, not just on certain topics. And if a personal relationship with the Almighty was indeed possible for me, then God couldn't be an appendage to the bond of community; relationship with him would have to be the primary life source before all other relationships. The friendship my parents had with God was an authentic, vital relationship that covered the whole gamut of life, not just one part labeled "religion". If I was going to have personal friendship with my Maker, then it had to be like theirs. It had to be real and all-encompassing, or not at all.

Side-by-side with a general distaste for the church world was this unmistakable enthrallment with the Scripture and with the main character of its salvation story. I always loved Jesus, even as an agnostic. Throughout my agnostic seeking, Jesus always stood out to me. In the garden of available worldviews, isms, religions, ideologies, and philosophies, Jesus was *different*. Growing up, I saw quickly that no other name got the rise out of people that Jesus' name did. This world undeniably treated Jesus' name differently than any other. Even before I was a believer, he captivated me.

Enter the specter of doubt. Was it a literal demon, attempting early on to unhinge me? Or was it my own naturally critical mindset? Or was it a bit of both, with the former playing on the latter? I'm not sure.

As mentioned earlier, I began asking the God question at an early age, and I recognized that everything depends on the answer. If I have a Creator who designed me for a loving relationship with him, then building that friendship is crucial to life's purpose. If there is right and wrong, if there is an afterlife, if I am accountable for the way I live my life, then *all of that impacts how I live right now*. But what if, when I die, I will simply blink out of existence with no awareness that I was ever here?

All of this existential turmoil was indeed a lot for a little second-grader. But this burden wasn't constant, at least not throughout my elementary-school years. My doubts and fears surrounding God, purpose, and the afterlife filled me with a most dreadful anxiety, but only periodically, in an otherwise happy childhood.

When I was five years old, my family moved into the house that I would call home for the next thirteen years, until I left for college. It was a beautiful Tudor-style A-frame with extensions, located atop one of the foothills of the Appalachians in the Chestnut Ridge—fairly close to Frank Lloyd Wright's famous Fallingwater—in Acme, Pennsylvania. My brother and I discovered fishing ponds, heavenly patches of wild blackberries, raspberries, and strawberries, and vines for swinging over ravines and playing Indiana Jones. There was a gorgeous brook a short hike away that our cousins affectionately named Murphy Mountain Waterfall. We were truly blessed to grow up in a slice of woodland paradise surrounded by the dairy farmlands of western Pennsylvania. Home was a sacred space where the seven Murphys—Dad, Mom, Sean, Sarah, Shaylyn, Jessamyn, and I—could grow close to God, nature, and each other. Forest adventures, fishing for small but delicious bluegills, swimming and playing "dive for quarters", gardening, outdoor barbecues in the summertime, winter sled-riding, epic Easter-egg hunts, and an abundance of love all made for a joyous boyhood.

As for periodic anguish over questions regarding God's existence, I kept the whole agnostic ordeal a secret from my two brothers, my two sisters, and my parents. I turned instead to extended relatives for help. One time, back when the crisis began, my paternal grandparents, Grampa and Nanie, visited along with their youngest, my Uncle Tim, who was still very much a Protestant at this point in his life. During their visit, I pulled Nanie aside to ask her how she could be sure that God was real. She laughed out loud at the question. "Oh Ian, I know he's real the same way I know you're real, because we know each other." It would take years for me to grasp what she was talking about. At the time, I was sorely disappointed in her response, which was honestly no help to me. I then turned to Uncle Tim, who refreshingly understood exactly where I was coming from.

After comforting me with the unique assurance that comes from uncles, he confidently went after the source of my doubts. He didn't go there defensively, but offensively—as one who has truth in the face of error, as light in the dark. That confidence itself helped as much as the content of his words. "Ian," he said, "God is real. But let's imagine for a moment if he wasn't, and let's imagine that life came about with nobody designing it, with nobody guiding the process. That would mean everything's a random accident. Does that make sense of the world? Really think about it. Use your human reason. *Does that make sense?*"

I imagined trying to say that nobody created our piano. How would I explain how it got here? I would have to say it was an accident. But would that account make sense—that all those purposeful parts came together by accident, with nobody guiding the process? The piano was obviously *somebody's* creation, even though I had never seen its maker with my own eyes. Then I thought about human reason itself. I was thinking about these questions with my *mind*. Does human reasoning look like it's just an accident? Or is it amazing, more like a piano?

My logical brain purred with relief, that is, until Uncle Tim left. The good mood of a fun family visit was over, I no longer saw and felt Tim's confidence, and those scary questions reared up again. The doubts were even worse this time, especially when school exposed me to the claim that this scientist named Charles Darwin was able to explain how human beings came about—in a way that didn't necessarily require any God. So, still in the second grade, I started reading excerpts from Darwin's *Origin of Species*. The fact that Darwin believed in God was of little comfort. Through evolution theory, was it possible, however unlikely, that things even more complex than a piano could nonetheless have happened by mere accident?

My next visit with Uncle Tim happened that summer. I pulled him aside, and told him I was freaking out. "Let's reason about this, Ian," he said. "Could something as complicated as the human eye happen by natural selection alone? Darwin himself called that idea absurd! He's right, it *is absurd*."

Across the next couple of years, Uncle Tim took me under his wing. He gave me books, and each one took a battering ram to the fortress that the devil was trying so relentlessly to build in my mind. During his visits, Uncle Tim and I would go for treasure-hunting walks either in the woods or along the train tracks near Grampa's house. He helped me find a buffalo nickel and an old rare medicine bottle, and all while talking about God, life, and everything. During our hikes he would take the Bible out of his backpack and show me some fascinating passage.

"Think about what happened to this guy—what a life!" he said about "cool" Moses. "Imagine growing up in a palace as royalty, then finding out that you have the same heritage as the slaves, then leaving, and then having to go *back*. Look what this guy went through, and look what God used him to do. Wow!" About Saint Paul he said, "Check out this letter he wrote—while *in jail*. Whoa." Tim made it real. The Bible stories lost their religious veneer and became riveting accounts of real human lives, people who had true encounters with the living God.

For Uncle Tim, the enchantment of camping on a perfect summer night with your friends, the fiercely competitive fun of a Monopoly game, the usefulness of a utility knife, the quality of King Crimson's music, the glorious taste of pepperoni, and the coolness of Moses were not separate, isolated realities. To Tim, all reality was God's. For him it wasn't "first Jesus, then the fun". With Tim, Jesus *was* fun. Like my parents, Tim had a friendship with the Lord that wasn't fake, wasn't compartmentalized, and encompassed everything. If I were going to have a relationship with God, it had to be like that.

And right about the time when I would become convinced, an Uncle Tim visit would end. While I was around him, all of Tim's confident assurance about God and his love somehow transferred to me. It made the stark cold and dark of my doubting stand out all the more after each goodbye, like leaving the light and warmth of the fireplace and walking outside into the sting of a cold winter night. "But how can Uncle Tim be so sure? What if God doesn't exist? What if Jesus was insane? What if he was lying about who he was? How can Dad, Mom, Uncle Tim, and Nanie really know ... how can they *know* that they're not basing their lives around a fairy tale?" I would ask myself.

After every move toward faith, the enemy tried to push me back in the direction of despair. My reading of the Bible continued through these years, now alongside my reading of various scientists, both Christian and non-Christian. Oh how I wanted the Gospels to be real! As J. R. R. Tolkien once said, "There is no tale ever told that men would rather find was true."

I needed more input, so during another visit to see relatives, I turned to my great aunt. Auntie Jo-Jo was one of only a few Catholics in the family, and while she probably didn't know it, she was my favorite aunt. I was curious about her take on the God question, so I pulled her aside.

"Auntie Jo-Jo?"

"Yes, love," she answered.

"Do you believe in Jesus? Do you believe he was who he said he was, that he is Lord ... that he was truly God with us, that he is risen from the dead, that he was resurrected? Do you have a personal relationship with him? I mean, do you really believe this?"

"You're damn straight I do," she replied, in a precious and thick New Jersey accent.

I asked, "But how can you know for sure? How do you know God exists?"

She appeared confused and troubled by the question, as though the very thought of denying God's existence could be entertained only if there was at least some level of madness at play, possibly diagnosable. With a puzzled look on her face, she answered, "So what you're trying to say to me is that there's all this amazing stuff, but *maybe nobody made it*? Let me get this straight, there was this big explosion in outer space, and then you accidentally get love, and beautiful sunsets, and butterflies, and right and wrong, and flowers, and music, and people? What's wrong with you? Four seasons and crops, the right sunshine and air, sorrow and laughter, and oceans—all from an explosion? What the hell is your problem?!" I sat there. I remember blinking a couple of times, but saying nothing.

She wasn't done. "Of course somebody made it, and that somebody obviously made us free to choose," she continued. "But I just don't understand how someone couldn't choose him. How could you not choose him? God showed us who he is, and he died for us, because he loves us *that much*! He really loves us goofy people! How could you reject that? God introduces himself to the world, and he hangs on a cross for you. He went through that for you. And he forgives you so you can have life. How could you not love that? What the hell is wrong with you?"

I would call this harsh variety of evangelization an attempt at *conversion by concussion*, and I'm typically against it—with the sole exception of Auntie Jo-Jo. She made it work.

At twelve years old, I was on another woodland hike with Uncle Tim when he sat me down for a serious talk. He got the Bible out of his backpack. It was respectfully protected by a handkerchief, which Tim reverently unwrapped as though the Bible itself was the most prized of all his treasures. He opened up to Saint Paul's Letter to the Romans and read various parts to me.

There was no fake religiosity in Tim's recitation. These were the real writings, of a real man, who really lived—an eyewitness of the risen Jesus. I experienced the Holy Spirit moving through Saint Paul two thousand years ago, especially through the way in which Uncle Tim read his words. He read slowly. Every word mattered. Tim stripped the account of all its churchy dressing and I heard it clean.

"Nephew, I know you struggle with doubts about the Lord, and you aren't alone in that. But you have to make a decision. At this point, not making a decision is making one. You can't stay luke-warm. You can't stay on this fence.

"Listen to what Paul says, 'For since the creation of the world God's invisible qualities—his eternal power and divine nature—have been clearly seen, being understood from what has been made, so that men are without excuse' (Rom 1:20, NIV). Then here, he writes, 'But where sin increased, grace increased all the more, so that, just as sin reigned in death, so also grace might reign through righteousness to bring eternal life through Jesus Christ our Lord' (Rom 5:20–21, NIV). And finally, he says, 'Don't you know that all of us who were baptized into Christ Jesus were baptized into his death? We were therefore buried with him through baptism into death in order that, just as Christ was raised from the dead through the glory of the Father, we too may live a new life.... For the wages of sin is death, but the gift of God is eternal life in Christ Jesus our Lord' (Rom 5:20–21; 6:3–4, 23).

"Ian, would you like to be baptized a Christian?"

On July 25, 1986, Pastor Charles Rizzo baptized me, along with my two brothers and my two sisters, by full immersion in Grampa's pool. Unforgettable. For the next several months, I was on fire with faith. The enemy's inevitable counterattack was severe.

My seesaw-wrestling with doubt about the God question and all of its ramifications worked on me like emotional, psychological, and spiritual labor pains. The stress squeezes got more intense and closer together, as though the overall crisis was swelling toward some climactic moment. Whether that moment would be good, or not, remained to be seen. This time when my doubts returned, they took me to an unprecedented place of turmoil. It got so bad, that I remember renouncing my Christianity to God in prayer.

I cried out, "Are you there? Are you real? As of right now, I am no longer a Christian! Not because I don't want to be, but because I don't believe it. The gospel means nothing to me unless it's actual reality. It's either true, or it's not. And if it's not, then like Paul said to the Corinthians, 'Let us eat and drink, for tomorrow we die.' Everything hinges on this. Jesus, if you never defeated death, then it's all a temporary accident. If you did, then *you are the Lord.* How can I know if it's true? Were you a con artist? Were your apostles deceived? Were they liars? Did you deceive my family? Or were you telling the truth? Am I even talking to anybody right now? Did my baptism mean anything? *Can I trust you?* You let Paul see you. You let Thomas have proof; do you love me any less?"

I paused, took a deep breath, and then concluded, "As of right now, I am officially an agnostic. If you're really there and you can hear me, please help."

The year I was fourteen was the worst year of my life. It's a rough one for a lot of people, I think. In the eighth grade of Mount Pleasant Area Junior High School, I was a mess. I was a wreck—miserable, depressed, and still trying to hide the entire six-year struggle from my immediate family. I stared out the window of the school bus, wondering whether life was an accident. I looked at the lockers in a haze, wondering whether all of my learning that day would matter. I looked at my friendships through a blurry and despairing lens, questioning whether relationships with other people were only temporary things. Day after day, I would get home from school, go up to my bedroom, get into bed, and curl up in the fetal position with unbearable anxiety.

One afternoon, I was curled up in bed, looking at my bedroom dresser, when I simply couldn't take it anymore. I prayed, "God, if you exist, then I need to *touch the spiritual realm for myself,* in order to have faith. If you don't exist, then I'm talking to myself right now, and nobody's listening. Amen."

As people sometimes say, "Be careful what you pray for because you might just get it."

4

Be Careful What You Pray For

Have you ever looked at the world around you and surmised that it's crazy? Have you ever watched the news and concluded that this world has gone stark, raving mad? At the same time, have you noticed that the darkness "out there" also lurks within yourself? The realization is enough to lead a person to the brink of despair. But what about the beauty and the mystery of life? Have you not also thought that we must be meant for something good but that we are broken and in need of healing? If you answered yes to these questions, then you understand the turmoil I was experiencing as I lay curled up on my bed, crying out for answers. At fourteen years old, I was aware that something was terribly wrong with the world and with me. Was there anything or anyone capable of healing us all?

I noticed that most people had something in their lives that provided them with a form of worship. Maybe they didn't go to church but to rock concerts or sporting events, where they gathered with others, lifted their arms, sang songs, and sought to be part of something greater than themselves. But the adoration given to musicians, athletes, and even movie stars always struck me as quite silly. Famous talented people may deserve our admiration, but certainly not our worship. The idols of this world did not impress me.

Jesus did impress me, not that his purpose in coming was to make sure Ian felt impressed. In addition to the authority and authenticity of his words and actions, everything answered to him. The weather obeyed him. Sickness departed from him. The demons submitted to him. He had the power to forgive sins. He walked on water and turned water into wine; observably, the elements themselves served him. Apparently, there was something more powerful than death for even *it* was overcome by Jesus, as witnessed in the miraculous raising of Lazarus and in his own Resurrection. I don't know what unsettled me more: that Jesus possessed the power to raise Lazarus or that Jesus never used that power to procure his own earthly advancement. The Bible reports that onlookers were *amazed and afraid*. It's no wonder. It's as though the computer programmer had shown up, walking around in his own program and commanding it from the inside.

In reading about Jesus' life and encountering his words, I was always struck by how much he was not like other religious leaders. Others taught *what* could save me. Jesus said that *he* could save me. Others taught good news. Jesus said that he *himself* was the good news. Instead of flying the "be true to yourself" banner, Jesus preached that in *dying to self* one finds life. He didn't appeal to earthly precedents, but spoke with his own authority. He never seemed concerned with securing the favor of others. And he taught love for one's enemies— earthly princes definitely didn't come up with that one. I saw that Jesus goes beyond anything produced by men.

Jesus didn't advance a self-serving agenda; he was a humble servant who ultimately surrendered his life. With Jesus it wasn't some alleged discovery about the great mystery of reality. With Jesus, that mystery had shown up from the other side of the veil, to make itself known. This wasn't an alleged deity or divine essence that a human mind purportedly figured out; this was the great mystery showing up and *disclosing himself to us*. This revelation went way past any human discovery, however accurate, because it transcended what we can learn by our own abilities—this was the great mystery revealing to us who he is. With Jesus, it wasn't over-stated speculation about how reality works. On the contrary, reality answered to him.

Jesus asked the question: "Who do you say that I am?" I pictured him approaching me—with just the two of us there and nobody else—looking at me, then asking: *Ian, who do you say that I am?* Whenever I envisioned this encounter, I would feel something. I would begin to tremble. Yet I wanted more proof, and I prayed those fateful words asking to touch the spiritual realm.

One night, I was awakened by an invisible, sinister presence. Wide awake, I leaned forward a bit, looking up at the area in front of the door where I knew it was. I was fully aware that I was no longer alone, and that *something else* was there with me in my bedroom. I couldn't see it visibly, but I could tell where it was. It's as though it was cloaked, but its cloaked presence left a haziness just enough to be detectable. Its malevolence was palpable. It felt evil.

Hovering above me in front of the door, it spoke. The speech was not audible; it was *clearer* than that. This preternatural entity was able to plant messages directly into my mind. Its telepathic form of communication left no room for misunderstanding. I had never experienced anything like it before. The way in which it talked to me was distinctively different from the occurrence of my own thoughts. These were intrusive messages, transmitted with perfect clarity. It said, "I just woke you up. I am here. I intend you harm." I could sense its wickedness, its desire to hurt me, and its hatred for all people.

Then I asked it a question. This decision was stupid. I ought to have realized, especially from my reading of the Holy Scriptures, that you do not engage these things in conversation. Let's take a lesson from Eve: don't talk to snakes; it generally doesn't go well. Nevertheless, I was insatiably curious, so I asked, "Why can't I see you?"

It answered me, "I have the ability to travel invisible to your human eye, but I am here. I am about to show you. I want you to die."

The cloaked entity began moving toward me. By watching the hazy trace of its presence, I was able to follow its movement through the air. It moved away from the door into the middle of the room, still hovering above me in a singularly intimidating way. For several seconds, it moved back and forth in a manner that disturbingly resembled the motion of a dancing cobra. It soon moved directly above me, descended down on top of me, and then it gripped me *physically*. With this sudden exertion of tremendous force, it pushed me downward, with me lying on my back against the bed; and then it started crushing me to the point of suffocation. The demon pressed down onto my body, while forcibly locking my legs together, and trapping my arms against my sides. I tried desperately to break its grip, but no amount of human strength was going to make this thing budge. I got the distinct impression that it could have eviscerated me, but wanted me to suffer first. Slowly and decisively, its hold intensified. And the more tightly it squeezed, the harder it became for me to breathe. It was utterly terrifying.

At the same time, it was undeniably fascinating. I watched the physical compression that was being exerted by an invisible entity with intelligence and will, one that could communicate mentally, and I was amazed. This experience constituted a tangible contact with the spiritual realm. Like the Apostle Thomas, I got to touch it. I was now physically accessing an invisible reality with my natural senses. Now I knew that there was more to reality than meets the eye. Now I knew there was something on the other side of the veil. There *is* a bigger picture! But tragically, I wouldn't live to tell anybody. People would assume that I had died in my sleep. Nobody would know that I had been murdered.

I fought back with all my might, frantic to save my life, but these efforts were of no use. The only part of my body free from its grip was my head, so I moved it back and forth, in desperate hope that I might somehow loosen its hold—also to no avail. It was as though a boa constrictor had wrapped itself around its prey. At this point in the attack, I knew that I would soon lose the ability to inhale. So I used my last breath to call for help, but with so little wind in my lungs, my voice didn't carry. I was now suffocating in the painful and horrifying grip of the enemy's final squeeze, unable to breathe at all.

I thought to myself, "All right, if this thing exists, then so does God. And if this thing can communicate telepathically, then I am pretty sure God can hear my thoughts—which is very important, because I have no air left to say anything to him out loud." As I look back at my thought process, I cannot help but be amused that I spent this life-threatening moment analytically reasoning about God's capability to hear words that aren't spoken audibly. During periods of faith across my agnostic seesawing, I prayed every night, and it was always silent—but I had never given it a second thought. God's ability to hear my thoughts was simply not a topic that I had ever wondered about before getting suffocated by a specter. All of a sudden, this particular divine feature was of central importance. I knew what to pray.

"God, I know you're there, and I know you can hear me. I need your help. To the thing that is crushing me, I command you: Go away, in the name of Jesus."

At that name, the thing was gone! It released me instantly, fleeing in panic out of the house. I was no longer scared of it, but I was in awe of the one it feared. I sucked in a gulp of exquisite air, threw off the covers, and leaped out of bed. I raced down the hallway into my parents' room, woke them up, and told them everything that had just transpired.

"I always knew something like this was going to happen to you," Mom said.

"What? You knew that one day, dark, invisible, demonic assassins were going to come to your son in the night and try to kill him? Mom, that information goes on the list of 'stuff to tell Ian about'."

"Like you would have believed me?" she answered. "My little doubting Thomas, no, you needed to see this for yourself." And I knew she was right.

"How did you know that something like this would happen to me?" I asked.

"During my pregnancy with you," she began, "demonic forces tried to strangle me to death, and I knew that they were attempting to prevent you from being born. Evidently, there was already an anointing on your life that they were aware of, and threatened by. I got rid of them the same way you did."

"I don't know about all that. All I know is, I need Jesus," I said. So Dad and Mom prayed together with me at that moment, as I asked, "Christ Jesus, come into my heart, forgive my sins, and lead me to everlasting life." I continued on silently, "God, you heard me. You let me touch the spiritual realm for myself. Like the Apostle Thomas, I received the evidence I requested from you, and I cannot thank you enough. You're real! The grace of my baptism was real! Who do I say that you are? *You are Lord.* I permanently surrender my life to you. Thank you for what you went through for me to make it possible. Thank you for your mercy. Thank you for saving my soul. And thank you for literally saving my life. For the rest of all eternity, I belong to you. I am officially a Christian!"

No words can describe the love, hope, joy, and peace that washed over me in that sacred moment. That weekend, Mom and I drove out to New Jersey for a special weekend trip. I spent the whole weekend with Uncle Tim, and we went on the best hike yet.

Jesus is called the Alpha and the Omega, the beginning and the end, God with us, and the firstborn from among the dead. And no one can explain him away. Cutting through all religious agendas that attempt to tame him, and through all the futile efforts across history to discredit him, there he is. Not doctrines about him but he himself, with love, power, and life for whoever wants it. The invisible presence, the one that had communicated its hatred while attempting to crush me to death, *fled in terror* at the name of Jesus. Whatever that thing was, it answered to Jesus, which had made Jesus and his Resurrection real to me.

If you are reading this now, it's no accident. If you are struggling as I did, consider that God has heard you. If you hear your Shepherd's voice, you don't have to wait—you can give your heart to Jesus this very moment.

5

Getting a Hippie to Church

Leaving agnosticism to embrace Christ was a healing relief for me as well as an exciting adventure. My agnosticism had been marked by the anxiety of wondering whether my life was nothing more than a random accident, which would be snuffed out in the end by time. My personal relationship with Jesus Christ was in many ways the opposite. I hadn't solved the mystery of life, but I had met him and decided to follow him. Everything was different after that.

Once agnosticism was officially behind me, God didn't just encounter me intellectually. God is far more intimately concerned with and involved in our day-to-day lives than we could possibly imagine, as he would show me over and over (and over) again. He would also reveal his personality, including his sense of humor. He's hilarious. Freshly rescued from the anxious grips of skepticism, I was fed sweet, creamy spiritual milk. Loads of answered prayers, frequent miracles, and amazing graces filled my early walk. They say that if you want a prayer answered quickly, ask a newborn Christian to pray for you, because God is likely saturating the infant with an abundance of faith-building *yeses*. There is truth in that.

When God answers prayer, even seemingly insignificant favors can become for somebody an extremely important display of the Lord's reality and active presence. I experienced such a miracle with regard to my very first official girlfriend. In particular, within a year of my conversion, I had my first kiss. The kiss was not itself the miracle, although it felt like one at the time. Objectively speaking, it was the worst kiss of my life, but all I was thinking was, "Holy smokes, I'm kissing!" This relationship was a summer fling with a girl from Waldorf, Maryland. A few months later, I was in the ninth grade at Mount Pleasant High School. Ambition kept my mind on grades, but

young love gripped my heart. I wanted to see the girl again, badly.
So I silently asked God for a special favor. I prayed, "Lord, could
you score me a lift to Waldorf, Maryland, and back for the weekend,
so that I can kiss that girl again?" A moment later, I said farewell to
our friend Jim who had been visiting the family that Friday. As I said
goodbye, I learned that he was leaving for a weekend work trip. I
asked, "Where are you headed?"

"Waldorf, Maryland, just for the weekend. Wanna join me?" he
said.

Time stopped for an instant as I stood there bewildered and
astounded. Only minutes after praying, I had the ride I had requested.
It felt surreal.

Jim saw the astonished expression on my face and asked me
about it, and I told him about what I had prayed a couple minutes
earlier. Also a Christian, Jim said that he didn't believe in mere
coincidence and was thrilled to be a part of God's answer. My dad
and mom were both excited for me and told me to pack a bag. My
older brother, Sean, who had been watching this exchange, coined
the term "Ian luck".

Ecstatically I went on a fantastic road trip with Jim to Waldorf
that weekend. I surprised the girl, and was able to kiss her again. It
was our last kiss because her family moved overseas a few months
later. Aside from the puppy-love drama, I had experienced something far more important than early lessons in romance. I saw that
the Lord wasn't only real, he was also in a true relationship with me.
He heard my prayers, involved himself in my day-to-day affairs, and
was a ready help in times of trouble. My cross would come later, but
it looked as though God first wanted to show me his trustworthiness
and extraordinarily personal care.

In addition to special moments of God's intimacy, my newfound
commitment also required some regular, ongoing formation in
the faith. Yet my opportunities for Christian community occurred
through only a couple of infrequent channels. One of these was
during routine family trips to New Milford, New Jersey, where both
sets of grandparents lived. Upon every arrival, we would find my
maternal grandfather, "GingGing", waiting for us in a lawn chair
a couple of blocks away from his house—so that he could greet us
from the street in grand fashion. No matter the weather, he would

always be there to deliver his distinctive street-side salutation, and then he would chase our car the rest of the distance to his driveway. "There's no such thing as a GingGing, and I'm it," he would explain. It was some of the only physical exercise he got, so we visited as often as we could, which was twice per year: in the summer and at Christmastime.

This biannual trek to see relatives was nothing short of legendary for clan Murphy. From GingGing's greeting to Grampa's pool, from outings with Aunt Lori to spaghetti dinners at Auntie Jo-Jo's, from hiking with uncles to hanging out with our adopted cousins the Christiansens, we savored every enchanted moment. Whenever we stayed at our grandparents' houses during those celebrated July and December visits, I genuinely enjoyed going to church with Nanie and Uncle Tim—the Maranatha Church of the Nazarene in Paramus, New Jersey. The head pastor there, Charles Rizzo, was the minister who baptized me in Grampa's pool when I was twelve years old.

Pastor Rizzo, an old classmate of my parents from New Milford High School, had a dramatic and miraculous conversion to Christianity after a markedly rough past. Placing aside all their reservations about institutionalized Christianity, my parents never missed a chance to see Charlie. As he explained in his powerful testimony, he used to steal guitars for drug money. "I was pretty terrible back in high school," my dad would tell me, "but Charlie was too bad even for me."

Dad once showed me Charlie's ghastly photo in his old high school yearbook. I thought to myself, "If God can save that guy, then nobody is out of reach." And God more than saved him; the Lord unleashed a missionary powerhouse like Saint Paul. Charlie Rizzo was among the finest homilists I had ever heard. He was real. I absolutely loved his no-nonsense preaching style, and his sister Jan was an equally amazing teacher. Whenever we were in town, I would attend their Sunday morning service famished for Scripture study. And they would feed me a feast.

In addition, their church hosted a Friday service for Jewish Christians, which I attended with my Nanie. I also listened to recordings of sermons throughout the remainder of the year, by way of the Maranatha Church tape ministry. I was a sponge, and the Rizzos were the perfect instruments at the perfect time. The excitement of July vacation and the magic of Christmas blurred together with an enthusiasm for the house of God, but I got to be in that beautiful place just a couple weekends out of the whole year. And a sapling can't grow healthy if it's only watered once every six months.

Aside from New Jersey trips, my other infrequent avenue for experiencing Christian community was church camp every June. This particular camp was run by the Christian and Missionary Alliance denomination, which I met through the Leeper family—dairy farmers who lived a mile up the road from our house in Acme, Pennsylvania. The Leepers were the best neighbors, and they loved the Lord with all their hearts. I worked on their farm in the summer and felt like a member of their family. Their son, Bryan, was my age, and he was a good friend.

I was eleven years old when Bryan Leeper introduced me to the Christian and Missionary Alliance church camp in Edinboro, Pennsylvania, near Lake Erie. I went faithfully every summer for the next ten years—first as a camper, then eventually as a counselor, as soon as I became old enough. I even attended during my agnostic crisis, for the fun, for a girl named Amanda Crisp, and always in hopes of throwing more answers into my bottomless pit of spiritual questions.

I was a bit of a misfit at camp, because I wasn't part of the evangelical culture that had nurtured everybody else there. Planting someone with no church membership into a Christian and Missionary Alliance summer camp was a recipe for nonstop comedy. Like a Bob Marley song at a Puritan picnic, I didn't quite fit, but the situation would undoubtedly make for some good television. I imagine the Lord saying to me what Gandalf said to Bilbo: "This will be very good for you, and most amusing for me." One time at camp, the mischief came over me in the dinner line, while the minister was saying a blessing over the meal.

"Lord Jesus, we pray in your matchless name here today. Lord, we just want to thank you, we just want to praise you, we just want to extol your holy, matchless name," prayed the minister.

Filled with monkey business, but also honestly having no earthly clue what he was saying, I whispered to my friends Amanda and Mauré, "Why do they keep calling Jesus a mattress—apparently one with holes in it?"

"Ian, shut up," Amanda whispered firmly, punching my arm.

"I'm serious. They keep calling Jesus a mattress. Why?"

"Ian, knock it off."

The preacher went on, "We just want to thank you, and we just want to worship you, and just want to ask your blessing over this meal ..."

I asked, "And why do they keep saying the word 'just'? Technically, it doesn't make any sense. They obviously don't want 'just' to thank God because they *also* want to worship him and get a blessing out of him, too."

"Ian stop it," Mauré said, with a snicker cracking through. Now I had them.

"And Lord, we're just gathered here together on this beautiful day in your holy and matchless name," continued the long-winded preacher.

"He did it again, and I don't like it. Jesus isn't just a mattress," I said, peeking at Amanda, who was now laughing so hard that she was shaking yet trying not to burst out audibly.

Mauré explained, "He's saying 'matchless', not 'mattress'. Jesus is 'matchless', as in *unable to be matched*." She thought her explanation would make me be quiet, but it only encouraged me.

"Oh. But nobody says that. How could that possibly be authentic? Imagine me at home saying, 'Hey Mom, these Cheerios are matchless. I'm just gathered here, and my breakfast knows no equal.' Nobody talks like that."

"I'm going to kill you after this prayer," Amanda said.

"Well, that gives me 'til tomorrow," I retorted.

I think the community there found me refreshing. And I loved them like family. They preached at us for three hours a day, which for many people would be a week of hell. But I couldn't get enough of it. I showed up every June evidently starving to be fed spiritually, and I absorbed the refreshment as a dry garden welcomes the new rain. Even if they sometimes utilized goofy, off-putting jargon, they were talking about Jesus.

Every summer at church camp, I learned more about the God who saved me. I learned more about that mystery which is never solved, but with whom I have friendship. At camp, I learned about how God revealed himself to the world gradually, through relationships. I learned about the *covenants*! As I look back at the broken road that led me into the Church, I simply cannot fathom the love of God, who went out of his way to provide numerous lifelines of grace throughout my growing up.

Having anti-establishment Woodstock parents, church simply wasn't part of my life outside of New Jersey trips and summer camp. In fairness to my dad and mom, I knew full well that they would have taken me to a church every week if I had asked. But in a glorious battle between my hungry-for-Scripture spirit and my love-to-sleep-in flesh, the flesh won. Church was fun when Christmas was in the air, but sustained commitment was hard. In the end, God knew that the only way to get me into a church every week would be through a girlfriend.

After my Waldorf girl moved away, I quickly set my sights on a Mount Pleasant High School cheerleader named Marie. She didn't seem to see me in the romantic way, but I swung for the fence anyway, a real cheerleader being the ultimate prize. As I had told my father at the playground back when I was four years old, I was going to swing the highest and the fastest; this pursuit was no exception. My ambitions also led to my winning the election for student council vice president in the ninth grade. I ascended to the presidency when the president got detention, which suited my ego nicely.

It may not seem too far-fetched for the student council president to get the cheerleader, but I wasn't the popularity sort of officer. Rather, I was the nerd kind, whom the class elects because they actually want the work to get done, and cheerleaders were typically off the market for straight-A students. I was convinced the only reason that girl from Maryland had liked me was because she didn't go to my school, and thus had never associated me with the stigma of perfect report cards. But after months of nervous hint-dropping and romantical research through mutual friends, and after a failed courtship with a girl named Kristi, I finally asked the cheerleader Marie to be my girlfriend. To my elated surprise, she said yes. She also said that she had impatiently been waiting months for me to ask her. Guys can be oblivious sometimes.

In the tenth grade, I was elected class president, I won second place at the Pennsylvania Junior Academy of Science, I got the lead role in the high-school play, and I was selected to play the baritone horn at both county and regional band festivals. Mount Pleasant's marching band was my favorite pastime that year, and Marie and I were an iconic high-school couple. She also told me that she was a brand-new, born-again Christian. She made me join her Pentecostal church as well as her youth group. She made sure that I attended three church services every week. And many of our dates included reading and discussing the Bible together. God certainly knew what he was doing. In truth, if it had not been for Marie, I wonder if I would have fallen away from the faith altogether. While I was getting tossed about amidst the carnal delights of realized ambitions—success in academics, high-school politics, music, romance, and acting—my Christian commitment was grounded by a beautiful community of zealous Christians.

I resented attending three Pentecostal church services each week in my already busy life as an extracurricular junky and insatiable perfectionist, but I would do anything for Marie. To keep myself sane, I had to be important to those church people, too, so I became their organ player in the worship band. My multifaceted and not-entirely-benevolent motives aside, the truth and beauty of the hymns sunk in, and my love for music, and for making music with others, grew through that experience. Among my favorite experiences at church were the occasional Wednesday evening services in which the pastor would skip the sermon, and we would play music the entire time. The pastor played the electric bass as skillfully as my dad and my brother Sean. And the church band's electric guitar player could have made a living with his talent. I tried to keep up, watching the guitar player's hands to know what chords to play on the organ, and we had a total blast together, playing hymns in a way I never imagined they could be played.

Marie's dad was the youth minister, and between him, my growing friendship with the Lord, Marie's growing friendship with the Lord, and my parents' excitement for my Christian faith, a secure foundation was in place. Through the worship band at the Pentecostal church, three services a week for the next few years, and through recordings of Charlie and Jan Rizzo's talks, my childhood love of Scripture took permanent root.

6

I, Like Thomas

Through the eighth, ninth, and tenth grades, I developed an interest in Christian apologetics. When I first learned the word "apologetics", I didn't like it, because I thought it implied that I was apologizing for my faith in the sense of saying that I'm sorry for it. I was relieved to learn that the term meant *defense*. The field of Christian apologetics was a defense of the faith, which showcased evidence that substantiates Christianity. As a former agnostic, I was captivated by it.

Shortly following my conversion in the eighth grade, I talked to Pastor Charlie Rizzo as well as a counselor I knew from church camp about my previous agnosticism. Both of them introduced me to the same book to help bolster my newfound faith: *Evidence That Demands a Verdict* by Josh McDowell. I poured over the evidence for the historicity of the Scriptures, the reliability of the Gospel accounts, and the reasonability of faith, with a mind bent on absorbing as much as possible. Then I moved on to other names in Christian apologetics: C. S. Lewis, Paul Little, and Lee Strobel.

Researching the field of Christian apologetics was like exploring a mine glinting with riches everywhere. Among my favorite discoveries were the first-century Christian martyrs. These early Christians did not die for an idea they were convinced was true, as noble as that can be. They died claiming that they had seen with their own eyes the resurrected Jesus. They were *eyewitnesses of an event that took place in the course of human history*.

Saint Peter, shortly before his crucifixion, wrote about having watched Jesus' miraculous Transfiguration along with James and John. He explained that their accounts were *not* cunningly devised fables, but that they had witnessed the majesty of God. He talked about it as a fact. Peter was either telling a bold-faced lie or telling the truth. I found it very difficult, especially in light of Peter's own crucifixion, to accuse him of deception, because he was willing to be crucified upside-down for his faith in the Lord.

Familiarity can breed a sort of numbness to the claims of the New Testament, but to me the implication of the scriptural record was clear. If it was true, then God has truly shown up. The Nativity, the Transfiguration, the Resurrection, Christ's Ascension, and so on— all are presented as actual events that took place right in front of real people. Paul talked about the Resurrection as a commonly known fact, the way people talk about a presidential election. He was able to say, and I'm paraphrasing, "If you don't take my word for it, just ask any of the hundreds of other people who saw the risen Lord." I had to be honest with myself that people don't talk like that about a hoax. And people don't suffer and die for something which they know didn't really happen.

Christianity didn't sound like a fraud. One of the Christian Gospels was written by John, who followed Jesus from the start of his public ministry and was at the foot of the Cross when he died. Luke, another Gospel writer, was a medical doctor working as a historian to document the life of Christ and the growth of the early Church. Paul, who wrote many of the New Testament letters, had persecuted Christ's followers until a mystical encounter with the risen Lord that left him blind. Paul wrote some of his letters from prison, where he was suffering for his faith in Jesus. He eventually was executed for being a Christian. These were real people, and they suffered so that I could hear their testimony. I could doubt the Resurrection, but I couldn't doubt that they believed it really happened.

Some of the miracles of Jesus and the early Church were confirmed by non-Christian writings from that time. Reading them I was even more convinced of the trustworthiness of the Gospels. Although the difficulties of faith in Jesus are great, the absurdities of not believing in him seemed greater than ever.

Most of all, I had no way to account for Jesus himself unless the Gospels were true. Jesus was either the Son of God, a liar, or a nut. But Jesus' deeds, words, and miracles made no sense to me whatsoever coming from a liar, and they made no sense coming from a madman with a God-complex, either. The most sensible conclusion was also the most fearful: that Jesus was who he said he was, which would explain everything, including why an invisible spiritual entity would run away terrified at his name.

Even though I was no longer agnostic, I would occasionally experience doubts. I felt like the Apostle Thomas, who had witnessed the walking on water, the loaves and the fishes, and the raising of Lazarus with his own eyes, but still needed more "proof". I really like Thomas. I've heard him picked on for his doubts, by people quick to echo, "Blessed are those who have not seen, but still believe." Yes indeed, such people are blessed! Thankfully, there's room in heaven for me and Thomas too. He makes me feel understood and not alone in my spiritual struggles, and he shows me a God who meets people in their need. And God patiently continued to do just that, whenever doubts would resurface. God met me where I was, using apologetics as an effective instrument in growing my Christian faith.

After time, I came to understand that my notion of "proof" had been problematic all along. The idea of "proof" or "certainty" turned out to be merely another kind of faith: faith in my own way of thinking. As an agnostic, I thought that if I could see it and touch it with my five senses, then it was real; if not, then it didn't exist. If I didn't currently possess in my five senses a way to access the data, then I *concluded* that the data wasn't there. What a sweeping claim of blind faith I had been making.

I had been like a baby in utero saying, "I have searched and searched throughout this entire, known, dark, watery universe, and I have found nothing to persuade me of the existence of some alleged 'Mom'. It's going to take *proof* to persuade me that Mom really exists." In the end, I wasn't going to find God in my own thinking, like the unborn baby isn't going to find Mom inside the womb. God is bigger, and I would sometimes feel him pushing back against my feet when I started kicking.

In addition to strengthening my commitment to Jesus, the study of apologetics cultivated the ongoing conversion I needed. Formerly, in the desire to satisfy my criteria for "proof", I hoisted myself over reality, trying to understand and feel in control. I had faith—but it was in *myself.* My trust was in my own thought processes. But through studying apologetics, I could no longer presume such a self-sovereign posture toward reality. Instead I realized that I am dwarfed by the mystery of a transcendence that is bigger than I am. I located my security and significance less and less in my own cognition, and more and more in God's Word. My purpose wasn't to be found in my own thinking, but in another's, through a relationship. What I was able to discover wasn't as important as what had been revealed, or rather who had been revealed. *Having control* gave way to *being the beloved*. It was no longer about possessing the truth; it was about the truth possessing me.

The study of Christian apologetics filled me with childlike wonder, helped me when I doubted, strengthened my faith, and fostered ongoing conversion in my spirit. But perhaps the most significant layer of all to my profound enjoyment of the subject was that it became instrumental in my love of neighbor.

My heart broke for other skeptics out there who desired some proof. I empathized with their plight, and I sought out the seekers and invited them to come and see that the Lord is good. I told them my own testimony. I told them about miraculously answered prayers in my own life and in others' lives. I talked about the daily friendship I had with God. And I applied copious amounts of apologetics to the whole enterprise. I had a burden for atheists and agnostics, especially the ones who were really seeking and searching. I knew what it was like to grow up outside the sense of safety that a church environment can offer. I knew what it was like to ask the hard questions that many people felt they weren't allowed to ask. I knew what it was like to look around at the world and sense that something was very wrong with it, and that whatever the original plan, obviously something had gone horribly amiss. I knew what it was like to feel lost and meaningless, with no clue what the point of it all is.

As somebody who had formerly designated himself as a bona fide agnostic, I could meet agnostics where they were. I understood their questions and concerns firsthand. And I had found enough evidence in apologetics to justify for anyone the leap of faith in Christ.

7

Divine Set-ups

My first attempt at evangelization happened shortly after my conversion experience, with my eighth-grade science teacher, Mr. Mills. He was teaching Darwin's theory of evolution as an account of human origins, with no mention of the Creator. I understood firsthand what it felt like to wonder if I'm merely the accidental and temporary result of a giant explosion, and my spirit stirred with the desire to tell him about God. I decided to approach him after class. My heart pounded through the rest of that day's lesson. I started sweating. A swarm of butterflies took up residence in my stomach. I second-guessed my decision as my mind began detailing all of the righteous reasons for doing nothing. In the end, one simple question made the difference. I asked myself, "Do I love this person enough to make sure he knows that he matters?" And my answer was *yes*. My hands left fog marks on my desk when I finally peeled them off. It was one of the scariest things I ever did, but by the grace of God, I walked up to my teacher after class.

"Mr. Mills," I started, "you've been explaining human origins as if human life is an accident. I don't think it's an accident. I don't think we're just the result of mutations. I don't think *you're* just an accident. I believe Jesus loves you. Is it okay if I talk to you a little bit about this?"

With a smile as large as his heart, Mr. Mills responded, "You bet it is, I would love that! This is important, what class do you have next?"

"Just study hall," I said.

"Perfect," he said. "I have next period off. Here's a pass, give it to your study-hall teacher, and ... do you know where the teachers' lounge is?"

"Yes, by the office," I answered.

63

"That's right. Give your study-hall teacher this pass, and then meet me in the teachers' lounge," he said.

It may as well have been a private invitation to the Oval Office. The teachers' lounge, at least to this eighth-grader, was a place of power and secrecy. Usually forbidden to students, the teachers' lounge was a hallowed space where grownups swapped stories about us and determined our fate. And I was about to *go inside*.

Mr. Mills sat down in a big easy chair across from me, and we had a great talk together about the problems with, and the limits of, evolution theory. The other teachers there seemed to enjoy watching an engaged student with real interest, something I wouldn't understand fully until I became a teacher myself. In a fantastic conversation with Mr. Mills about the great mysteries of existence, he became less teacher-like and more fatherly. Then he said that he believed in God.

He explained, "Ian, *if* evolution is how we got here, then I think someone had to guide it. I don't think it could be an accident. Chance mutations don't account for the wonder in the world, God does. I believe in him. What really matters to me is that one of my students really cared about me. You wanted me to know that I'm not just an accident, and that I matter, and talking to me took guts."

Beyond putting me at ease, his words inspired me. I discovered that not only was this endeavor less difficult than I had feared, but that people enjoyed talking about the meaning of life. Most of all, I saw that people need to know that they are genuinely cared about.

Encouraged by my encounter with Mr. Mills, I decided to reach out to my social studies teacher, who was among the best teachers I have ever had. He also was teaching human origins according to evolution, while making no mention of the Almighty. When I said that I wanted to talk to him about it, he lit up with childlike joy.

After our conversation he said, "Ian, would you mind giving a talk to the whole class tomorrow about this? Your thoughts can contribute to our whole learning community. I know it's scary, but I know you can do it, and I think it's very important. What do you say?" (I am a teacher now because of that moment. God bless good teachers!)

"A classroom presentation?" I thought to myself. One-on-one conversations were scary enough; talking in front of the whole class would be terrifying. Furthermore, what would this talk do to my reputation among my classmates? My good grades had already put me in the nerd category. Giving a presentation that wasn't an assignment would make me look like a teacher's pet. But then I thought of my friends in that class. "They just heard that they might be nothing more than cosmic accidents. They need to hear that they don't have to be scared that they're accidents, because God is real and loves them. Do they mean enough to me that I would take the risk to tell them that their lives have meaning beyond survival of the fittest?" That night, I prepped my first official *talk*.

The next day in social studies class, the teacher opened with the announcement that I had an important message to deliver. I walked to the front, looked at my peers, and swallowed. I had everyone's attention and was sweating profusely. Then I thought about God, and why this opportunity mattered.

"Hey, thanks for hearing me out," I began. "I know that it can feel pretty scary to think about why we're here and what happens when we die. Anyway, the topic is really important to me, and I want to talk about some of the things we've been looking at in class.

"See, here in the *Origin of Species*, Charles Darwin admits that the human eye is too complex to have arrived strictly by way of natural selection," I explained. "In fact Darwin says that it would be 'absurd' to say that, but our textbook doesn't mention this."

I went on, "We see that this false missing link between apes and humans was actually built around the tooth of one extinct pig; this other fossil includes multiple fragments of bone from across a distance, so I guess whoever Lucy was she blew up. And this one turns out to have been the skull of one animal fused to the jawbone of a different animal to invent the skull of a missing link that never really lived. If these half-species between man and ape actually existed, why would they have to make *fake* fossils and *lie* to us? These scientific hoaxes like 'Piltdown Man' happened, but our textbook doesn't mention them. In fact, some of these confirmed frauds are actually still published in our textbook as science. Here's a picture in our textbook of an alleged half-bird, half-lizard missing link. Now let's talk for a minute about the issues with a half-bird, half-reptile lung— issues that, again, our book doesn't talk about."

I instructed them about early complexity in the fossil record. I talked about evidence of design in biology. I showed them faith-based assumptions within scientific methodology, but without using the term "methodology". I talked about what was missing from our textbooks.

"I can't tell you what to believe," I concluded. "That's your choice. With our textbook leaving out so much information, I wanted you to see this other research, so that you can make a more informed decision about what you believe. I hope that you might consider that God could actually be real. I believe in Jesus, and that he loves you. I really believe that. Thanks to our teacher for giving me this chance, and thanks again for listening guys." As I sat down, everybody was clapping.

My teacher was glowing. He thanked me then said, "Class, this wasn't just an example of critical thinking and extra information. This was, at the same time, a demonstration of freedom of speech and freedom of religion, a public exercise of our constitutional rights! Our veterans risked and gave their lives so that we can live in a country where *that* can happen."

After both classroom presentations, individuals started to approach me with their spiritual questions, and word spread that I had a message worth hearing. My unofficial ministry to skeptics was officially underway. Some classmates were sincerely interested in hearing about my faith. But others were belligerent, and one of these was my friend Ron.

Ron and I both played the baritone in the school band. He was brilliant and hysterically funny and a senior who could drive. Lucky for me, he took me under his wing. With Ron, it felt like I had a personal body guard, a mentor, and a driver all at the same time.

One Friday night, as Ron drove me home after our marching band's halftime show, he and I were enjoying one of our many comical talks until the conversation took a serious turn. I don't remember how the subject came up, but Ron started arguing with me against Christianity, and he got angry. I was already intimidated by his seniority, so his temper made me feel quite uncomfortable, nervous, and afraid. I prayed, "God, please give me the words."

The next thing out of my mouth was "Ron, see the steering wheel you're holding?"

"Yeah, what's that got to do with anything?" he said.

I answered, "Did somebody make it?"

"Of course somebody made it," he answered, frustrated.

"Have you seen the maker?"

The look on his face changed. "*No*," he admitted, thoughtfully.

"You believe in the creator of that steering wheel because it has grooves for the purpose of gripping, and it functions in coordination with other parts," I continued. "It was obviously designed. And you trust in the existence of its designer, even though you've never seen that person, because it's reasonable. Now think of your own body. Your ears are grooved to collect sound. You have a network of cardiovascular vessels . . ."

Eventually I concluded, "Ron, you just insisted that your body might be an accident. But then you professed faith in the creator of the steering wheel, which is much less complex than the human body."

Ron pulled over, stopped the car, and gripped the wheel as the color washed out of his face. After a long silence, he said, "I just converted, and I prayed. I am officially no longer an agnostic."

This first experience of witnessing a person's conversion was as encouraging as it was amazing. I am sometimes asked how many people I've converted, and the answer is zero, because I can't do that—only the Holy Spirit can do that. And it's incredible to watch the Lord move a soul to connect with him in prayer, and to recognize the love of God for the first time.

My first experience of rejection was also important for me. After a long discussion with another agnostic friend of mine, he said something I'll never forget: "You have successfully answered every one of my questions. In addition, I cannot answer any one of yours. Yet I remain a non-Christian."

"Why?" I asked him.

"Ian, your experience of spiritual warfare is truly amazing, and I know you're not crazy, and I know you're not lying to me," he said. "What happened to you indicates that there is invisible, spiritual reality, and in your case, it answered to the name of Jesus. I don't listen to that flippantly. I know what it means. And on top of what happened to you, logically speaking, human reason favors that I was indeed designed. And I may very well meet God, and have to account for my life. I choose to remain as I am because I want to be the god of my own life, and do whatever I currently feel like doing. I don't want to answer to somebody else. And I take full responsibility for my decision, including its consequences."

I saw that not only does the mind need to be persuaded, but also the heart needs to be awakened. I remembered Jesus' words about how a person could rise from the dead, and still some people wouldn't believe. When a man says that his mind is made up, what he really means is that his *heart* is made up. I also realized that as cold as my friend was, he was at least honest. God can work with that kind of authenticity.

In the eleventh grade, I was re-elected class president, played the baritone in the high-school band, and again got the lead role in the school play. My addiction to extracurricular activities extended to the county level as I became Mount Pleasant's representative to the Westmoreland County Student Forum, which convened monthly. I continued to attend the Pentecostal church thrice per week with Marie. And the time-honored traditions, like church camp in June, New Jersey trips to visit relatives, summer fishing in the nearby ponds, and our celebrated Easter-egg hunts, were all in play. All around, life was good.

Through all of it, God kept showing up with expressions of his extraordinarily personal care, sometimes in quite memorable fashion. One evening, at the request of the band director, I attended the girls' basketball home game. It was against an old rival, and Mount Pleasant wanted to boost our team's morale with an exceptionally large audience. Marie couldn't make it that night, but I was happy to sit in Mount Pleasant's gymnasium with the other members of the high-school band who had come to show their support. Our basketball players were truly outstanding, but no match for the rarest kind of superstar on the opposing team. She owned the court, and single-handedly annihilated Mount Pleasant's team.

During the game, members of the crowd, including some people sitting around me, began a mean-spirited chant that I won't repeat, naming the star athlete's jersey number. Not my proudest moment; I gave in to peer pressure and joined the jeering mob. I knew it was wrong, but in order to attain favor from those around me, I joined in anyway. I tried to take comfort in the fact that over a hundred people were committing the same sin I was.

Later that month I attended the Westmoreland County Student Forum. As I sat by myself waiting for the event to begin, a lovely girl showed up, sat next to me, and started talking to me. I was already spoken for, but her attention was exhilarating. She and I spent the whole morning ignoring the events on the stage and talking together.

"So what high school are you from?" she asked during lunch. "Are you class president?"

I responded, prioritizing my title over the location, "Yes, I'm the president of my class, at Mount Pleasant High School."

And that was the moment when the enchantment stopped. Her face fell. Her eyes filled up with tears. She quietly put down her fork.

"What is it?" I asked.

"Mount Pleasant, huh, I had a ... I had a bad experience there," she said.

I thought to myself, "It *can't* be, no, she *can't* be, the chances are *impossible*." I asked, "What high school are you from?"

"I'm the captain of our girls' basketball team," she answered, "and at our away game against Mount Pleasant, the audience started yelling lies about me. They named my jersey number, so that I would know that they meant me. It still hurts." The look on my face said everything.

"Were you there?" she asked.

"Yes, I was there."

She nodded back with understanding, and with forgiveness. I felt like I was looking into the face of the crucified Jesus, forgiving me from the Cross.

Sitting across the table from that girl, choking back my own tears, I told her I was sorry. Then I turned my heart heavenward and prayed silently, "Lord, you set me up. Don't ever stop setting me up. How can I tell friends and classmates to follow you, when I don't? Please forgive me."

Even after what that girl had been through, she still spent the remainder of the afternoon with me. We were getting along so well that in the back of my mind I was questioning my relationship with Marie. I knew that I would absolutely *not* be okay if Marie were enjoying the day with a guy she found charming, attractive, and Christ-like, wondering whether he would make a better boyfriend than I was. So why wasn't I following the Golden Rule, and being loyal to her the way I would want her to be loyal to me? I hid the incident from her, but I could not hide from the light it was shining on my duplicitous behavior.

8

You Can't Read That

I had more reasons to doubt my relationship with Marie than enjoying the day with another girl. I had been having reservations about the teaching at the Pentecostal church we attended. For example, it taught that if you did not possess the spiritual gift of speaking in tongues, then you had not yet been baptized in the Holy Spirit. One Sunday morning at Bible study, the pastor asked people to raise their hands if they could speak in tongues. Roughly two-thirds of the people proudly raised their hands high. Then the pastor asked the group that hadn't raised their hands, which included me, "What is wrong with the rest of you?!"

I had experienced gifts of the Holy Spirit, but speaking in different tongues was *not* among them, at least not in the way in which my church practiced it. I believed that the gifts of tongues and their interpretation were real; I simultaneously observed that they seemed to be among the easiest gifts to fake or mimic. My initial encounter with the gift of tongues was a disquieting experience. Back when I was five years old, we attended a charismatic church somewhere in western Pennsylvania at the invitation of some friends of the family. During their worship service, I heard grownups around me saying random syllables, and I thought that they sounded very silly. It sounded as though they were babbling and repeating the phrase "shock to take a bowtie" over and over again. Then during their children's church breakout session, our leader tried to train us, one syllable at a time, to speak in tongues. He wrote meaningless sounds on the chalkboard which he had us repeat. Even at five years of age, I found that strange. To survive the morning, I started intentionally speaking like the character Speedy Gonzales from Loony Tunes. The teacher thought I had the gift.

Peter and Paul both affirmed the reality of the spiritual gifts of tongues, and this was sufficient for me to believe in these gifts. Later, however, I learned that the Bible designates two different gifts regarding tongues. One gift refers to human languages, specifically to people hearing words in their own language even though the words had been spoken in another language. The other spiritual gift refers to people uttering languages not their own, which may include angelic speech. Since two different Greek terms both get translated into the same English word "tongues", some confusion has resulted. The Bible clarifies certain protocols for the appropriate exercise of such gifts—protocols which that particular church was not following.

Marie's church also ignored biblical wisdom for practicing spiritual gifts. Often during the worship services, multiple people would pray in tongues out loud, at the same time. The resulting sound of audible prayers in tongues, absent of interpretation, disintegrated into the sort of chaotic noise Saint Paul had warned against. And when our pastor publically shamed those of us who did not have the gift of tongues, he definitively missed the mark of mercy. Although I could forgive my pastor, I could not get past the contradiction between the New Testament teachings about tongues and the practices at this church.

The church also taught that all alcohol was "the devil's vomit". It explained Jesus' famous miracle at the Cana wedding as a case of some really delectable, nonalcoholic juice. Likewise, they explained Paul's instructions for Timothy to bring a little wine for his stomach as a reference to some tummy-warming, nonalcoholic juice. Juice is delicious, but I never knew any juice that helped people to forget their troubles for a while as described in the Proverbs: "Give strong drink to him who is perishing, and wine to those in bitter distress; let them drink and forget their poverty, and remember their misery no more" (31:6–7). The biblical text was undoubtedly referring to alcohol.

Troubled by these apparent contradictions between Pentecostal doctrine and biblical teaching, I asked the youth minister about them. It was a scary moment for me, especially because my youth minister was also Marie's father, and the typical response of church leaders to a person's questions was not an answer. Rather, the usual response to tough questions was for the minister to suggest in reply that the devil had deceived the person's wayward soul. I wasn't happy about the prospect of potentially being demonized by my girlfriend's dad, but

I really wanted an answer. He responded, "Yes Ian, that passage in Proverbs is obviously talking about alcohol. You see, those people, the ones in this particular verse, were lost beyond all hope, so the Lord is telling them that they may as well have some fun enjoying sin, before they burn forever in hell."

There were so many things wrong with his answer that I would need charts to explain them all. He contradicted everything he had ever taught me. I replied, "But sin is not a source of joy; it's slavery. And no one is ever 'beyond hope'. And it is not in God's will that any should perish. And the Lord would never, through inspired and inerrant Scripture, instruct people to commit sin." He then suggested that I had been deceived by the cunning of the devil.

Amidst awkward incidents and unsettling questions, I had to draw an important distinction between problems of *sin* versus problems of *doctrine*. Christianity is a hospital for the sick. So we shouldn't be surprised whenever the patients within the hospital, including ourselves, are symptomatic. Human folly is on display in every church, including the one I was attending with Marie. But sincere Christian love was on display too. Once at the Sunday evening service, a brave young teen stood up in front of the church crying. She confessed publically that she was sleeping with her boyfriend, was pregnant, needed Jesus, and needed us. The pastor embraced her, and the church rallied behind her to assure her that there is no condemnation for those in Christ Jesus. It was a beautiful night.

Another time, I needed to pray, and while kneeling at the prayer altar, Marie's dad joined me. When he prayed over me, I felt the presence of God galvanizing my faith. The fortification and the refreshment I experienced were real. That Pentecostal church created an atmosphere where such sweet and life-changing moments of grace could happen on a regular basis. How could I ever thank them for supplying my formation through those years, imbuing such a deep love for God? They were God's instrument, no doubt, and yet I could not be completely at peace with that congregation because of the doctrinal problems I was discovering.

I knew that other Protestant denominations held teachings different from the Pentecostals, and I knew that different Pentecostal sects were at odds with one another. Regularly in his sermons, our pastor would put down a nearby Pentecostal congregation that he derogatorily referred to as "the tin church". I never knew what the church's actual name was, but I had the clear sense that it was deemed by our pastor to be a house of deadly deception under the leadership of some false prophet. Reportedly, anyone who attended the *tin church* had fallen prey to the cunning of the devil. In the Bible, Saint Paul admonishes the Christian churches to "stop devouring one another", yet that's what our doctrinal differences were doing. I began asking myself how the same Holy Spirit could inspire different followers with contradictory information.

The various denominations seemed to have serious disagreements about every Christian doctrine. How and when to baptize, the gifts of the Holy Spirit, the nature of Communion, the question of eternal security, the relationship between grace, faith, and works, the place of justification, sanctification, and righteousness in the Christian life, and countless other doctrines were matters of serious and sometimes heated debates between the different denominations. Feeling troubled, I picked up a handbook of Protestant churches and was stunned to see over two hundred distinct denominations. Moreover, these various denominations were expressed across thirty thousand different individual churches with unique nuances and a host of doctrinal disagreements between them. The Bible says that there is "one body and one Spirit ... one hope ... one Lord, one faith, one baptism, one God and Father of us all, who is above all and through all and in all" (Eph 4:4–6). Through what I had become convinced was truly inspired and inerrant Scripture, the Lord calls his Church to strive to "preserve the unity of the spirit in the bond of peace." We are not supposed to divide. Rather, the Bible calls us to remain gentle and patient, "forebearing one another in love". It also calls us to speak the truth in love, but this is not an excuse for causing a quarrel, for "we are to grow up in every way into him who is the head, into Christ, from whom the whole body, joined and knit together by every joint with which it is supplied, when each part is working properly, makes bodily growth and upbuilds itself in love" (Eph 4:15–16). The Bible repeatedly calls believers to loving unity. It speaks of one body, one faith, and one baptism. It didn't talk about thirty thousand different bodies, faiths, and baptisms. How could I remain a part of a system of denominational fragmentation, when the Bible clearly calls for *unity* among Christ's followers?

During my junior year of high school, I experienced a spiritual struggle over the question of whether or not a Christian could "lose his salvation" (the question of eternal security). I trusted God. But I did not trust myself. The Ian I showed to those around me was a shinier fellow than the Ian who looked back at me in the mirror. If there was such a thing as sinning to the point of losing one's place in heaven, then I knew that I was capable of it. That scared the hell out of me.

My anxiety over the possibility of losing my salvation haunted me the same way my agnostic doubts had back in junior high. My pastor said that my name could indeed be *erased* from the Book of Life. But the Lutherans I knew assured me that it couldn't. I liked their answer better. But since they both couldn't be right, the opposing answers became as stressful as the question itself. The Christian and Missionary Alliance preacher told me that summer that my soul was safe. My girlfriend told me that it wasn't. Since eternity is a long time to burn, I became increasingly frustrated with the contradictory answers. And I was not content to quit on the question. I wanted the truth about my eternal destiny. I took no comfort in believing what I liked. I may like to believe that a million dollars are waiting for me on my bed, but that would be no comfort to me *unless it were the truth.*

Then one day I had an epiphany. "Wait a minute," I thought to myself, "just as Jesus had disciples, they too would have taken on their own students, especially since Jesus commissioned them to go out and make more disciples; and those students, the disciples of the original apostles, would have written stuff, too!" I was so excited about this realization that I remember leaping up from my seat to confirm my hypothesis. I raced from my bedroom to the phone and made a long-distance call to New Jersey, to the Maranatha Church of the Nazarene.

I kept on thinking about it. "This is huge. If the apostles' disciples wrote stuff down, and if those writings survived history as the Gospels did, by people copying them, and reading them, and spreading them around the Christian churches during the first centuries following the Resurrection, then I would have writings about the gospel teachings that were only one generation removed from the original eyewitness sources! Of course the early Christians would have copied and dispersed their work, because the apostles' disciples would have been important voices during Christianity's first years. I know it wouldn't carry the foundational authority that eyewitnesses rightly possess, but still, it would be so close to the source that it might help me discern what the earliest followers of the risen Christ believed about the doctrinal questions I have!" I was as excited as a kid on Christmas.

"Hello, this is Maranatha, Church of the Nazarene, how may I help you?" said the voice on the other end of the line.

"Hi, I have to be quick because it's long distance. Did the original disciples have disciples of their own, and did *those* people write stuff down? Like, did John have followers, and did they write about Christian teachings?" I asked excitedly.

"You shouldn't ask that," the person answered.

"But did they?" I repeated.

"That's a very dangerous question, and you really shouldn't ask that. If you want some good reading, check out C. S. Lewis," the person answered.

"I love Lewis. Just answer my question," I insisted.

"Well, yeah, you're right ..." the man admitted, hesitantly.

"I KNEW it!" I exclaimed. "Do we know their names? What was a name of one of John's disciples who wrote stuff down? I've got to start somewhere."

"Well, Polycarp, but you shouldn't read his work, or any of them. Stop asking about this," he said, sounding concerned for my salvation.

"What's the problem with it, is it not Christian writing?" I asked. "Did Polycarp start an early heretical cult or deny Christ to save his own skin or help Nero or something bad like that?"

"No, he was martyred, actually, just don't read it," he said.

"I'm going to need a reason, and even when you give it, I'm still going to read it anyway, so don't worry, the results won't be your fault," I assured him.

He replied, "Since it's so close to the original composers of the inspired text, it becomes too easy to read it like it's Scripture. *But it's not the Bible!*"

I answered, "Oh, I realize that. But just think how awesome it would be to read from somebody who knew the Apostle John personally! Wow! That's *cool*."

He answered, "You just shouldn't read it at all. Here, let me mail you some C. S. Lewis books."

I challenged him, "But C. S. Lewis also came *after* the original eye-witnesses, almost two thousand years after, so how come it's okay for people to read him, but not Polycarp, when neither one contributes to the Bible? C. S. Lewis isn't the Bible; how come I'm allowed to read him?"

At this point in our exchange, I felt annoyed and puzzled that he didn't share my enthusiasm. "The apostles' disciples could shed so much light on teachings, on personal growth, on church history ... I have never been more excited to read something since the Bible itself!" I affirmed.

"I'm sorry to hear that," he said, and then we said our goodbyes.

Bewildered by the whole conversation, I talked to the pastor at Marie's church that Sunday. He looked at me with a worried countenance and said, "Um, you shouldn't read that. Be careful Ian, the devil's crafty."

I wondered what on earth was going on with this inexplicable but common allergy. If Christians today wish to be as much like the original Christians as possible, then why not read what the original Christians wrote? The idea seemed simple enough. In fact, I felt cheated that nobody at any of my churches had ever told me about this dragon's hoard of treasure. I could actually read the writings of somebody who was personal friends with somebody who saw Jesus back from the dead with his own eyes—why did I have to figure this out for myself?

I asked one of the pastors I knew from my summer church camp about it. The minister replied cautiously, "Well, you need to be very careful here, Ian." I was stumped.

One day a package showed up in the mail from the Maranatha Church of the Nazarene in Paramus, New Jersey. I excitedly opened it to find a nice note, and a few C. S. Lewis books, which were all excellent. But the package didn't include any writings from the apostles' disciples—no Polycarp. When my dad asked me why the Nazarene church in New Jersey had mailed me a package of books, I let him know about my question.

"Did Jesus' apostles take on followers of their own, in obedience to the Lord's commission to go make disciples of others? And if so, did those people write stuff?" I asked.

A terrified look washed over my father's face, as if he were worried for my life. He replied with an intense sincerity, "Ian, those are very dangerous writings, they are not the Bible. Please trust the Nazarene Church, and read what they sent you."

"But what they sent me isn't the Bible, either," I said.

My dad didn't answer me but gazed at me with a look of concern until I said, "Okay."

It was a mystery why everybody was so frightened of these writings, but the fear got me and I stayed away from them. Ironic how the enemy uses fear to keep people away from what he's so afraid they'll see. Everybody's aversion spooked me for a while, but only for a while. My curiosity and excitement won out in the end, and one day I eventually read Polycarp. He sounded *Catholic*. "Maybe that's why everybody hates his writing so much," I thought to myself, "but this guy knew John—that's awesome!"

I felt stuck in my questions over doctrine and my unease over the division among the various Protestant denominations, but I did find one thing that all Protestants agree on—the papacy. Every Protestant denomination, by definition, rejects the pope's authority. So, in a sense, the pope is the single unifying element of all Christianity, Catholic and Protestant alike. As a result, the topic of *authority* became increasingly important to me. I sensed God was setting me up again.

9

Out of the Mouths of the Condemned

As I continued to witness my faith, I noticed the very different responses that the name of Jesus can elicit. When a follower of Confucianism heard the name of Jesus for the first time, her face lit up and she said, "Jesus, Jesus, Jesus ... it's so beautiful. I feel like I already know him, and I already love him. I just want to keep saying his name over and over again!" On the other hand, a stranger approached me and said, "If you mention the name of Jesus around me, I will kill you. Don't you utter it in my presence." On hearing the name of Jesus, some fall in love, kneel to his lordship, and follow. Others become hostile, as if something invisible but active in this world is threatened by Christ. Repeatedly, I saw Jesus' name illuminate the heart and draw out what's inside.

The only other thing that got a similar rise out of people was Catholicism. After the Bridegroom, the next most provocative thing is the Bride. As far as I was concerned, the Catholic Church was the enemy. Whenever Catholicism came up, I vehemently opposed it. I had nothing substantive to say, but I would glare. Whenever I heard mockery of Catholics, I shared in the derision of the Church.

My father loved Jesus, but he despised the Catholic Church. Based on some insidious Jack Chick tracts, which he would make us read and distribute, Dad called Catholicism *the Whore of Babylon*. I literally grew up hearing the Church called a whore. And he would refer to Catholics as *those cookie eaters*. That particular insult never worked for me. Whenever I heard the designation *cookie eater*, the phrase evoked images of cute little children eating Oreos, with chocolate crumbs all over their chubby, happy cheeks. Or I would envision the gluttonous Muppet, Cookie Monster. Nonetheless, Dad's loathing became my own.

The anti-Catholic sentiment was fairly common across my extended family, too. One of my favorite traditions during New Jersey trips was pulling an all-nighter with Nanie. Faithfully once per visit, she and I would stay awake all night catching up, snacking, playing cards, and swimming, and more than once these visits disintegrated into anti-Catholic gossip.

My grandfathers were Catholic, but most of my relatives were Protestants, several of whom had left Catholicism. Thus, we were all very surprised to hear that Uncle Tim had entered the Catholic Church. His fiancée, Stephanie, also converted, and the two of them were planning to have a Catholic wedding roughly a month prior to my high-school graduation. My father was beside himself, feeling confused, betrayed, furious, and worried about his children. During a game of cribbage, my dad gave me a stern warning.

"I know he is your uncle, and I know he is your godfather. I'm also aware of how much he has helped you in your own salvation," he began. "Ian, my little brother Timmy has been deceived by a lie. He is now in league with the upcoming Anti-Christ, and you need to pray for him! Make no mistake about it, if Tim deceives you—and don't you think for a second that it couldn't happen to you because Tim's smart, too, yet he was duped by Lucifer's masquerade—if he deceives you, and you partake in the idolatry of the Catholic Mass, then you will burn forever in the lake of fire prepared for the devil and his angels."

Then Dad gazed at me with those deeply caring and concerned eyes that he was able to make, and I said, "Okay."

Not long afterward, an English teacher I highly admired asked me to meet with him. Concerned that I wasn't being challenged enough, he invited me to attend, at no cost, advanced sessions under his personal tutelage. We would discuss some extra reading, beginning with the full-length version of Homer's *Iliad*. I dreaded the extra homework, but the special treatment made me feel special. I could suffer a little extra work in exchange for elevated status, but I absolutely could not stomach any risk to my first-place class rank. Precariously tied with my friend Dora, one little A- could drop me to the position of salutatorian. So I agreed to the extra work provided it wouldn't hurt my grade.

He replied, "So you'll accept the recognition, but you don't want the risk? If you take on extra responsibility and the appropriate honor that goes with it, then I believe that you ought also to adopt the corresponding level of accountability. If you accept my offer, your grade could be different."

"Then as much as I would like to, I cannot accept this arrangement. Without your assurance that my grade won't drop, I can't do it," I insisted.

"Ian, your class rank has become an idol for you, and it's hurting you. But I will work with whatever you're willing to give me. Your grade won't drop," he replied, handing me the *Iliad*. "You are now officially doing homework that's not for a grade, and that much is indeed a good step for you right now."

This teacher impressed me on numerous levels. He possessed a strength of character that transcended intellect or title. It was *solid*, and I desired it. He made me aware that recognition still mattered more to me than virtue. I thought to myself, "In just a short meeting, important truths about my priorities came to light. I am better aware of where I am spiritually, and where I fall short. He's right. There is another god in my heart, and while it only steals from me, *I still serve it*. He identified my idol. How did he do that? Who is this man?"

Thankfully, Homer's skill with words had me hooked, and the *Iliad* was an enjoyable read even though it was extra homework. Another English teacher on the faculty heard that I was reading it. Aware of my affinity for addressing classrooms, she invited me to teach the epic poem to her ninth-graders, under her supervision. I enjoyed that experience very much.

My tutor was excited to hear about my teaching opportunity in his colleague's classroom. For my next task, he invited me to employ my love of the theater by choosing a character from Shakespeare and, in costume, performing for another class he taught. After that, he asked me to read *The Brothers Karamazov*. My assignment was to identify an argument against Christianity embedded in the narrative and then locate the flaw in the argument.

The teacher asked me about my relationship with Marie. Relieved to have somebody to talk to about my questions and doubts, I opened up to him about some of my concerns about the Pentecostal faith.

"I had always thought that your Christianity was compatible with Marie's, at least you made it appear to be," he observed.

He was brilliant and wise, and he was also humble. He could see through me, affirming the best while indicating where I was missing out. For example, he noticed that I lacked a balanced schedule and that I hadn't been getting enough sleep. He wanted me to be my best self.

I was so surprised when I discovered that this man was Catholic. "Well that doesn't make any sense," I thought, "but I suppose that even a poor musician can play correct notes by accident on occasion." Despite the notion that my English teacher was in league with the imminent reign of the Anti-Christ, his lessons in integrity stayed with me.

I had another favorite influential teacher. This man taught history and social studies. He had a great sense of humor and the air of a no-nonsense New Yorker who knows what *real pizza* tastes like. He challenged our assumptions and made us think seriously about the messages we were absorbing from the culture around us, and I respected him for it.

Once he challenged the notion that individuals can be whatever they choose to be. He explained that talents are distributed across people the way varying functions are distributed among the different organs of the human body.

"We all need each other," he said passionately. "When you aspire to do only what makes you feel good about yourself, we all miss out on what you were uniquely and specially wired to be. And you miss out, too, on the vocation that will make you the most happy. If anybody wishes to challenge me, I welcome it, because it is important to me that you think about your gifts, think about how you are a blessing to human society, and think about your responsibility to your fellow human beings."

"I challenge you!" shouted a fiery Amy.

"I welcome it," he said.

Amy argued, "My friend is handicapped, and he wants to be a star quarterback in the NFL. He can be! He can be whatever he personally chooses to be!"

"No he can't," answered the teacher.

"Yes he can, he can be a superstar quarterback!" she shouted back.

The teacher answered calmly, "Not without the athletic ability that the post requires."

The student answered back, "Anything is possible for us."

He answered kindly, "No, it isn't. We are not omnipotent."

"Do you believe that God could heal my friend?" she asked him.

"Personally, yes I do," he said. "With God, nothing is impossible. Barring such a miracle, maybe your friend could consider the possibility that God has placed a higher calling upon his life than athletic celebrity. Since you asked me, that is what I believe."

I was captivated throughout that exchange and so were many others.

On more than one occasion this teacher challenged moral assertions based strictly on feelings. He explained that emotions by themselves can be misleading, and he required his students to provide sound reasons for their statements.

This teacher enforced a strict policy against tardiness. Across all of his history and social studies courses, everybody knew the penalty for showing up late. Specifically, the guilty student had to handwrite the current chapter of our textbook in order to square the debt of justice. One day, with three minutes between bells, I took the risk and bolted off for a locker run. I almost made it, but was exactly eight seconds late. When I arrived, my teacher was standing outside the classroom, leaning against the wall, wearing the grin of a man who collects student excuses as a personal hobby.

"Come on in," he said.

I took my seat as all my classmates stared at me.

"All right," he said, "I gotta hear it. What's your excuse for being late?"

I examined my conscience and realized that, even if I had made it back on time, respect for my teacher was not a thing one should place at risk. I thought about what I was learning from my English teacher and how I desired a virtuous character, not just shallow recognition. I answered, "There's no excuse. I made a bad decision. It was disrespectful, and I'm accountable."

I could tell that something serious was going through my teacher's head, but he provided no clue of what it was exactly.

"Write out chapter four by hand and give it to me tomorrow," he said.

"Yes, sir," I answered.

Chapter four was the lengthiest chapter out of that entire textbook. I know because I checked. But in hindsight, I didn't need to check. Of course it was. I finished at about 10:00 that night, shaking my cramped hand and thinking to myself, "I see why accountability is something that people might be tempted to dodge." But while my hand ached, something incredible was happening within me. My conscience was clean, and the integrity of my behavior made me feel like my true self. *Virtue* made me feel more human, I realized, than *recognition*. The approval of other people was *not* essential to what it means to be a person. Solidity of character was.

"Lord," I prayed, "I am learning more about you from my high-school teachers than from my pastor. When I go to these teachers at Mount Pleasant, I discover who I really am. I'm seeing what it means to die to self, wash feet, love you, love others, live free, and be a new creation. But then when I go to your house of worship, I hear about how that crafty devil deceived everyone at some nearby tin church. Dad says Tim's going to hell. But Pastor says Dad's going to hell, for drinking the devil's vomit with dinner. Whether or not I'm going to hell depends on which denomination I ask. Honestly Lord, I wish I could go to my two favorite high-school teachers every Sunday morning instead."

The next day at Mount Pleasant, I got to class early.

"You owe me a chapter," said my teacher.

"Yes, sir," I answered, delivering my handwritten copy of chapter four. It was thick.

"Is this all of it?" he asked.

"Every word verbatim; I'm sorry for what I did."

He smiled at me and said, "You are forgiven."

Then in his class lecture, he presented the way in which I handled the situation as an example of integrity, explaining how I had ministered hope and refreshment to his tired heart.

"Who is this guy?" I thought. In my curiosity I asked around, and I discovered that he was a Catholic.

"Not again!" I thought. "This makes no sense. It's one thing for a poor musician to hit the right note on accident sometimes. It's quite another when the poorest musicians are the ones who consistently play the symphony the best. How come the servants of the Anti-Christ, the ones who are destined for a never-ending eternity of anguish in a fire prepared for the father of all liars, are the ones bringing me the closest to Jesus Christ? Why would the serpent have his deceived puppets doing *that*?"

Back at home, I was comforted by the sounds of a wise, soothing, and motherly voice echoing throughout the upstairs of our house. It was one of my mother's best friends, Marilyn (Maggie) Prever. My mother was listening to one of her cassettes, and from my bedroom I soaked up every edifying word.

While gathering laundry, my mom found me listening. She said, "Instead of writing letters to each other, Maggie and I talk to each other this way. She says really good stuff, doesn't she?"

"Yes, she sounds like a strong believer," I noted.

"Oh, she is. She converted to Catholicism out of Judaism, accepting Jesus as the Christ who God promised to send to the world, the fulfillment of the Old Testament. You know Ian, it's funny, but the most mature Christians I know are Catholic."

Uncle Tim, Maggie Prever, my favorite teachers—all of the most advanced teaching was coming to me from the mouths of the condemned.

10

For Such a Time as This

Anxieties surrounding my relationship with Marie as well as my doctrinal questions about Christianity continued to gnaw at my conscience throughout my senior year at Mount Pleasant High School, but I distracted myself with an overload of extracurricular activities and Advanced Placement courses. I continued attending church with Marie faithfully, and now licensed to drive, I started bringing my little sister and brother, Shaylyn and Jesse, along with me to the services.

In the summer preceding my senior year, instead of visiting my relatives in New Jersey, I attended the Pennsylvania Governor's School for International Studies. During five unforgettable weeks held at the University of Pittsburgh, I performed comedy sketches as a character I invented called the Newsman. Through the generosity of the program's funding sources, we toured museums, met with leaders of the World Bank, and studied culture, religion, and political systems from around the globe. The Japanese language class was my favorite. The experience was all-around wonderful—until a group of people started mocking the name of Jesus.

To provide a virtual experience of international diplomacy, the Governor's School utilized a software package whose acronym was GSIS. Some people started calling it "Jesus", and the joke spread like a computer virus. It started with people saying that it was time to be with Jesus, that Jesus has things to teach us, and other puns like that. After a while, the jokes included mockery and even blasphemy. After my conversion experience, the misuse of Jesus' name always hit me in the gut. They were making fun of the one who had saved my life. I understood that I wasn't perfect, and I understood that not everybody had personal encounters that showed them in a tangible way that Jesus is Lord. But I *did* have such an encounter, and I felt a burden to put a stop to the widespread belittling of Jesus' name.

At one of our largest conferences at the university that month, all the students and professors were present along with other dignitaries from the city of Pittsburgh. At the close of the meeting, the president of the organization addressed some basic matters of housekeeping and scheduling. "Oh, and of course be sure to spend plenty of time with Jesus this week," she said, laughing at her own joke. So much for the religious respect and tolerance they were preaching in class. Apparently, respect and tolerance applied to everybody *except* Christians, who were alone subject to public ridicule. I raised my hand.

"Yes, Ian, does our resident newsman have something to add?" she asked.

I answered loud enough for my voice to carry across the large auditorium, "I don't appreciate our GSIS software being referred to as 'Jesus'. I mean no disrespect to you, but it is not appropriate to belittle the name of Jesus openly like that."

She responded, "I don't know what you are talking about, I am merely sounding out the letters of the acronym."

I couldn't believe she tried to play it that way. Nobody was merely sounding out the letters of an acronym. In truth, they were pronouncing the letter "g" by itself, and then adding the sound "sis" to sound like Jesus. Did I really have to explain that?

I prayed silently for wisdom, and then I answered, "You know what you're doing."

A long, awkward hush fell over the room. Finally she responded, "From now on, nobody is allowed to call the software 'Jesus'. Now we all have to pronounce each letter, calling it 'G,' 'S,' 'I,' 'S.' Because of Ian, nobody is allowed to call it 'Jesus' anymore. Does that make you happy?"

"Thank you," I replied.

I heard the audible groans of annoyance with me, saw hundreds of heads shake and eyes roll in contempt. But several students and professors approached me privately afterward, to express their appreciation for what I had done. The history teacher was particularly grateful, because the bigotry had been bothering her, too.

Several days later the president required every student to participate in various religious rituals, including a Voodoo ceremony, a

Hindu meditation, and a séance with dead ancestor spirits. When I refused to do these activities, the president explained that she wished to broaden my mind religiously. She had publically made a joke out of my faith convictions, and her announcement that *because of Ian, nobody is allowed to call it 'Jesus' anymore* had singled me out for group disdain; according to her, I was the one who required tolerance training.

She arranged a meeting between me and a Hindu priest and assigned me an essay in which I was to justify my refusal to pray to other gods. In the essay I attempted to explain the bigotry and the violence of mandating prayer, mocking a particular religion, and singling out its practitioner with public humiliation and a punishment essay. Beyond being unconstitutional, it was unethical. I wrote that I was happy to attend our religion classes and learn as much about all of God's children as possible, in order to understand their beliefs and practices better. Even when I disagree with another person's take on reality, I wrote, as a Christian I believe that God created that person in his image and likeness and that he can therefore teach me something about God. Finally, I argued that, while we may be required to attend class, it is illegal to require participation in religious practices. She would never *require* all students, regardless their religion, to pray the Our Father—or else do extra homework. Yet I was required to say Voodoo prayers and then punished for my refusal to do so.

While I disagreed with her giving me the punitive assignment, I saw it as a ministry opportunity. It may sound strange, but I really liked this woman. Aside from her mistreatment of me, I genuinely enjoyed her personality. In a wonderful and humble moment, she told me that she appreciated my convictions and my ability to articulate them in dialogue. She admitted that I really made her think. That essay took hours, but it was worth it.

My meeting with the Hindu priest, on the other hand, lasted only a few minutes. Wearing colorful robes, the man walked up to me to introduce himself. "Hello, young man. I understand that you are a Christian. I am a Hindu priest. While I have a particular devotion to the god Vishnu, I honor all the gods, *including yours*," he opened.

I didn't feel respected by that introduction. From his words, body language, and tone of voice, I felt as though he was hoisting himself above me with a more enlightened and inclusive religion than my own. He had also just embarrassed himself by advertising how little he understood my faith, for the God who said that *you shall have no other gods before me* would not be "honored" by being listed alongside Vishnu as an equal.

He continued, "You see, as a Hindu, I believe that there are many paths to one summit, and that every path is valid. I would therefore *never* call another person's belief *wrong*."

I prayed silently, and then I replied, "Jesus said, 'I am the way, the truth, and the life, and no one comes to the Father but by me.' And I believe him."

The Hindu priest became observably flustered then interjected, "No, that is wrong! That belief is wrong!"

I replied, "You just told me that you would never call another person's belief *wrong*."

His facial expression changed from flustered to stunned. He hit his forehead with his hand. He forcefully ran his fingers through his hair. "You're right," he stuttered. "My ... my God, you're right." Then he turned briskly away.

I called after him, "Sir, I am happy to talk with you more about all of this, please."

Without stopping, he muttered, "No ..."

With the sincere interest of a person who would one day become a university professor of world religions, I wanted to learn more about his beliefs and practices. And I wanted the chance to explain to him that I believe heaven will include multitudes of people who didn't profess Christianity during their time on earth, especially in light of Jesus' remark that whatever we do for the least of these, we do for him. I wanted to tell him that I totally understand if he had a bad impression of Christianity due to bad experiences with Christians who had perhaps been less than respectful to him.

Sadly, I never got to say any of that. Again, so much for *tolerance!* ("You keep using that word. I do not think it means what you think it means.") The organization president, who had watched the brief exchange, stood there silent. I looked to her for guidance, but she said nothing. She didn't appear angry; she seemed to be trembling. Something powerful had happened, and I believe she felt it.

In early August 1992, the Governor's School had reached its end. But the rising intensity of my unofficial apostolate followed me into the beginning of my senior year at Mount Pleasant later that same month. In particular, our high school invited career counselors to speak to the seniors during their social studies classes, in order to help prepare everyone for the life-steps following graduation. During her visit to my class, the career counselor opened with an ice-breaker exercise to get us thinking about our futures.

"I would like everybody to pull out a piece of paper, and on this piece of paper, please number one through five," she began.

We all did as she instructed, waiting with baited breath to discover what five items we would be asked to list.

She continued, "I want you to stretch your minds, and imagine that you have the ability to throw a party, a party of epic proportions. At your party, you get to hang out with five individuals of your choosing, no matter who they are. The only catch is that they have to be dead. They can be from any time period, but they can no longer be living. Go ahead, the less time you think about it, the better this exercise works."

After providing a moment for the class to finish, she looked around the room then called on me.

"You, you there ..." she said.

I asked, "Do you mean me?"

"Yes, what is your name?" she questioned.

"Ian."

"Ian, please read your list out loud to the whole class," she requested.

"The Apostle John, the Apostle Paul, Gandhi, Socrates, and Milton," I read.

The woman locked eyes with mine and glared at me as if I were a freak. Her face conveyed a special mixture of angry eyes and a condescending smirk. Then she chuckled. Eventually she spoke.

"Well, yours would certainly be a religious and intellectual party," she announced to the class in a patronizing tone of voice. She added, "I'm surprised that you didn't put Jesus on your list!"

"You said they had to be dead," I answered.

At that point, her glare became fierce. She shouted, "Somebody else! You, read your list," while pointing to one of my classmates. He proceeded to list five dead athletes.

"Thank you," she exclaimed, "that is a normal answer." Then she proceeded to tell the class that most dreams don't come true, but that we might plan for careers in sports medicine, so that at least we could be close to professional athletes someday. I don't know who dumped vinegar in this woman's cornflakes that morning, but it seemed to me that she sorely needed a hug.

During the fall of my senior year I applied to Carnegie Mellon University (CMU) in Pittsburgh, Pennsylvania. I thought my application was so amazing that my acceptance was a foregone conclusion. I was therefore devastated when I read the CMU rejection letter and realized that the admissions committee was not as impressed with me as I had been. Fortunately, I learned soon afterward that I was the co-valedictorian of my high school.

At high-school graduation, that special opportunity to talk about the gospel, which I have already described, was a defining moment for me. It rendered meaningful many of the trials of my life until that point. Through the attempted censorship of my commencement address and the variety of events and experiences that followed, I observed how my unique road to God had landed me in a position to tell people about Jesus. I felt like Esther from the Old Testament, who, when given the opportunity to defend her people from annihilation, said that her entire life had been *for such a time as this.*

Shortly after my high-school graduation, I received a personal phone call from one of the deans at CMU. "Ian, I followed your story on the news, and I am impressed," he said. "You remained poised and well-spoken throughout an exceptional affair. Your boldness epitomizes the spirit of Carnegie Mellon University. I pulled some strings, and if you'll still have us, there is a seat in the program waiting for you this fall semester," he said.

"Thank you, sir!" I exclaimed. "I can't thank you enough! I will spend the next four years at your institution making sure that you never regret this decision."

True to my word, I graduated rank one in my college at CMU four years later.

11

Prayer 101

After the intensity of the media blitz surrounding my graduation and the relief of having secured admission at CMU, our annual summer trip to New Jersey provided welcome refreshment. A newly-wed Uncle Tim still made time for glorious hikes along the train tracks of New Milford. Nanie and I pulled an all-nighter catching up on life and gossiping about Catholics, especially Tim. Attendance at the Maranatha Church of the Nazarene was extra special that July because the church had followed the news story about my commencement speech, and Charlie mentioned me in his sermon. And at eighteen years of age, I had just as much fun playing "dive for quarters" in Grampa's pool as I did back when I was six.

Another favorite tradition of mine during New Jersey trips was our visit with Bob and Amy, two of my parents' best friends from high school. They still looked exactly like their yearbook photos. Bob is the living definition of "boisterous", with his outrageous sense of humor and his brash, somewhat threatening presence that intimidated those who prided themselves on propriety.

During a barbecue at Bob and Amy's house, Bob said, "Hey Ian, get over here and sit down with me for a minute."

Holding up a copy of a newspaper with my photo on the front page, he said, "Look at this guy ... THIS GUY! Damn straight, it's a free country, way to go!" He continued, "I gotta say that I personally think Jesus is a crock of b. s., but this is my land, this is my property, and this is my house. And it's my constitutional liberty to say it at the top of my lungs: JESUS IS A CROCK!" I had observed before this that grownup men sometimes like to drink a couple beers and then talk about their territory.

"What I'm saying is that we're free here in America, and you took a stand for that. I don't believe in Jesus, but I *do* believe in freedom of speech and freedom of religion. You did something so important for our country, and I'm proud of you. You're my hero!" he said, locking me in a half nelson, and giving me head-noogies that pulled out a couple strands of my hair. Then he offered a toast, and made me drink an under-aged sip of beer with him. Of course, I conveniently failed to mention to my girlfriend upon returning home that I had consumed the devil's vomit while on vacation—and that I thought it tasted delicious.

Later that summer, my older brother, Sean, pulled me aside for a loving and life-changing heart-to-heart talk about my relationship with Marie. I talked to him about my doctrinal disputes with the Pentecostal church, and the resulting incompatibility issues that these disputes were yielding in my courtship.

"Yes, that's real, but there's a bigger problem than that. You're lying to her," he said.

"What do you mean?" I asked, already knowing what he meant, and that he was right.

"You know what I mean. I'm not talking about *being a Roman to the Romans*. I'm not talking about emphasizing points of commonality. I'm not talking about the wisdom of only revealing certain intimate secrets in their appropriate time to the appropriate people. What I'm talking about are bold-faced lies! You are intentionally misrepresenting yourself. You are deceiving her. It's hurting you, her, and your relationship."

My immediate response was to stare at his purple, fluffy carpet.

"Do you sometimes think that swear words are *funny*?" Sean asked.

I started to answer, "Well in the Bible—"

"Stop. Just stop. I'm not talking about doctrinal issues, I'm talking about lying," Sean rightly interrupted. "Do you?"

"Yes, sometimes I think swear words are funny," I admitted.

"Okay. Does Marie know that about you?"

"No," I answered.

"Did you drink some beer with Bob?" he asked.

"It was just a sip—"

"Stop," he interjected.

"Well in the Bible—"

"Stop. Did you?" he persisted.

"But Marie—"

"Did you?"

"Yes," I answered.

"Okay. Did you enjoy it?" he asked.

"Yes," I said.

"Do you believe that you ingested Satan's puke, to your own eternal detriment, by swallowing that sip of beer?" asked Sean.

"No, I don't," I said.

"Okay. Does Marie know that about you?" he asked.

"No, she sure doesn't. I tell her that I'm against drinking because it's what she wants to hear," I confessed.

"Right. Now you and I can both agree that she's wrong about the beer, but can we both also agree that you're wrong for lying to her? After years of dating, honestly, do you wish you could kiss her more than she allows?" he continued.

"Yes, and I lie about that, too," I said. "One time, I even told her that the devil was *crafty*, only because it would make me sound good to say it. I can't stand the word 'crafty'. I wanted to wash my mouth out with soap afterward."

"Right. Ian, do you love Marie enough to be straight with her about *what she's into* by being with you? This deception doesn't love her, it serves you. It's selfish, and isn't that an actual sin, according to the Bible? Isn't the devil defined as the father of deception? If you were straight with Marie about what she's into here, and she was truly free to choose you as you are, and *then* the two of you decided to break up due to incompatibility, I would support that! And if you were straight with her, and *then* decided to work through your differences, I would support that, too. But you and I do *not* do fake. We've always had a built-in alarm system for it. And I can't handle watching what this is doing to you. Because I believe in Jesus, too, I had to talk to you about this."

I think because of his extraordinary (and endearing) allergy to all things 'churchy', Sean spoke of his faith less than any other Christian I knew. But whenever he did, it was the most important to hear. That life-changing conversation encouraged me to start being straight with Marie about who I really was, and those conversations with her *didn't* go well. The freshman year at our respective colleges meant the slow, painful, but ultimately healthy disintegration of our romance. As my younger brother, Jesse, has said so well, "It's not the last straw that breaks the camel's back; it's the last mile." While our ultimate break-up was emotionally charged with some not-so-benevolent moments for each of us, Marie and I quickly forgave one another for all of our *stuff*. In the end, we parted as friends.

In a word association game, if you say "college", then the first word I think of is "all-nighter"—and not the fun kind playing cards at 2:00 in the morning and snacking on shrimp with Nanie. In my first semester at CMU in the fall of 1993, I faithfully pulled at least one all-nighter every week doing homework following the wake-up call of my first "D" grade on an exam. Class rank remained an idol for me. At freshman orientation, a speaker asked all high-school vale-dictorians in the crowd to stand up. When I stood amongst hundreds of other rank-one champions at the starting-line of this new rat race, I thought to myself, "I'm going to swing the highest and the fastest." And a bad grade would soon reveal just how hard I would need to work at it.

They say college is a time and place for *questions* and *discoveries*. My chief question entering the university was this: "Does everybody feel as completely terrified as I do, and like me, is continuously expending energy to appear otherwise? Or, am I the only one who feels this dreadfully overwhelmed?" My chief discovery was the "freshman fifteen", which refers to the fifteen pounds of weight-gain that happens to many college first-years. If you are a scared-to-death college student reading this now, please know that you're not alone.

The day my dad and Sean dropped me off at CMU was unforgettable. I had grown up surrounded by the Appalachian foothills; now I was surrounded by skyscrapers and crowds of people representing cultures from around the world, as though the big fish from a small pond was suddenly tossed into an ocean filled with sharks and countless other creatures never before seen. It was scary. My first day in the city, I dodged an attempted mugging, which didn't help. If it hadn't been for my five weeks in Pittsburgh one year earlier, I wonder whether it all would have been too much.

My heavenly Father saw my needs, and quickly provided me with a few more sweet tastes of infant milk to assure me of his perpetual care, protection, and guidance. One day early on in the semester, I was walking along Craig Street when I prayed, "God, my next pay-check from my ten-hour-per-week work-study job doesn't arrive until this Friday, and I need just a couple bucks for the bus to get me through the rest of the week." At that very moment, a gust of wind blew a crumpled-up ball of cash uphill on the sidewalk of Craig Street. It bounced against my shoe. Yes, I prayed for money, and immediately a literal *ball of cash* blew up to my feet. I said out loud, "You've got to be kidding me." I watched it happen with my own two eyes, and I still couldn't believe it. I reached down, picked up the gift, and unrolled six mashed-together dollar bills that were, of course, *exactly* enough. The countless times since then that I have prayed for cash, the answer has consistently been no every time. However, it only has to happen once to *know* that God hears prayers. Beyond the immediate practical help, the real grace was a tangible reminder that my Lord would never leave me or forsake me, as he had promised.

In another special moment, I had realized too late that I needed to add one more class to meet the credit requirement and to qualify for my level of financial aid, and only one class fit my schedule—but the class was full, and had a wait-list over ten students long. I prayed for the Lord to get me into that particular course. Shortly after praying, the professor called me and said that, even though he wasn't supposed to go to the end of the wait-list, he felt like he was supposed to add me to the class.

In a dorm-room Bible study, I prayed, "God, please send a non-believer into this group right now, so that I can tell him you're real." At that very moment, a young man walked in and sat down with us. He said, "I'm not a Christian, but may I join you today? I want to hear about God."

God continued to emphasize his closeness. On the eve of a major test, I played Monopoly instead of studying. Unprepared for the political science exam the following day, I sat at my desk with pencil and bluebook in hand, feeling panicked. I prayed for the Holy Spirit to give me a get-out-of-jail-free card, even though I surely didn't deserve one. The first essay question asked what the "critical number" from our reading was. I hadn't done the reading, so I guessed "three", and then basically wrote a paragraph about how "three" is critical because it's important. The next question asked what the most important half of the budget was from the reading. I hadn't done that reading, either. I guessed "the bottom half", then basically wrote a paragraph saying that the bottom half was more important than the top half because the top half was less important than the bottom. The last question also asked about a reading I hadn't touched. "What did the author argue about social security?" I guessed, saying that the author thought we should abolish the system even though it's called the "third rail" of politics. They were all *wild guesses*, except for the fact that I felt strangely nudged in each response. In fact, during the exam, I had initially written a paragraph guessing that the author argued *in favor* of the social security administration. The spiritual nudge that I had received felt so strong that I literally tore that page out of the examination booklet, then started fresh guessing the opposite—that the author sought to eliminate it.

A couple days after the exam, the professor of that class called me up personally. I figured I was about to get chewed out, especially for my answer about "the bottom half", which could easily have been construed as my having made a joke of his exam. As it turns out, the critical number *was* three. The most important half of the budget *was* the bottom half. And the author had indeed argued that social security ought to be abolished, even though it's deemed the "third rail". I received the only perfect score in the class. The professor had called me to personally congratulate me and ask me to consider making political science my major. With the sole exception of my Ph.D. comprehensive exams years later, God responded to all subsequent requests for test answers with a no, resulting in my first and only "D" on another test shortly thereafter. But again, a miracle only has to happen once to show that God indeed hears our prayers, and *cares* more than we can imagine.

In the end, his no was just as crucial as the previous yes. Like Charlie Rizzo once said in a sermon, "God is not our cosmic butler. He's not a wish-granting genie. He is Lord." The miracle answers to prayer remain annoyingly rare, but are utterly amazing whenever they do happen! It's no coincidence that I was given this unique series of sweet, creamy milk feedings during my freshman year. The undeniable reality of the sheer power of prayer which God revealed to me during these formative months inspired and cultivated in me an enduring prayer life, one that I desire for every follower of Jesus Christ.

Praying in the lounge of my dorm in early October, I said, "Lord, your Word says that you *tell us what to pray for*. What do you want me to pray for right now?"

Then the strongest kind of heart burden washed over me for the soul of Bob, my parents' entertainingly brash friend from New Milford. I prayed, "God, Bob needs to know you. He's *precious*. I can't imagine heaven without him there, and I want more than anything else in this moment for Bob to come to a saving relationship with you now, on this side of eternity. I know he is the most unlikely of converts; I recall him shouting to the world how you're just a 'crock'. What on earth could persuade him? Father, I ask that you use Bob's two little girls, Ashley and Melanie, to lead him to your Son. In Jesus' name, amen." I didn't think much more about that prayer once the regular all-nighters started.

In one of my philosophy classes, I had an experience similar to the one I had at the Governor's School for International Studies, in which I was given a punishment essay for talking about Jesus in class. In a private meeting after class, the professor said that he believed all Christians were close-minded and that he wanted me to write a ten-page essay on Aristotle by the next day. He didn't answer my questions nor did he converse with me. He just assigned a lengthy essay, with only one night to write it. I could have complained, and I would have been within my rights to do so. But God nudged me to another option: *show excellence*. I pulled an all-nighter and became a lifelong fan of Aristotle—especially his *Nicomachean Ethics*, which I would one day come to teach as a professor in my own philosophy courses. After reading my essay, the professor gave me a sincere apology for his bigotry, asked my forgiveness, and told me that the excellence of my paper's scholarship forced him to rethink his assumptions about Christians.

Another professor and chair of his department told me that, although he was an agnostic, my classroom witness and performance had him considering Christianity. "The worldview that Jesus Christ revealed may in fact be the truth. I already find Christian scholarship far more reasonable than the atheists I study; thank you for making me think," he said. At least some of the freshman terror began to subside as I saw that I could continue my outreach to doubting Thomases.

One of the ramifications of parting ways with Marie was that she had been my anchor to a church community. God was quick to replace that lifeline with a new one. Pastor Salvatore "Sam"

Brunsvold was a graduate student in theology at nearby Duquesne University, and he worked as a campus minister for both CMU and the University of Pittsburgh. Sam pulled me out of the crowd during a student club fair as though he was led to do so. Or perhaps I looked as lost and scared as I felt. Whatever Sam's reasons for reaching out to me, he was one of God's greatest gifts. He befriended me, plugged me into a local "non-denominational" Christian church, and took me under his wing. He remained my personal mentor during the next four years.

Sam's Friday evening gathering of Christian university students, held at Pittsburgh's Cathedral of Learning building, was the best part of my week—and the extent of my social life. Through those meetings I made some lifelong friends, including a red-headed guy named Nate, who shared my personality in numerous ways, including my sense of humor, disdain for anything fake, love of missionary work, struggles in the dating world, and animosity toward Catholics. Sam's Friday evening gatherings were eventually followed regularly by a night out with Nate catching up over hot wings or cheeseburgers.

With a shared heart for evangelization, Sam and I teamed up on a biweekly study, which he led, entitled "Meeting Jesus". It was a series designed for introducing nonbelievers to Jesus in a safe space, based upon the book *Your Home a Lighthouse* by Bob Jacks, Betty Jacks, and Ron Wormser, who advised having an ashtray available at the Bible Study. Sam created a disarming climate absent of agenda. Without any pressure, people could truly make themselves at home and ask all of their hardest questions. Sam was a shining example of Christian charity. He demonstrated authentic love for God and neighbor, and he was the ideal instrument for leading a group designed to introduce people to Christ. I brought numerous doubting Thomases to the meetings, and one after the next chose to give his heart to Christ.

Late one night, Pastor Sam opened up to me about his concerns regarding my inordinate regard for class rank, just as my high school English teacher had done. He observed that my Christian commitment was a seesaw, while my commitment to getting top marks was unshakeable, and all I felt during that entire conversation was how Sam loved me as though I were family. We continued to have regular one-on-one meetings at Duquesne, where I also sat in on classes he was teaching as part of their graduate program.

I asked Sam if it would be okay to read the writings of those, like Polycarp, who followed the original apostles. Sam said, "Yeah, you should definitely read that stuff. Read Clement of Rome, Ignatius, and Polycarp, the ones who knew the original apostles. *Fascinating.* Then also read the guys who knew *them!*"

"Strange," I thought, "he's the only minister who has ever said that. Well, he *is* going to Duquesne University, a *Catholic* school. Maybe they're brainwashing him. But at least somebody else out there realizes how cool it is to read the writings of the apostles' disciples."

Sam thereby reawakened my interest in the Church Fathers and gave me a sense of "permission" to keep digging. I found out that Clement of Rome wrote a letter to the church in Corinth, as Paul had done. "This really happened ... these were real people ... this is marvelous!" I said to myself as I read it. I then turned to Clement of Alexandria, Cyprian, and John Chrysostom, who remains my favorite preacher of all time. His eloquent compositions demonstrate why he was named Chrysostom, which means "golden tongue". As I read Ignatius of Antioch, there was that recurring, gnawing observation, "He sounds Catholic, too. But history connects him to Peter, and it looks like this guy knew John personally—wow!" Then I entertained the unspeakable: maybe Uncle Tim and Scott Hahn got it right.

That's when I recalled that look in the eyes of my dad and his threat of eternal damnation. "How come the response to my considerations of Catholicism is never intelligent dialogue but fear," I asked silently. But the fear was nonetheless very effective. I quickly returned to the safety blanket of mocking Catholicism and gossiping about Catholics with my friends.

The highlight of the whole school year was a trip home shortly before Christmas break, when my mom invited me to join her for a special weekend trip to New Jersey. "Bob wants to talk to you, is that okay?" Mom asked. "Yeah, that's great! I love the Bob show. He's hysterical." With his having called me his *hero* earlier that same year, I was already looking forward to whatever he wanted to talk about. When we arrived at his house, Bob raced toward me, and lifted me up off the ground, greeting me with a wonderful chiropractic crack of my back.

"You were right!!" he yelled at the top of his lungs. "You were right about Jesus! Everything you said was right, and I am so sorry for not listening to you, Ian. I got saved, I'm a Christian; so is my wife! Thank you for giving me the good news."

It was one of those moments that stays with you, one of those moments in which time slows, and for one stretched second, you could swear that you actually feel the earth turning. Heaven celebrates every time somebody accepts God's offer of friendship; I felt like an integral part of that angelic celebration. I asked Bob, "How did it happen?"

He answered, "It was the strangest thing. Back sometime in early October, Ashley and Melanie approached me out of the blue, and they asked me to tell them who Jesus was. I knew who I thought he was, and if I was wrong about that, I would take my licks—in this life and the next, you know? But I would be damned if my two daughters, the best part of my whole life, would take my licks because I got it wrong. I told them I would have to research it more for myself, and then get back to them with an answer. So I looked into it seriously, and boy had I been WRONG. Jesus *is* risen from the dead, and he is Lord. Then my wife converted too. Finally, I went to my girls and said, 'You wanted to know who Jesus is? He's God! He loves you, and he wants a personal relationship with each of you.' Somehow it was like they already knew. We're regular churchgoers now, the whole family—that's a hoot. Can you believe it?"

It immediately struck me that back in early October, I had asked the Lord what he wanted me to pray for, and was then moved to ask God to use Bob's two little girls to lead him to Christ. That is *precisely* what had taken place. That prayer-nudge had been so strong and specific that it was impossible to explain what had happened as a coincidence. The event became for me its own apologetic defense of God's existence and love, a lasting witness that testifies to the undeniable reality of prayer.

Bob started crying and said again from the bottom of his giant heart, "Thank you."

12

Dinner in the Household of Saint Enda

Having found my groove, college was going strong. For better or for worse, I remained a grade junky. But Pastor Sam graciously remained a lifeline to grace, and ministry was flourishing. From the Meeting Jesus study to the Pittsburgh Food Bank, from befriending beggars on Craig Street to bringing blankets to the homeless, there was no shortage of service opportunities in the area.

With encouragement from Sam, I started teaching at different Bible studies, leading youth retreats as a keynote speaker, and giving church presentations. With the permission of the University of Pittsburgh and the help of the sponsoring organization's outdoor sound equipment, I gave a street-side message for Easter that drew hundreds of listeners. I was giving talks on a fairly regular basis to student groups at the University of Pittsburgh. I delivered a lecture at CMU that drew a particularly large crowd. I was even invited to speak on a couple radio programs. People said they enjoyed all the comedy and narrative in my presentations, as well as the information. But more importantly, they felt loved. You can't fake actually *caring* about the people you're addressing. I really cared, and people could always tell. My presentations would draw a number of agnostics and atheists who, like me, genuinely sought as much truth about the great mystery of life as was available—and I watched in joy and thanksgiving as many of them accepted Christ. It was a powerful time of realizing vocational *purpose*. The more I gave talks about the good news, the more I knew that I was born to do so.

My junior year of college, I travelled to Ireland, the home of more than half my ancestors, for a study-abroad program. No words can do justice to the beauty of the Emerald Isle, where a number of gorgeous

landforms—breathtaking mountains, prairies, forests, and beaches—
are all condensed onto one island. It truly is a green gemstone, and
no photograph, movie, or calendar could ever do it justice. My year
there was an adventure of epic proportions.

I was enrolled at the University of Ulster in Coleraine, Northern
Ireland—established in the middle of the farmland between the cities
of Belfast and Derry, so that neither city could *claim* it. The tensions
of Ireland's Troubles were high during that 1995–1996 school year.
Surrounding the annual "orange marches", a long-standing truce
broke in the summer of 1996. I witnessed fire-bombings and armed
soldiers patrolling the city streets. But at least Coleraine gave me the
finest cheddar cheese I have ever tasted.

I quickly discovered how deeply divided Catholics and Protestants can be in Ireland. I'll never forget being shunned by a group
of friends in Portrush when they discovered that I was a Protestant.

"You lied to us!" shouted one of them.

"What do you mean? How did I lie to you?"

"You told us your surname's *Murphy*!" the girl exclaimed angrily.

Eager to resolve the situation, I answered, "But it *is*! My last name
is 'Murphy'. I wasn't lying to you."

"Murphy's a Catholic name, but you're a Protestant." And with
that, I was officially and permanently kicked out of their apartment.

The categories of *Catholic* and *Protestant* were uniquely *charged*
terms, which incorporated history, heritage, politics, identity, and
social memory in a way previously unfamiliar to my American mindset. Providentially, I sensed the need to bracket off my own anti-
Catholic hostilities.

I also discovered how much the Irish people drink tea. The study-
abroad organization wisely placed us with host families for our first
weekend on the island, announcing an annual competition for the
fastest offer of tea. The student who currently held the record had
been offered tea within the first four minutes after meeting his hosts.
The honor passed to me when I was offered tea within the first
four seconds.

"No, thank you," I said, "I don't drink tea."

At those words, the father of my host family looked deeply
offended. After a long pause, he said, "Coffee then?" in a tone of
voice that suggested I had given him the *wrong* answer.

Three hours later, the mother of the family said, "No more coffee. That was one-time-only, for politeness. You're drinkin' some tea with me now!"

I obeyed. As soon as the pure amazingness that *is* Irish tea hit my taste buds, I exclaimed, "This is *incredible!*"

"You say that like you're informing me. I already know that," she said with a grin.

My host dad chimed in, "To be fair, we sure can't blame you for *thinking* that you don't like tea, in light of the fact that your only experience has been American tea. United States tea is *bollocks!* You dumped the good stuff into the Boston Harbor, and you never got it back."

Before I left for Ireland, Sam Brunsvold beseeched me to find a Christian group during my time abroad. He sensed that if I lost Christian community, then I would *be* lost. I promised him that I would, and I wasted no time in getting to know the campus ministry staff at Ulster. What an eclectic and *fun* band of misfits they were! The group was headed by a Roman Catholic priest and a nun—two of the most amazing missionaries I've ever had the privilege to serve with. The rest of the team included an Anglican, a Lutheran, and a charismatic Evangelical. They bickered in front of students. As was common among the Protestants I knew in the States, the only thing uniting them was their shared opposition to the pope.

In spite of their quarrelling, the Protestant ministers were brilliant and talented. There were characteristics in each one that I came to treasure, making it difficult for me to choose which group to join. Each of the pastors on staff held his own respective weekly gathering. With the exception of the Catholics, I tried and liked each option. I became anxious to settle upon one of the groups and commit to it, in order to help me form some friendships in a place where I had arrived knowing *nobody*. Several months into the year, I was still floating from one weekly fellowship to the next, so I prayed for God to lead me to the community that he desired me to be a part of. At a spiritual retreat held near the Giant's Causeway along the salty north coast, I received my answer.

On the opening night of this weekend getaway, I was initially hanging with the Evangelicals. They loved that I had played the organ for a *real Pentecostal church in America*. After a while, the Evangelical preacher started complaining about how the Anglicans "didn't have the Holy Spirit" because they couldn't speak in tongues. The gossip session became so uncomfortable that I quietly walked away from the group. I then walked over to the Anglican crowd. They were protesting together against the Lutherans for aligning a Christian community around a protest. So I meandered over to the Lutheran group to find them laughing at the charismatics for how ridiculous they sounded when speaking in tongues.

I knew that I certainly wasn't innocent of the sin of backbiting; I had done so plenty of times myself. But in this particular experience moving from one group to the next, I felt as though I was being given a tour of sorts. It felt as though God was trying to show me something. As a last resort, and with nowhere else to find fellowship, I finally walked over to the priest and the nun, to hang out with the Catholic students. They were all talking about the love of Jesus Christ. I made a conscientious decision in that moment to place my own allegiance with the priest and the nun, and I joined the Catholic student group. I *never* told my dad.

The Catholic weekly fellowship at Ulster felt different from the other groups. It was uniquely *rich* and entirely Christ-centered. The content of their discussions revolved around character, integrity, and virtue—the same *substance* for which I had become hungry ever since my two Catholic high-school teachers had given me a taste. Unlike my Portrush friends who had kicked me out and shunned me for being a Protestant, the Catholics who attended this student gathering simply loved having a Protestant in the mix. And there was plenty of tea.

One of the guys sitting next to me at their Friday evening meeting said, "Ah, a Protestant named 'Ian Murphy'. It's a unique thing, ya know; like gettin' to see a rare animal."

I laughed out loud.

He asked, "Is your grandpa Catholic?"

"Yes, he is, but his wife, my 'Nanie', is Protestant," I explained.

He said, "Their marriage is a picture of the island itself. I think you'll become Catholic one day."

I laughed even louder. "No offense, but it will be a cold day in hell before I become Catholic," I said in reply. "My dad would probably say that I'm going to hell just for being here at the Catholic student organization."

"Well I sure hope not," he said. "If you're going to hell just for sittin' with me, it doesn't bode well for my own soul. I think you *will* become Catholic. Tell you what, if you do convert someday, then do me this favor: I want you to think back on this smirking face."

In one of my spiritual direction meetings with the priest, a young woman walked into his office, sat down, and admitted to him that she just had an abortion. I got up to leave, but she looked up at me and said, "No, please stay, I need as much help as I can get right now."

The priest asked her, "Why did you come to me?"

"Because I need to change my life, and I knew that you would be the only one who would be real about this, and tell it to me straight," she answered.

With intense care in his eyes, the priest spoke with her, and seemed to know details of her situation before she revealed them. He lovingly instructed her in the sacramental steps for moving forward and connected her to available therapeutic support. At the end of their conversation he said, "God LOVES you, unconditionally. And his favorite thing in the whole world is a *repentant heart*. I will help you through this. Go in grace and peace, and sin no more." The freedom and the gratitude that washed over this girl were visible. I also got to help her, and that wasn't the last time she would invite me to sit with her during counseling appointments. I wondered why God had orchestrated my being there. All I knew at the time was that it was extraordinary to watch this man minister God's love to his heartbroken daughter. It was as though the priest was standing as a visible representative of Christ to her.

Inspired by the potent ministry God was doing through them, I asked the priest and the nun to *please* put me to work. They wasted no time. University talks, church talks, retreat talks, and peace-building missions filled the year. Impressed by their trust, I asked the priest why he was providing so many opportunities to a Protestant speaker. Seeming confused by the question, he answered, "You're my brother in Christ."

Speaking engagements took me all over the island. Castles, graveyards, rainbows, cliffs, a cave near the ocean, and a cracked bedrock beach each filled my soul to the brim with wonder. All of Ireland evoked this wondrous sense of an alluring enchantment ... something *beautiful*, which I could also hear mysteriously embedded in the music. My favorite of all sites was the Nuns' Walk of Portstewart, a winding, ocean-side path, illumined by a moonlit mist that crawled throughout the air during nightfall. It was an undeniably sacred space, yet it had been named by a Dominican order of sisters—by *Catholic nuns*. It was as though the beauty of Catholicism transcended the witness, the artwork, or any doctrine, and seemed to saturate the creation itself. Far away from the glare of my dad, I continued to encounter the Catholic-sounding testimony from the early Christians. And when I finally finished *Rome Sweet Home*, I was unable to debunk it. One tiny bit at a time, my animosity against the Catholic Church not only melted away across the year, but was replaced by something else that I dared not admit to myself—an *attraction*. My journey experienced a crucial shift that year: rather than running *away* from the doctrinal problems I had noticed in Protestantism, I was moving *toward* the beauty of the Catholic Church.

On one unforgettable trip to the west coast of Ireland, I took the ferry in Galway out to Inishmore, one of the Aran Islands. My heart and mind were alert to this ever-increasing pull toward the Church. It was a fine time for me to retreat to a quiet place, far away from comfort zones and fears, in order to reflect and pray about everything stirring within me. Inishmore, an island off an island, was the remotest place I had ever been—an adventure perfectly suited to my needs. The sun was glinting on and off that afternoon, ducking behind dark clouds that never broke into rain that day, and then reemerging to light up the landscape once again. The cool and comfortable breeze was strong and constant, as the shadows of clouds moved across the green countryside. The wind smelled of a characteristic mix of salty ocean air with the whisper of burning peat from some distant fireplace. Hiking all by myself that afternoon, I felt as though I was being led.

Eventually, I stumbled across the remains of an early ninth-century church known as Teaghlach Éinne (Saint Enda's Household). It was a small and intimate church named in honor of a trailblazer for Irish monasticism who, several centuries earlier, had established a monastery at that site. The roof of the church was missing, yet its surviving stone walls emanated a sense of timeless strength and protection. The remains appeared sunken down into the earth a bit, which may have contributed to the walls' preservation. The ancient graveyard, along with its stone crosses marking the resting places of its dead, filled my soul with reverence. While walking through the ruins, I reflected, "Way back in the *early 800s*, the followers of the risen Jesus gathered together *right here*—long before there was an America ... and long before there were *Protestants*." The Christians who attended this church may very well have included my own grandfathers and grandmothers, and they were *Catholics*. It was no accident I was there. I had been led there by God's providence, invited to dinner at the household of Saint Enda.

I stood inside the structure staring at the altar when the sun peeked out again. The sunlight lit up the floor and cast cross-shaped shadows from the gravestones onto the surrounding grounds. I imagined the church at the peak of its glory, and time began to shrink. I thought to myself, "The people who had once worshipped in this place believed in the Incarnation and the Resurrection of Christ, just as I do. They carried the good news of what God had done for the world through their own time period, and I stand here a Christian because of their faithful perseverance." My heart swelled with gratitude for the faith of those who had gone before, as though I could feel their love for *me* in that moment. And I remembered that the Book of Hebrews says that they're cheering me on to finish the race strong. In that moment I could almost hear them.

I suddenly realized that, up until this epiphany moment, I had envisioned the body of Christ's followers as an entity that had been comprised of the earliest Christians, was followed by a millennium-and-a-half "blackout" period, and then magically reappeared in the Protestant Reformation. I preferred to think of myself as a relatively intelligent person, but I had to admit that this idea of a "disappearing, reappearing Church" was *ridiculous*. Just as the Church didn't stop with the apostles, it didn't stop with Cyprian and then pick back up with C. S. Lewis. "Why did it take my having this experience to recognize something so obvious?" I asked myself. "It's as if this encounter with the landscape and the ruins was a conduit for grace into my life!"

The question led me to consider that maybe that's what the sacraments are all about—grace being communicated through physical signs. The people who worshipped in that place celebrated the Mass. "If the Eucharist is inherently evil as my dad insists, then how do I possibly account for the people who sat right here and *received it*?"

I asked myself. Then I thanked God that they did receive it, in that very place. My own existence and salvation resulted from the Catholic faith of my ancestors.

When I returned to the States, I brought a few Irish treasures along with me. I smuggled in my last bricks of Coleraine cheddar, some proper tea, several bags of Tato brand salt-and-vinegar crisps, and some Irish coins. I also brought home a lilt in my speech. I never adopted the brogue, but I picked up the Northern-Irish *lilt*, in which one's tone of voice goes up at the end of most sentences. In the United States, it makes every statement sound like a question. It was obnoxious, and it took a couple months to wear off. Most importantly, I kept with me a newfound appreciation for Christ's Church. And while my heart was bursting with the love of the whole family of God across the ages, I knew that these recent convictions could not remain a secret forever.

13

The Weight of the Cross

After an unforgettable year in Ireland, I returned to Pittsburgh to start my senior year at CMU. The best part of my homecoming was that Pastor Sam and I were back together again. The one-on-one mentorship meetings, the Friday night gathering at the Cathedral of Learning, the retreats, and the Meeting Jesus study were all back in full swing.

Through Sam's team of missionaries, I became close friends with a number of extraordinary people. We thoroughly enjoyed one another's company, bonding in the crucible of young adulthood. In college, your declaration of a major might determine your career, how much money you earn, where you live, and who your lifetime friends will be. The person you date might become the parent of your own children or the next catastrophic break-up, or perhaps both. In the pressure cooker of life-changing decisions, Sam's flock huddled together. We held one another up and kept each other laughing.

Sam was a *remarkable* shepherd. Still a young adult himself, he was just a little further along in life than we were. He had a career and a family, but was pursuing a graduate degree at Duquesne. He still liked to do young-guy activities like shooting hoops with us, yet he always retained his dignity. He placed as much emphasis on orthodoxy (right *belief*) as orthopraxis (right *practice*).

"Right belief is important!" Sam would explain. "Whatever you believe to be true about reality, humanity, and purpose will steer your life. Are you content holding to lies? The truth matters. It's important to seek truth and to be aware of what you believe."

Sam would also say, "Right practice is important! God is love, and we reflect that image, so putting love into practice is the heart of our calling. You are Christ's hands and feet! Make sure that whenever people encounter you they encounter *him*—they encounter love."

Through Sam, I came to see the both-and of belief and practice. To believe God is love but not to love, is to reject God. As I came to summarize it, *truth* minus *love* equals *rightness*; it's not enough simply to be *right*. Sam not only taught me the essentials of my faith, he lived it. In his flock, we got out there with him, entering into the chaos and meeting people's needs.

At each Meeting Jesus session Sam avoided a tendency, common among many people who study the Bible, to debate matters of doctrine on an intellectual level. Rather, Sam *entered* into the Gospel accounts, and he took all of us along with him. For instance, in discussing Jesus' miracle at the wedding in Cana, Sam invited us to envision ourselves there. With an abundance of knowledge about the history, customs, and cultural context of Jesus' day, Sam set a vivid stage that worked like a time machine. We heard the music and smelled the food. We felt the stress of running out of wine, as though it were happening at our own wedding reception. We considered the intriguing dialogue between Jesus and Mary and what it would mean for Jesus to display his power in public for the first time. We realized that those who witnessed the miracle were real people, just as hungry for truth, meaning, and purpose as ourselves. We wondered if we had been there, would we have been amazed and afraid, pondering with hope whether this could in fact be the Savior God had promised.

Reading and receiving Scripture in this way is very different from *analyzing* it. Through Sam's study, people were indeed feeling the power of God by *meeting Jesus*.

Toward the end of the fall semester, Sam offered to hire me as the ministry's full-time intern. The position, which would begin after graduation, came with free housing. Convinced it was God's direction for me, I wholeheartedly accepted, saying, "It would be my honor to keep working under your leadership."

Sam said he was overjoyed by my answer, but then he gave an ominous warning: "Keep on the full armor of God and watch out for any kinks. The enemy's backlash against what God's been doing in Pittsburgh can be ... Well, it can be severe."

"What do you mean?" I asked.

He responded, "You know what I mean. You of all people know."

"Is everything okay?"

"Not too long ago somebody threw a rock through my living-room window," Sam said.

"WHAT?! What are you going to do?"

"I'm going to keep doing what I've been doing."

"Is it safe?"

"No, urban ministry isn't safe. Bearing a cross can be a literal reality for the followers of Christ. Jesus gave his life for me, and I'm willing to give him mine."

In January 1997 I began my final semester at CMU, as well as the next cycle of Meeting Jesus sessions. I was so overloaded with academic work, however, that I was totally unprepared for the Meeting Jesus session on January 28, as was the rest of the team. I hadn't invited anyone, and no "seekers" showed up; Sam spent the hour preaching to the choir. At the close of the meeting, he implored the team to step up the effort to invite people. "I know how busy life gets," he said, "but there is a spiritual war out there. Never lose heart, and keep the salvation of your neighbors a priority. That matters forever."

He closed the session by putting his hand down on the table, and one after another we stacked our hands on top of his. With our hands united, we all promised to step up our effort and commitment to invite new people to the next study.

Afterward Sam reminded me how he was counting on me to bring people to the series. Smiling, he encouraged me by saying how much he was looking forward to the summer, when I could be fully devoted to the ministry. He offered me a lift home, but I told him that I could use the walk. It was the last time I would see Sam alive. When Sam returned home that night, someone shot him in the head in front of his house.

Sam's murder overwhelmed me with grief and fear. At the office a couple days later, I could barely bring myself to dump the cold coffee in his mug. The murderer was still at large, and I was afraid that if the person knew about my upcoming role with the ministry, he would kill me too. As a result, unlike my last experience with a media blitz, I didn't want to be in the spotlight. I asked another person on the team to be our unofficial spokesman, and I was so proud of this new Christian when he told the television news crew: "Jesus taught that the greatest two commandments are to love God with all your heart, and to love your neighbor as yourself. Sam lived that." I was proud of him but ashamed of myself. I felt like Peter saying, "I do not know the man" (Mt 26:72).

Because Nate had been elected the president of Sam's student organization, he stepped up to help with keeping Sam's ministry alive, and so did many others. During the memorial service held by the team, I committed myself to continuing the Meeting Jesus study, as Sam would have wanted, and other team members agreed to share the responsibility of leading the remaining sessions. We finished the series at the end of the spring, and one more precious soul accepted Christ. That man's baptism was a celebration not only of new life in God but of Sam's enduring work. For me, however, it marked the end of my relationship with his ministry.

As the organization that had employed Sam sought his replacement, they cancelled my upcoming full-time internship. Of course I understood that until they hired a new campus minister they did not have a role for an intern. And besides, Sam's replacement would no doubt chart a new course. But it meant that I had no job waiting for me after graduation, and no direction for my future.

Throughout the breakthroughs that rescued me from agnosticism, I was repeatedly struck by how Christianity's first martyrs died not simply for *ideas*, but for miraculous *events* they saw themselves, like the Transfiguration, the Resurrection, and the Ascension. But while looking into the open casket at Sam's wake, at the reconstructed ear covering the gunshot wound, I was struck by the reality of Christian martyrdom. It was one thing to serve Jesus when it meant reading the convincing evidence of courageous people from two thousand years ago, basking in fame, or enjoying spiritual experiences during an overseas adventure. It was quite another thing to serve Jesus when it might cost me my life. I had embraced God's many blessings, but I refused to embrace his Cross.

He who tries to save his life will lose it, Jesus said. And that is exactly what happened to me. I ran from the Cross, and my life spiraled downward. I no longer prayed the way I once did. I put aside Christian reading. I stopped sharing my faith and giving talks. I buried all memory of the insights I had received in Ireland. I even skipped my own college graduation. I turned completely inward and began eating and drinking excessively.

I got a job as a secretary, moved in with two former team members, and refused their sincerest attempts to help me. For the next two years, I indulged in random diversions. Lacking commitment and discipline, I simply lost myself in whatever escape suited my fancy at the moment, especially unwholesome dating. I sank into a dark and barren place of self-destruction. In the journey of life, I went from being a destination-driven *pilgrim* to an aimless *wanderer*. If you've ever been to the wasteland of hopeless wandering, then you may have seen some of my old footprints in that place—they go in circles.

I was thoroughly miserable. In one of my worst moments, I kissed a girl who was already spoken for, engaged to another man. When she confessed our affair to her fiancé, he became understandably *upset* and claimed that if he ever saw me again, he would kill me. I didn't know whether it was merely angry words, or if he was capable of carrying out his threat. But I didn't stick around to find out. I quit my job, said goodbye to my friends, and left Pennsylvania for a new beginning in another state. I showed up at my sister's doorstep in Austin, Texas, with nothing except two bags of clothes and ten dollars in my front pocket. Graciously, she and her husband took me in. Texas would remain my home for the next five years.

14

Rilian's Plight

My memoires of my first couple years in Texas are somewhat blurry. The backsliding, which began after the death of Sam, extended into a long spiritual winter of sloth and depression. When I was living as a faithful, albeit flawed, Christian, almost every day was a story worth retelling. I had been walking in friendship with my Creator, and that relationship was the source of my substance and growth. In contrast, during these dark years my life was like a directionless blob of happenings. I quit doing ministry and stopped going to church. I packed on weight until I plateaued at three hundred pounds. I took up cigarettes, and started chain smoking two-and-a-half packs every day. And while I always had a fondness for money, it became my idol. After staying with my sister for several months, I rented my own apartment near Austin—my latest launching pad for the pursuit of one unfulfilling escape after the next.

For employment, I entered the sales world, where my ambition shifted from outranking my classmates to exceeding sales quotas. I started out by selling computers, and then landed an executive-level position selling cell phones. I recall purposely talking a customer into an inferior option that won me a higher commission. As if that wasn't bad enough, I proceeded to *boast* about it to my manager while he gave me an affirming pat on the back. It's alarming how one's conscience can grow numb to the vilest of deeds. It was as though the enemy wished to make a mockery of my best gifts, as I went from teaching people out of love to manipulating people for mammon. The money was a sharp hook, to be sure. Worse yet was the hook of pride. Even more than the money, I reveled in the thrill of the sale and of going over quota. Still in my twenties, I was already earning a six-figure income and squandering every cent of it on "fun", like the Prodigal Son had done with his early inheritance. Without God as my center, my life shriveled to a mere *existence* that resembled a photocopier on repeat—each day looked like any other. I was in hell.

This season of my life is best described in the words of Dr. George Worgul, who would later become one of my favorite professors at Duquesne University. His phrase *hedonist flight of forgetfulness* captures my experience perfectly. I had indeed been *fleeing*, running away from God, into self-indulgent distractions and numbing agents. And there was a *forgetfulness* to it—as I momentarily forgot who I really was. My flight away from God, in whose image I'm made and without whom I can do nothing, had simultaneously been a flight away from myself.

I did have periodic moments of lucidity, in which I would briefly remember myself. But, as soon as my memory returned, I would become overwhelmed by the prospect of change. A number of vices had become habitual, and the force of habit was considerable. In one of Saint Augustine's vivid and chilling scenes from the *Confessions*, he describes his sleeping soul being stirred awake. As his bleary eyes begin to peel open, his personal demons are seen standing over his bed, intent on keeping him down, eager for him to slip back into the nightmare. They whisper, "Are you trying to get rid of us?" That's precisely what it was like. The moments of clarity would pass as I fell back into the gravity of old habits. My residence, career, and schedule revolved around an entirely new lifestyle. "How could I possibly change all of that?" I would think to myself. "How could I crawl out of this hole, a hole which I dug myself, when I am already in so deep?" And with that despairing thought, I would quickly race to the next empty diversion.

I felt like the character Prince Rilian from C. S. Lewis' book *The Silver Chair*. Deceived and ensnared by the spell of the Emerald Witch, Rilian became her willing slave. Formerly destined for a life of fruitful service, he now spent his days in a cave along with others whom she had enslaved. But periodically, the prince experienced episodes of clarity when the daily spell of the wicked enchantress would wear off, and he would momentarily remember Aslan, himself, and his true calling. The witch made certain that, during such moments, the prince was strapped to a chair—bound with chords that he had *allowed* to be tied.

I was also experiencing a worsening homesickness for God. It would become so unbearable that I would resolve to do anything necessary in order to be healed. But whenever any sense of hopeful determination would surface, the witch had an answer for that too. I would suddenly become dreadfully frightened at the prospect of returning to God and facing the full reality of what I had done with my life. I thought that God would be furious with me. I had been given so much. I had received an abundance of grace including tangible encounters with the spiritual realm, direct and miraculous answers to prayers, the finest mentor a person could hope for, a loving family, and the privilege of bringing other souls to Christ. Instead of responding to those gifts with gratitude, humility, and continued service of the Lord, I simply left it all behind in order to indulge myself. "God must be outraged," I would think to myself. "How could he ever forgive me?" I pictured him holding a club, thumping it against his hand, waiting to punish me, and regretting ever choosing me as his servant. Was I thinking those thoughts? Or was a different entity speaking them to me: "God could never forgive you. You can never change. You're mine now."

With no sense of purpose, depression set in. The sadder I felt, the more I turned to my plethora of vices that, in turn, only made me feel more depressed. The slow-moving traffic jam to the office was a daily reminder of my plight. I would open the car window, suck down one cigarette after the next, and hold my forehead in my hand while crawling at a glacier's pace—only to reach a cubicle that looked more like a prison cell each day.

Stuck in exceptionally bad traffic one day, I asked myself, "Will I spend my whole career in a cubicle, with one *decade* blurring into the next?" Stuck in the highway congestion, the hour seemed to stretch. I began to think about my apartment complex, and how closely it resembled a beehive. "I work laboriously every day for the queen bee, returning nightly to my little spot in the nest," I thought. "We each keep an individual cut from our own sales, while one very rich queen gets a cut of *every* bee's sales."

At that point, the traffic jam felt more like a cattle drive than a row of vehicles. Being an expressive fellow, I decided to communicate my feelings publicly. I snuffed out my cigarette, stretched my head out the open car window, and began *mooing* at top volume—just like a cow. Having grown up around dairy farms, I was able to reproduce the bovine noise with accuracy.

Apparently, I wasn't the only person who felt that way, as the guy in front of me instantly started laughing and yelled back, "I know what you mean, dude! I feel the same way." Then he started to moo out his car window, too. The lady behind me was next to join in. This whole row of traffic totally *got it*, and within seconds, nearly twenty different drivers were mooing at the top of their lungs. Now at least the situation *sounded* honest. If only I had caught it on my cell phone, that moment might have been YouTube gold. It provided a cathartic release for all of us.

When I eventually arrived at work, I was called into a morning sales seminar. I sat next to one of the managers, feeling frustrated that I was missing live sales calls, when a person dressed up in a large, mascot-style cow costume walked into the room to initiate the meeting. It was another one of those time-stopping moments. After driving into work feeling as though I was part of a figurative cattle drive, my shift started with a literal cow putting me to work.

"No, it can't be; this is impossible. Am I dreaming?" I thought, sitting there in a state of stunned disbelief. I don't subscribe to coincidence, and I was already aware of the Lord's sense of humor. "God," I prayed for the first time in too long, "I hear you. I think you're reaching out and trying to show me something because I'm looking at a cow right now after mooing out the car window on my way here."

The giant cow then wrote the word "moo" on a piece of paper and held it up to one half of the crowd. It was clear what they were supposed to do. They obeyed, and half the room began mooing. I honestly wondered at this point if I were in one of those dreams which seems so real that you're convinced it is until you wake up. But this was no dream. The only thing sleeping was my spirit, and the experience was jostling my soul awake into one of those rare moments of clarity.

"You're not mooing loud enough," said the cow, using obvious body language to convey her ideas. Then the cow said that only the most spirited mooers would receive the free T-shirts that she was about to start tossing. Next, the cow lifted up the "moo" sign to my half of the room. I sat there with my arms folded, refusing to comply.

You might be saying to yourself, "What's the big deal? Didn't you just moo that very morning? Now you could get a free T-shirt." But that morning, I had mooed of my own volition. It was a free-will moo. I do *not* moo on command. In order to preserve the last taught thread of my human dignity, I wouldn't embrace an identity among the herd. I remained silent, until the manager seated next to me turned to me and said in a thick Texan accent, "I don't like your attitude. You had better start mooin', son, or *it's your job!*"

So I stood my ground, right? I firmly planted my feet, and honored God's clear communication, right? Wrong. I said in reply, "Yes, sir," then mooed with gusto, in fear for my job. As hilarious as that entire morning was, it felt in the end as though I had sold one more piece of my soul to the queen bee, in exchange for that week's paycheck. I didn't even catch one of the free T-shirts. Afterward, my spirit quickly returned to its slumber.

God didn't give up on me. He simply kept throwing life pre-servers into the water until I grabbed one of them. In fact, rescuing is one of his specialties. My ultimate wake-up call came one day when the boss hired an Elvis impersonator to run our morning's sales meeting. Hiring this performer was a thoughtful gesture on the part of management, granted. And the artist's Elvis routine pro-vided the sales team with an entertaining break from the daily grind, which I appreciated. This entertainer was more enjoyable to watch than the giant cow had been. However, the disproportionate man-ner in which my coworkers responded to the Elvis performance was among the strangest things I've ever seen. You would think they had seen the Lord.

One woman described in detail how deeply *meaningful* the fake Elvis was to her soul. She also attached an Elvis quote to her cubi-cle wall and explained how she found his words inspiring. Another person claimed that the impersonator had *brought him true happiness* amidst the pain of his recent divorce. Right when I thought that things couldn't get any weirder, my favorite coworker, Bill, pulled me aside with a clown-like smile on his face. He proclaimed, "Elvis gave me purpose."

I thought to myself, "Entertaining, sure, but 'meaningfulness to one's soul, happiness, and purpose'? They're talking as though they've found God."

Bill continued, "My life's been in a real funk lately. I admit I've become full-blown depressed, even to the point of *contemplating suicide*. But Elvis pulled me right out of it!"

I walked back to my cubicle with my spirit stirring within me. I saw that all people have a God-shaped hole within them, which only *he* can fill. People were made for a loving covenant with their Creator. People were made to know and be known by God in an *intimate* relationship—as his child, as his brother or sister, as his friend, as his bride, and as his temple. If they don't know God, that hole is still there. As nature abhors a vacuum, they will attempt to fill it with *anything*.

I pondered, "My coworkers might be filling their God-shaped hole with the wrong things, like Elvis impersonators, but at least they're trying to fill it. I actually know who the answer is, but I've been actively running away from him ever since I lost Sam."

I placed my hands down on my desk with a rekindled determination. "That's it. I'm back," I said. And with that, glassy-eyed and emotional, I marched back over to Bill's cubicle.

"Bill," I said with my voice cracking.

"What is it, Ian? Sit down, talk to me," he answered.

I replied, "I need to tell you about Jesus Christ, the *real King*."

He answered kindly, "I'm an atheist, but go ahead."

I then delivered an impassioned presentation of the gospel, including my own testimony.

I finished my appeal saying, "You're my best friend in this place, and I can't handle the thought of you wanting to take your own life. Jesus knows firsthand what that degree of anxiety feels like. The New Testament records Jesus feeling *pained unto death*. He understands. He loves you, and it is his heart's desire to save you. Whatever you got from Elvis won't last, and it won't satisfy. But if you drink of the water I'm telling you about, you will never be thirsty again. Jesus is real. Give him a chance, please, so that he can show you he's real, just as he showed me."

With tears of joy, Bill accepted Jesus as Lord and Savior. He was baptized a few weeks later, by full immersion in Lake Austin. At the outdoor ceremony, the preacher of my new church read a letter to the congregation that I had written to him. It specified how, in the end, Bill was the one who had ministered to me.

Bill said, "I can't believe how many years I've wasted not knowing God, but I won't waste one more day. Now the first thing I think about when I wake up in the morning, and the last thing I think about before I fall asleep each night, is how God is real, loves me, and saved my life. It's the best news I've ever heard. I didn't know a person could be so happy!"

A powerful reversal happened that day in the office when I found my courage, walked into Bill's cubicle, and presented the gospel to my coworker. After that spiritual awakening, I entered into an intense time of prayer, self-reflection, and examination of conscience, in which I admitted that I had quite a bit of cleaning up to do. I gave my life back to Jesus.

When I asked Christ back into my heart, I discovered that God wasn't waiting with a club. He was waiting with a hug. As soon as I took one step his direction, my heavenly Abba leaped off the porch where he had been waiting, watching, and hoping the entire time. He ran the rest of the distance and caught me, squeezing and rocking me in his arms. With the relief of a parent upon the return of a kidnapped child, he cried, "Don't you do that to me! Don't ever run away from home again, my precious baby." In other words, I felt a Father's love. I realized in my rescue that I hadn't merely fallen in love with God's blessings across my life. I loved *him*.

The Lord proceeded to use those dark years for his redemptive purposes. He showed me how deep the rabbit hole of sin and ignorance goes, and how radically dependent upon him we truly are. He showed me the lie of self-sovereignty—the lie of following our own way, the lie of playing God. It's a lie we were all born into, and turning to our Creator for life means dying to that misplaced sense of trust we place in our own way of thinking. If we want to live, then there are things that have to die. We must have our own understanding turned on its head, over and over again, and nothing does that for us like our sufferings.

I learned that being made into the likeness of Christ is a process; after being convicted of my need for salvation, I must pick up my cross and follow him. He revealed to me how bearing a cross is not just a metaphor. If I am to follow him to life, then I need to die to self. I finally saw this surrender as good news, for I had done it *my way* for the past several years, and those years had proved utterly empty.

Giving my life back to Christ filled me with purpose and happiness, as the blood of the Lamb washed me clean.

I said earlier with regard to my backslidden years that, according to Jesus, he who tries to save his life will lose it—and that is exactly what happened to me. Jesus also said that he who loses his life will find it. That also happened (and continues to happen). In order to leave behind enslavement to selfishness and advance in the love that God has for me, I needed to lose my vicious addictions. I have repeatedly needed to shed my own shortsighted assumptions and to allow my current way of thinking to die, in order to grow into the fuller and more accurate perspectives that God reveals. As a Christian I must continually die to self-centeredness in order to lift up God and neighbor more—even to pray for those who persecute me. I have desired more than anything a flourishing life of happiness, love, and freedom. Figuratively speaking, I was just "dying to live". As it turns out, that was literally what Jesus was asking me to do.

Saint Augustine describes in his *Confessions* how he turns to God in repentance: the virtue of self-control says to him, "Why do you stand upon yourself and so not stand at all? Cast yourself upon God and be not afraid; He will not draw away and let you fall. Cast yourself without fear, He will receive you and heal you."

He's right. God *will* receive you. When I finally took a knee, the Great Physician cracked his knuckles and went straight to work healing and restoring me. It never ceases to amaze me how much I'll exhaust myself in resisting repentance, only to find again how happy and immense the mercy of God really is.

15

Brother Ian

After I gave my life back to God, one of the first things I realized was the need to transition out of the phone sales job, which was *not* my calling, and back into teaching and ministry, which *was*. To help accomplish this necessary change, the Lord sent me the right people at the right time.

The first new lifeline to grace that God sent me was my younger brother, Jesse. Having recently graduated from Mount Pleasant High School, Jesse decided to move to Texas and become my roommate. He had been growing in his own close walk with the Lord throughout adolescence. Now entering into young adulthood, he was a bright and vital witness of a life lived to the fullest. He shared my passion for the performing arts, including both music and acting, having taken lead roles in school plays as I used to do. Jesse is among the funniest people I know, and he made me laugh every day.

My second lifeline to grace was my new mentor, Dr. Maurice Carver, one of the most accomplished and brilliant individuals I would ever have the honor of knowing. My brother Jesse discovered him first. Not long after moving in with me, he came home from work one day bursting with excitement. "God nudged me!" he exclaimed. "He set me up in a meeting today with this cool girl at Target's snack shop. I noticed her reading this book about professional counseling, and I felt moved to talk to her. She said that the Holy Spirit must have sent me over to her so that she could tell me about her night classes at a Bible institute! It's like a college, but they can't call it that yet, because they're still in the accreditation process—they just started out. I'm gonna visit the school tonight and check it out. Wanna come?" he asked.

Exhausted from another over-time day selling phones, I said, "Maybe another time."

Jesse came home later that night glowing and bounding with excitement. "I enrolled!" he exclaimed.

"Whoa," I blurted, "you enrolled in a Bible institute tonight? That's big. What about tuition costs?"

"It's free," he answered happily.

"Free? Not-yet-accredited? Because you met some girl at Target today? It sounds suspicious. Are you *sure* about this?" I asked, feeling concerned. "I know about the guidance of the Lord, and if this is from him, then that's great. But I can't help wondering if the school is legitimate. If they don't charge tuition, how do they pay their faculty?"

Jesse explained, "They don't. Their whole faculty volunteers their time and service. It's a Christian mission to offer an education to people who otherwise can't afford one. Isn't that awesome? Just meet the president of the institute. As soon as you meet him, it will all make sense. This man exudes leadership. You'll catch his vision, and you'll understand. They could use you! I bet they would let you teach. You've been talking about a career change. It wouldn't hurt to have a little post-graduate on your resume, now would it?" said Jesse, with a glint in his eye.

I listened night after night to Jesse's passionate explanations of the biblical counseling material he was learning. A couple of weeks after his classes began, I decided to investigate for myself.

Talking with the president, Dr. Maurice Carver, I soon realized that I was in the presence of greatness. I was captivated as he relayed to me the school's history. As though I had found my next Meeting Jesus study, I desired nothing more than to teach Christology and apologetics courses for the institute.

I begged him, "Sir, I know that I have only an undergraduate degree, but it's from Carnegie—"

"You're hired," he interjected. "When can you start?"

Pleasantly stunned, I replied, "I can get you my transcripts and resume right away. I should have brought them with me tonight."

"I don't need them," said Dr. Carver. "All I need is the fact that two minutes before you knocked on my door tonight to meet me, I was in a prayer meeting with a couple of the other faculty members.

We prayed together, 'Lord, we need one more instructor. If this school is your will, then please send us another teacher *tonight.*' Two minutes after our prayer meeting was over, you knocked on my door. The Lord just hired you. I'm only an instrument. How soon can you begin?"

Wasting no time, I dove right in and was soon teaching several different free evening classes for the institute. I also adopted Dr. Carver as my new mentor. In addition to his being the most accomplished person I had ever met, he was the most humble. According to earthly measurement standards, he had more right to brag than anybody else I knew. Yet during years of friendship, he has never boasted, not once.

"How many times, exactly, have you been personally invited to the White House?" I once marveled. "That's huge!"

"Three—but no, it's not huge," he answered. "What's big in the eyes of men is different from what's big in the eyes of God. God is no respecter of persons in the way that fallen humanity is. Each individual child is equally precious to him. What God values is a repentant heart. People really repenting is the big deal."

Dr. Carver's combination of brilliant theology with loving practice reminded me of Pastor Sam's harmony of belief and action. Being around Dr. Carver felt like being around Sam, which makes sense in light of the fact that the same Lord was present in both of them.

I began at the institute by teaching Christology and apologetics. Eventually I added a Christian history course too. I had forgotten how much I loved giving talks. I didn't know that a person could have such a fulfilling and enjoyable time working. "If only there was a way to do this for a paycheck," I thought to myself, still selling phones during the day. The contrast between my day job and my evening job was growing more and more evident, and where I belonged was becoming obvious. One day Libby, my Catholic sister-in-law, said, "Ian, you weren't put in this world to sell phones."

Those words hit my soul as though the Lord himself had spoken them to me, and the truth of those words set me free. I finally announced at work that I was quitting my job. Then I went straight away to Dr. Carver's office.

"Murphy!" he bellowed, as was his typical greeting. "What brings you here at this time?"

"I quit my job. I want to be a teacher for a living. I never want to step foot into a cubicle again, for as long as I live," I said.

He replied, "I have been waiting and praying for this day. Get in the car. There's no time to lose."

Dr. Carver then drove me to a nearby Baptist university, where I enrolled that very day in a graduate program. It was an abrupt transition, but God provided my needs through another series of sweet, creamy milk feedings in order to strengthen my spiritual legs. Asleep for three years, I hadn't used them in a while, and apparently they had atrophied. With the providential help of a student loan consolidation, a scholarship, and some financial aid, my master's degree was quickly underway.

The graduate program blessed me with another dream-team faculty, every bit as gifted and influential as my high school teachers had been. I needed three years to finish the ordinarily two-year program because my undergraduate degree was in social history; my extra two semesters of graduate school consisted entirely of prerequisite courses in theology. I was therefore surrounded by undergraduates in all my classes the first year, which was loads of fun. I was like their Sam Brunsvold—not a full-fledged adult, but a little further along in life than they were. I reveled in the position of role model, leading student study groups, organizing local ministry endeavors, and driving a carful of classmates down to the Bible institute, where they enjoyed sitting in on the classes I taught.

My study groups were exam preparations, prayer meetings, missionary training, and hang-out sessions all at the same time. College traditions quickly formed around crab feeds, card games, and coffee shops. Strengthened by all the love and support, I finally quit smoking. Having tried and failed numerous times before, I had started to wonder whether it was possible. But God's grace proved to be sufficient. He also had plenty of grace for my family and friends, who had to put up with a cranky bear for roughly two months.

I added a New Testament concentration to my master's program and began studying Greek. My professor, Dr. Paul Johnson, was the head of New Testament studies and became my academic advisor. He was a gifted teacher, and he opened my eyes to how much an understanding of the Greek language can unlock deeper layers of meaning in the Gospels. For instance, he explained that in the Bread of Life Discourse from John chapter 6, when Jesus says, "I am the bread of life", the word "I" in the original Greek text was implied. Yet it had been added for emphasis. Thus Jesus was really saying, "I myself am the bread of life", as if to make clear that he was not speaking figuratively.

Dr. Johnson added himself to the list of heaven-sent mentors, and he became a dear friend. Providing fatherly guidance, he helped me to discipline myself and to regain my integrity. He asked me in one of my meetings with him, "Which verb is passive, Ian, 'speak' or 'listen'?"

I answered, "The verb 'listen' is the passive one."

"Wrong," he said. "That's the common misconception. Not only are *both* verbs active, but listening is much *more* active than speaking is, for a couple reasons. First, whenever I'm speaking, I already know what I mean. But when I'm listening, I may misinterpret the speaker's meaning. Consequently, I must expend greater energy in order to give my neighbor the respectful attention he deserves. Second, the listener must also actively fight off the temptation to formulate a response while the speaker is still talking. Listening is extraordinarily active. If you do it correctly, then you'll break a sweat."

He modeled this active listening every time I met with him to discuss my questions or to ask for his advice. And when he spoke he would say, "Ian that is the stupidest course of action you could possibly consider", or something along those lines if that's what I needed to hear. And I was able to hear it because I knew I was *loved*. I knew I was loved because he had "broken a sweat" listening to me.

Learning from Dr. Carver and Dr. Johnson, teaching classes at the institute, and enjoying my coursework all made for a spiritual springtime. The long, dark winter was behind me. Best of all, I was about to become a pastor. The administrators at the university introduced me to the Baptist General Convention of Texas, which gave me a license to preach in their affiliated churches. This licensure afforded multiple opportunities to preach at local services and tent revivals, and I quickly found myself giving talks with the same frequency I had enjoyed during my time at CMU. Before long, I was a popular interim pastor for a number of congregations.

One particular church kept calling me back week after week to cover its Sunday morning worship service. It had 250 members, a thriving group of on-fire youth, and an overall spirit of zeal that I hadn't experienced since leaving the Pentecostals. Their love for God and each other was so manifest that when they asked me to become their head pastor, I was beside myself with joy. I accepted the post without reservation.

The congregation affectionately referred to me as Brother Ian, a name that spread rapidly to almost everyone who knew me. When my friends used the title, it seemed as though they got a kick out of it. When church members used it, it implied the deepest respect.

The church was in a small town, and during my first week there I was given a royal welcome. The congregation hosted a magnificent housewarming party when I moved into the parsonage. They showered me with gifts, hugs, and the best chicken and dumplings and zucchini bread I've ever eaten. The local paper ran a story about me, and the local tailor gave me a new suit. I was invited onto the football field at the high school's Friday night game to be introduced to the community and to pray with the players. From my first moments in town, the local gas station owner never let me pay for my own tank.

This church practiced the virtue of generosity to an amazing degree. To this day I haven't seen its equal. The congregation not only paid me a salary that far exceeded a *justice wage* but they were funding the building of a new church in the area for Hispanic immigrants. The church quickly put me to work at the construction site with hammer, nails, and calking gun in hand.

Soon I was leading three services a week and the youth group. New families started driving in from as far as ninety minutes away to hear what they called "preaching that's funny, entertaining, and life-changing, all mixed together". Every Sunday there were conversions and recommitments after the altar call, and I baptized five precious souls within my first few months as head pastor. My cup was overflowing with blessings.

It seemed I had found my vocation at last, and my ordination ceremony was a momentous occasion, where even the toughest of Texas deacons was caught drying his eyes as though he were attending a wedding. But there was just one small problem: at this point in my rekindled walk with the Lord I was nearly convinced that the Catholic Church contained the fullness of truth.

16

Wrestling with God

From the time I began reading *Rome Sweet Home* in 1993 until I entered the Rite of Christian Initiation of Adults (RCIA) in 2003, I had been studying Catholicism, but my pilgrimage to the Catholic Church was much more than a mental exercise. Jesus never said that it is out of the overflow of the *head* that the mouth speaks. The spiritual journey is ultimately about the state of one's heart, and the human heart is a complex thing.

Awareness of the truth is of little benefit unless a person is actually transformed by it, and for me the process of both learning the truth and being transformed by it took time. I am comforted by the fact that the God of Abraham didn't deposit a list of claims into the world and say, "Believe everything on this list in order to be saved, or reject it to your own demise." The heavenly Father revealed himself to his people across time, through an unfolding relationship. My own relationship with the Almighty has taught me why he calls his people "Israel", which means "struggles with God" or "one who has striven against God", for I have had plenty of struggles. As anyone who is married can tell you, for love to be real, you *will* wrestle.

As I continued my study of Christianity, one of the things I had to wrestle with was the dawning realization that almost everything I thought I knew about Catholicism was wrong. As much as I respected the Protestants who taught me along the way, I increasingly came to see that the following claims they made about the Catholic Church were false.

- Catholics worship Mary.
  In truth, the Church deems the worship of Mary to be a heresy.

- Catholics worship statues.

    Actually, the worship of statues would constitute idolatry according to Catholicism.

- Catholics worship dead people.

    Catholics honor those members of the Body of Christ who have died and gone to heaven (called saints) and ask for their prayers, just as we ask our brothers and sisters on earth to pray for us.

- Catholics believe the pope to be the head of the Church.

    What the Church really teaches is that Jesus Christ is the head of the Church while the pope serves as his representative on earth.

- Catholics think that through their good works they can earn their way into heaven.

    The Church teaches what many Protestants believe—that the death of Jesus paid for our sins and opened heaven for those willing to accept him as Savior and Lord.

- The Church tells people *not* to take their sins to God.

    In reality, the Church makes continual appeals for people to confess their sins to God and to receive his mercy through the sacrament of penance. In addition, *taking one's sins to God* is one of the first things that Catholics do at Mass.

- Catholics don't read the Bible.

    Actually Catholics hear readings from the Bible at every Mass. Also, the treasured writings of the saints and the catechism itself are full of quotes from the Bible.

The more I learned about the teachings of the Catholic Church, the more troubled I became. If Catholicism were as evil as Protestants claimed, then why would they need to invent falsehoods to make their case? Or were Protestants just unaware? Either way, I realized that for centuries Protestants had been putting the Church *on trial* and playing the role of the prosecuting attorney. I was alarmed to discover that the name "Satan" means "accuser of the brethren". I was even more alarmed to realize that I too had been adopting the position of the enemy of God by standing as the Church's *accuser*. I also had to admit that in doing so I had not been motivated by a desire for the truth. Instead, my heart had been driven by a vested interest in the Catholic Church being wrong. After all, by the time these realizations were really sinking in, I was an ordained Baptist minister. If Catholicism was true, then I stood to lose everything.

I thought back to when I first encountered the *Denominations Handbook*, which God had used to propel me toward the early Church Fathers. This handbook had listed more than two hundred different denominations, which amounted to thirty thousand different churches that frequently opposed one another. However, the Lord had instructed his followers to stay unified in the bonds of peace, and he had paid dearly for this peace. Moreover, the conflicts and the divisions in the Body of Christ had created massive confusion, and God is not the author of confusion.

I was an ordained minister about to finish a master's degree in theology, and yet the burden of figuring out for myself which teachings were true was too heavy for me. In a word, it came down to *authority*. Did Jesus leave authority on this earth for his people? Wherever that authority was located, it could not be seated in a system of protest and fragmentation, not when the Bible commands unity.

These reflections about *unity* and *authority* led to related observations. The first of these was that, as a Baptist, I practiced my own version of everything that I *thought* I rejected in Catholicism. For instance, I thought I rejected the *liturgy* of the Catholic Church. Then I realized, while preaching at the Baptist church, that we had our own liturgy. There was a definite sequence of events at the worship service. There were rituals. There were designated times to stand and times to kneel, times to pray and listen, and times to sing hymns. We had our own version of a liturgy; it just looked different, that's all.

Similarly, I critiqued Catholicism for following the *traditions of men*. To me, the Bible by itself was enough. Yet, ironically, *sola scriptura* isn't in the Bible. In fact, 1 Timothy 3:15 refers to the *Church* of the living God as "the pillar and bulwark of truth". In reality, *sola scriptura* was a tradition of men—one that contradicted the Bible.

As Baptists, we also practiced a democratic voting system to deal with disputed matters. I was offered the position of head pastor as the result of a majority vote, which is *not* how pastoral leadership positions had been appointed in the New Testament churches. Unsettled, I asked one member of the choir why she voted for me to be their head pastor. She answered, "You were the funniest of all the preachers we were looking at." The compliment aside, I found it highly problematic to select shepherds based on popularity and the ability to tell jokes.

According to this ballot system, the Lord revealed his will in the present moment through a majority vote. When, across all of Judeo-Christian history, do we see the current majority get it right? The norm is that of our patient God commissioning a lone prophetic voice against the masses who catch up to the revelation in subsequent generations. The Baptist polling system was yet another tradition of men, and *not* one with biblical warrant.

As Baptists under the Baptist General Convention of Texas, we held to an understanding of the *priesthood of each individual believer* that clearly wasn't the scriptural understanding of the phrase; we preached the *autonomy of the local congregation* which also wasn't biblical. These, too, were the traditions of men. The more I looked, the more traditions I saw.

Another thing I thought I rejected was apostolic succession. Based on my father's prejudice, I assumed that apostolic succession stopped with the New Testament churches. My dad would fume over the Catholic claim that the pope was the successor of Peter, saying, "Catholics made that up so that they could control people and usurp more power." I would answer all fired up, "Yeah!" While a pastor, however, I learned that Baptists have their own line of succession. They trace themselves back to the Anabaptists of the sixteenth century, who they claimed were the spiritual descendants of the first Christians. Liturgy, tradition, and succession—as a Baptist I had all three.

There were other epiphanies. I didn't like that Catholics had bishops. But didn't we Baptists have our own version of *overseers*? I didn't like that the Catholic Church claimed Jesus was truly present in the Eucharist. But as a Baptist I emphatically preached that Jesus was *truly present* in our community because Jesus said, "For where two or three are gathered together in my name, there am I in the midst of them" (Mt 18:20). Christ's presence was *not* representational; the Lord was literally *there* in our midst in a special and miraculous way. I didn't like the sacraments, but didn't we practice the two *ordinances* of baptism and the Lord's Supper?

We didn't have the sacraments, but we had ordinances. We didn't have the pope, but we had the Bible Answer Man. We didn't have a bishop but we had the Baptist general director of missions. We didn't have confirmation, but we had tent revivals where we encouraged people to make a decision for Christ at the age of adult consent and receive the Holy Spirit. With our own version of everything, we had become experts at reinventing the wheel.

Through wrestling with the Almighty, he showed me that I already practiced everything that I *thought* I was against in the Catholic Church, in some form or another. But two more important epiphanies were yet to come.

17

How to Give Catholic Homilies as a Baptist

As I've come to see over and over again as a professor, one's philosophical assumptions exert a tremendous influence on every part of a person's life. Which assumptions are the more influential: the ones of which we are aware or the ones we don't even know exist? I would answer that the assumptions of which *we are not aware* are the ones exerting the greatest impact, because they run about within us unchecked.

In my case, without realizing it I had come to embrace a number of modernist assumptions that were exerting a tremendous influence over my thinking. Not enough can be said here about the limitations and the distortions of the truth caused by a strictly modernist view of reality, but one of these is compartmentalization. Saint Thomas Aquinas would one day give me the language for understanding that reality occurs as a *whole*—not in disconnected compartments.

During the period of history we call the Enlightenment, men of learning began to specialize in narrower and narrower fields of study. The great universities founded in the Middle Ages had different scholars teaching medicine, law, philosophy, mathematics, and so on, but over time these branches of learning subdivided even more. The trend has continued to our own day to the point where an undergraduate can major in such narrow fields as biomedical informatics or sustainable food systems.

There is nothing wrong with deconstructing a grandfather clock to see how the individual mechanisms work. However, it seems that across the ages we have forgotten to put the clock back together again in order to see the whole. The problem of compartmentalization has become so extreme that many people think religion and science oppose each other. They do not see that the truth is a whole in which its various parts exist in harmony with each other. In truth, there is no competition between studying the Artist and studying the canvas, paint, and brushes that the Artist used.

As Saint Thomas Aquinas explained, we differentiate *to unite better*; we draw distinctions between the different aspects of reality in order to understand better how they occur as a whole. Before I encountered Aquinas, I thought that math was math while music was music. Now I appreciate how mathematical music is and how a brilliant calculus formula can be a song—a work of art in itself.

Whenever I viewed Christianity through this fragmented view of reality, a host of unnecessary questions and problems arose, problems that never actually existed in the first place. I tortured myself with questions about faith, works, grace, justification, sanctification, and salvation. Trying desperately to work out where each one fit into the way of Jesus, I found myself lost in a labyrinth of doctrinal disputes that, not surprisingly, had fragmented the Church itself into a myriad of factions.

After pulling an all-nighter with some graduate students, in a failed attempt to figure out the distinctions between grace, works, faith, and more, I visited Dr. Johnson. I walked him through all my unresolved questions as he nodded and said, "Mmmm."

I concluded, "So the best I can come up with is that the process of sanctification starts after the moment of salvation stops, while justification happens at the end of our sanctification. But that doesn't exactly add up because there seems to be justification present when we're saved, and Paul uses the progressive, ongoing aspect of the word 'saved' as opposed to the simple aorist past tense—therefore, salvation is itself a justifying process, not a 'done deal'. In the end, I don't know where to draw the line between these separate things. So I just hate my whole life right now. I'm finished, please respond."

My mentor replied, "That's really stupid. You're not, but what you said at the end is. Ian, you were on the right track there for a moment, especially in observing that salvation is a 'justifying process'—that's right. But then you said that you didn't know where to draw the line between these 'separate' things. I had no idea you were such a modernist."

He could have spelled it out for me, but like the finest teachers he provided exactly enough for me to draw my own conclusions.

He continued, "Let me ask you this: Can you claim credit for your ability to have faith in God?"

I answered, "*No*, that capacity is a *gift*."

"Right," he affirmed. "So I suppose you might say that faith itself *is* a grace?"

The light bulb went on, and kept getting brighter. Faith *is a grace*. Faith is also something we *do*, a *work*. At the same time, the ability to do good works is a grace, which is received abundantly through the practice of our faith. Faith, works, grace, justification, sanctification, and salvation are not the isolated entities I had assumed they were. They each hold special importance in their own right; they are intimately tethered in an inextricable way. They occur together. They are even *present within* one another, as the lung already has within it capillaries that are part of the cardiovascular system, while the heart already contains within it oxygen receptors that are part of the respiratory system. "The different parts aren't 'separate', in the first place!" I realized. "They're all connected, mutually interdependent, and present within each other. Their agency occurs in union." Dr. Johnson had put the clock back together, and now it worked. The peace I experienced was indescribable.

The second epiphany happened when I studied the Church's liturgical calendar and discovered that I had been unknowingly following it ever since my conversion experience when I was fourteen years old. Every year during the time leading up to Easter, I had been moved to take on a spiritual purge. I would make sacrifices. I would reflect prayerfully on those who had fallen asleep in Gethsemane during the Lord's great hour of need. I would ponder how, in my own way, I had been among those who shouted *crucify him*. I did these things based on nothing more than spiritual nudges—long before I knew what Lent was. Similarly, during the weeks leading up to Christmas, I found myself celebrating with excited anticipation both the first and the second comings of Christ into the world—long before I had ever heard the word *Advent*. One day, I found myself overwhelmed with thankfulness for the divine mercy of God, only to discover later that this particular day had been designated Divine Mercy Sunday on the Catholic calendar.

My desire for these practices couldn't be explained by my exposure to Scripture or Protestant theology. The phenomenon was truly mystical, something arising from my union with the Lord, which connected me with his Church. Here is another example. Once when I was asked to give a talk I was led to three specific Scriptures. I based the lecture on those verses and found out afterward that I had "accidentally" chosen all three readings from the Catholic Mass on the day of my talk, down to each chapter and verse. Discovering this special intimacy with the Lord and his Body was as humbling as it was uncanny—it was *beautiful*.

Through the Holy Spirit I sensed that there was more to a celebration of the Lord's Supper than symbolic representation. During a Communion Service, the Lord spoke to my heart and said, "This is sacred. I am present in this." At another Communion Service, when the minister said that what was about to happen was *purely representational* and that any claim to the contrary indicated the worst sort of idolatry, the Spirit said quietly, "That's not right. I *am* in this, more than they know."

After all of these realizations, I found myself defending the Catholic Church while I was still a Baptist pastor. One church member approached me and asked, "Brother Ian, why do Catholics keep Jesus on the Cross? I thought he rose from the dead! *Why are they keeping the Lord earthbound?*"

I responded, "Do you put up a Nativity set at Christmas?"

"In my opinion, every self-respecting Baptist should have a Nativity set. Yes, I do," he answered proudly.

"Is baby Jesus in the manger?"

"Well of course he is! It's not a manger scene without baby Jesus in there."

"Why are you keeping the Lord earthbound?"

I could see the light come on. As though an unnecessary weight had lifted, he said with relief, "Well I never thought of it like that. Thanks, Brother Ian!"

Another person approached me and asked, "Does a Catholic believe that he is saved?"

I answered, "Your question is flawed."

"No it's not!" he blurted. "It's a simple question, and you just admitted that the Catholics can't answer it."

I responded calmly, knowing firsthand where he was coming from, "No, the question is in fact flawed." Then I waited.

Eventually, he couldn't resist. "Okay, how is my question flawed?"

I explained, "According to the grammatical aspect applied to the Greek term for 'saved' in the New Testament, salvation is an ongoing reality. It's a *process*. Therefore, to answer your question, a Catholic Christian would say, 'Yes I'm *saved*. Yes I *am being* saved. And yes I *will be* saved.'"

"Oh my God, that's right," he said thoughtfully.

"They get a lot of things right," I replied.

On another occasion, I was asked to give an Easter talk for a large venue. I gave my talk on the humble and loving role model that my Blessed Mother was to me. I also defended her in class when an ill-informed student began to mock her. I appealed to Luke's Magnificat, and because it was Scripture, my classmate retracted his comment. In a profound reversal, this student who previously mocked Mary now honored her by practicing the humility she modeled for us. Moved by the incident, the professor asked me to pray for the whole class.

In one more example, one of my professors approached me privately with a special request pertaining to his theology course that I was taking at the time. He said, "Ian, as you know our class is about to give public speeches as part of the final-exam grade. I know that each student is allowed to choose one of the topics from the syllabus, but I am asking that you cover the topic of the Catholic view of *sola scriptura*. I fear the other students might be scandalized in researching that subject. I can trust you, our resident fulltime Baptist pastor, to do fairness to the Catholic position, without getting misled."

"I would be happy to," I answered, as the mischief descended upon me.

The day of my graded speech, I stood in front of my classmates and opened by engaging the room in a sort of Socratic dialogue, which drew my colleagues right in. The professor loved it, at first.

"What does *sola scriptura* mean?" I asked.

One of my friends chimed in, "It means that the Bible alone holds authority in Christianity, as opposed to attributing authority to both the Bible and tradition. Tradition doesn't hold authority in Christianity. Only the Bible does."

I replied, "Thank you. So what I hear you saying is that, according to *sola scriptura*, the Bible by itself is authoritative—*not* Church tradition."

"Precisely," she answered.

I proceeded, "I want to make sure that I have fully heard you. You're claiming that Christians ought to attribute authority to the Bible, but they shouldn't attribute authority to Church tradition. Is that what you're claiming?"

She answered, "Yes, that is exactly what I'm claiming. And I believe it."

"Is there a list in the Bible of the documents that should be included in the New Testament, and a list of the documents which should not?" I questioned.

The student answered, "No."

"How was the New Testament canon selected?" I asked.

"By early Christians who decided which documents held the authority of eyewitness accounts or the authority of researchers like Luke who took the time and effort to interview the eyewitnesses— as opposed to secondhand or thirdhand resources, which although valuable, do not possess the weight of the primary-source material," she said.

I encouraged my friend, "Well said! The historian in me really appreciates your articulation."

"Thanks."

I continued, "So, the documents of the New Testament canon were selected by early Christians?"

"That's right," another student agreed, with the whole class nodding.

I said, "So, there is no canonical list in the New Testament. Rather, the New Testament's documents were compiled by the Church. In other words, we all agree that it was *Church tradition* that determined which documents constitute the New Testament."

I paused as the faces throughout the room indicated the forming of new mental connections, as well as the suddenly unsettled emotions that resulted.

I concluded, "Therefore, there is *no such thing* as *sola scriptura*. If you attribute authority to the New Testament canon, then you have simultaneously *already* attributed authority to the Church tradition that selected it. *Sola scriptura* is impossible by definition. I'm sorry if the idea of ascribing authority to Church tradition makes you feel uncomfortable, but in trusting the canon, you've already attributed authority to Church tradition. Don't feel bad, you just honored the Bible. After all, in the third chapter of Paul's first letter to Timothy, he calls the *Church* the pillar and bulwark of—"

"Stop!" my professor shouted. "You get an A+. Now go back to your desk, before you convert every one of my students to Catholicism—and get me fired."

"I'm finished," I said, taking my seat.

By this point my sermons at the Baptist church had become Catholic homilies in disguise. No one caught on because I replaced Catholic buzzwords with their closest Baptist equivalent. I substituted "Communion" for "Eucharist" and "ordinance" for "sacrament". "Penitential observance" became "voluntarily giving up stuff", while "seven deadly sins" became "seven sins that can kill you". I recommended sixty minutes of devotional time rather than a Holy Hour, and I talked about Peter instead of Saint Peter. As long as I carefully selected my terminology, I could preach all the Catholic doctrine I wanted. And they loved it. Church members said they had never heard such rich substance in all their lives.

Of course, those linguistic nuances sometimes matter a great deal. The Eucharist is more than what many Protestants mean by communion. Even a commonplace word like *community* carries important connotations that are missing from the closely-related-but-still-not-exactly-synonymous term *fellowship*.

"Are you lying to your sheep?" my conscience asked.

I would speedily answer, "Nooo ... no ... I'm just ... I'm ... *Shut up!*"

Like my agnostic crisis and my spiritual winter, I again stood at a crossroads. The new issue was *ecclesiology*, the true nature and expression of Christ's Church. If the Catholic Church was what it claimed to be, then I had to become Catholic. If Jesus had left authority on this world for us, against which the gates of hell would never prevail, and if the Church was truly a hospital for the sick that—despite our shortcomings, even through our shortcomings—demonstrated God's love for all people, then joining was the next step. I had to convert to Catholicism for the only reason *to* convert: because it's true. Doing so, however, would mean the loss of my livelihood, my network, and my reputation. In addition, there would be the inevitable consequence of confusing, scandalizing, and likely *losing* a number of close friends. Then there was my dad. *What would he do?* That was one of the scariest questions of all. The solution was obvious—I could keep my Catholicism a secret! That solved everything. As my imaginary courtroom trial came to its close, the verdict was in: I needed to become a closet Catholic. How does one live persuaded by the truth of the Catholic Church, while working as a fulltime Baptist preacher? The answer is simple: by living a double life.

18

When Parents Pray

As I said early on in my story, I am one of nine converts to Catholicism in my family. As Saint Augustine credits his mother's prayers for his entry into the Church, I credit the prayers of my two Catholic grandfathers. Displaying the power of fatherhood, Grampa and GingGing stood their ground as faithful Catholics in a religiously divided family. My grandfathers were best friends for most of their lives. They even served as altar boys together at a Catholic parish in New Milford, New Jersey, long before Grampa's firstborn child married GingGing's firstborn child.

Grampa was Catholic while his wife, my Nanie, attended Charlie Rizzo's Nazarene church. Similarly, GingGing was Catholic while his wife wasn't. My maternal grandmother, known affectionately as *Pamah* instead of *Grandma*, had joined the Jehovah's Witnesses.

My dad had been born Catholic, but later left the Church. Jesus met him in early adulthood through some very cool urban ministers who helped draw my father back into Christian faith. Whenever Dad told the story of his dramatic conversion story, I would picture the missionaries as urban pirates. I imagined these gruff and salty dogs, who sailed about the city streets in their church van and set the land-lovers free from that evil establishment we call the government—by introducing them to Jesus. Dad remained a Protestant Christian his whole life.

Thankfully, my mom rejected the Watchtower Society, which is essentially the heresy of Arianism wearing a new dress—there is nothing new under the sun. But like my dad, my mom also left Catholicism. Jesus met her, too, and the intimate friendship she's had with him ever since developed on the Protestant side of the divide.

The only other Catholics in my family of whom I was aware, besides Grampa and GingGing, were GingGing's sister, my great-aunt Jo-Jo, and her husband. In other words, the Protestants in my family largely outnumbered the Catholics.

One time, GingGing opened up to me about the tension of living in a spiritually divided marriage. "I am committed to my wife until death do us part. I love her, and I will never break that commitment," he concluded, after describing his heartache to me in detail. He maintained a special devotion to the Blessed Mother. After he died, he was buried with two personal treasures from his earthly life: a pack of cigarettes and his rosary. GingGing once told me about a dream he had in which he was present at Christ's crucifixion. "I was there," he explained. "In my dream, I saw our Lord's love for us with my own two eyes. The next three days were the happiest of my whole life. It went *way* past any earthly happiness. I tasted the joy that awaits people in heaven. His followers have more to look forward to than I could ever put into words, son."

GingGing introduced me to Mozart. He also recorded himself singing the Our Father. I would play this recording often, especially during times when my life got rough. When GingGing gave me his "how to be a man" speech, I was in awe of his humble strength of character. Similar to the two Catholic teachers who had inspired me in high school, he had that quiet, solid integrity and I wanted it.

Grampa remained stoically quiet about any tensions he experienced from living in a divided household. But I sensed it whenever he invited me to Mass. He would say, "Ian, would you like to come to Mass with me today?" I would reply, "No thank you," with a touch of arrogance. Grampa would say nothing in response, but the look on his face conveyed a mixture of heartbreak and hope. Every summer and every Christmas without exception, he invited me to Mass. Although I turned him down every time, he never stopped asking.

Like the two rooks on a chessboard, who together are even stronger than the queen, these two men spent most of the game sitting in the background—only to decide the victory in the fullness of time. They never stopped praying for us. Then, one at a time, we started coming home.

Grampa and Nanie's youngest, my Uncle Tim, was the first convert to Catholicism. Tim's wife, my Aunt Steph, joined him. After that, my Nanie became Catholic. Shortly thereafter, my sister Shaylyn entered the Church.

Shaylyn asked me, "Ian, did Uncle Tim give you *Rome Sweet Home?*"

"Yup," I said.

She replied, "You should read it."

My older brother, Sean, the one allergic to all things churchy, was next. Holding to our family's Irish tradition of marriages between Protestants and Catholics, Sean was Protestant while his wife, my sister-in-law Libby, was Catholic. Libby had been patiently fielding all of his questions about the Church since their courtship.

Years into their marriage, during the time when I was still working as an interim pastor for a Baptist church, I visited Sean during a pivotal time in his life. He had enrolled in RCIA, but a couple of unresolved issues had him questioning whether he would actually enter the Church that upcoming Easter. Sometime around midnight, while the rest of the house slept, Sean and I had a life-altering conversation.

Sean said, "Every time I have a question about the Catholic Church, and I mean *every single time,* they always have the answer. None of what I thought about Catholicism was true. None of it. This is the one lighthouse that rises above all the others. It goes back to Jesus, and it remains united amidst differences. I know you're a Baptist preacher, so I hope this doesn't offend you, but it's like all the younger Protestant break-out groups of Christianity stand in the shadow of this one lighthouse. It's like Catholicism is the gold standard, and I've been settling for bronze and silver when I could have gold."

I responded, "Sean, I know. In secret, I'm almost convinced, and I've reached those same conclusions myself. Maybe I'm already convinced but won't admit it yet. Please don't tell Libby. She'll know I'm a hypocrite for keeping my job. And whatever you do, *don't tell Dad.*"

"Tell them what?" he said with a clever smile.

"Thank you," I responded emphatically.

Sean continued, "You know me—I say you should be real about what you believe. If you're convicted that Catholicism is true, then you should enter the Church. There, I said it. But you need to come to that decision in your own time. I know it's been a long process for me. I *understand.* I bet you can help me with my last two questions."

"What are they?" I asked.

"The first one is this: I don't like that, if I become Catholic, then I *have* to believe the words of every self-proclaimed prophet who comes down the pike. I realize that individuals experience miracles all the time. I have no problem with that. I once saw an angel visibly, with my own two eyes. I had asked God to protect our house, and he allowed me to see the angelic guardian standing at his post by our front door, plain as day. I'll never forget it. *I know* it happened, because it happened to me. But here's the thing, I couldn't exactly *demand* that somebody else *has to* believe me—someone who's never met me and doesn't know whether or not I'm trustworthy. There are also liars out there in the world, counterfeits, and mentally ill folks, too. Individual reports of the miraculous should be up to my own discernment. If it's real, it's real. If it's not, it's not. But don't tell me that God makes my receiving of the Eucharist contingent on my personal opinions about purported events. The Church can't tell me that I have to believe in these private revelations."

"They don't," I answered.

"They don't?" asked Sean.

"They don't," I repeated. "You *do* have to believe in Christmas, Easter, and that Christ is really present in the Eucharist in order to be Catholic."

"Certainly," Sean said. "That's obvious by definition. It would make no sense for an atheist to believe in God, but then claim to remain an atheist. No, if he believes in God, then he's not an atheist anymore—simply by definition. If I'm going to be Catholic, then that means I accept the fundamentals of the faith, of course."

"Exactly," I affirmed. "But when it comes to claims of private revelations, it's up to your own individual discernment."

"Let me get this straight: I could read a miraculous personal testimony published in the parish bulletin last week, deem it to be complete hogwash, and I'm still allowed to become Catholic?" Sean asked.

"That's right," I said.

"Well that was easy," he said. "See, they always have the answer. So maybe they have one for my final question too."

Sean proceeded to explain that he simply could not fathom how molecules that constitute the mixture of bread turn into the molecules of human flesh.

Sean complained, "The people who teach RCIA at Libby's parish claimed that the substance of the bread is changed. The *substance*? It's *substantially* him? If it was really flesh molecules, then people would get sick when they digest it. As a physician's assistant, I can prove it. That belief sounds like ... like ..."

"Like hyper-materialistic superstition?" I interjected.

"Yeah. Like that," Sean agreed.

I asked, "Sean, do you think that the word 'substance' is a synonym for the term 'material building blocks'?"

"Yeah, I suppose that's how I've been thinking about it, anyway," my brother answered.

I explained, "Substance is *not* the same thing as material building blocks. This is a tendency we've inherited from modernism and postmodernism, which, for all of their good points, can be very limited in what they consider. Contemporary worldviews since the Enlightenment tend to emphasize only one part of reality: the part to which our five senses currently have access. Modern thought can do a great job in its focus on the physical aspects of the universe, sure. The problem occurs when it ignores the rest of the picture. In reality, the sensory data makes up less than 1 percent of the total picture. Your working definition of the term 'substance' is falling into a materialistic worldview that reduces the whole of reality into one small part, the part we can see. But there is so much more to reality than just what our five senses can access. It's like assuming the tip of the iceberg is the *whole* iceberg—ignoring the gigantic part that's unseen."

"Keep going," Sean said.

I continued, "Like an iceberg, most of reality is invisible. In fact, the most important parts are the invisible ones. Can you look at *music* under a microscope?"

"I can look at the particles that make up the paper upon which the musical score is written, but not the music itself," Sean said thoughtfully. "In this case, the substance of a song is something I can hear or experience, not reducible to paper particles. Substance is not the same thing as material building blocks!"

"Excellent," I said, realizing that I may be one of few Baptists preachers acting as an evangelist for the Catholic Church.

I continued, "If it helps, think about the difference between a *corpse* and a *body*. The two may contain the same physical building-block particles, but they are different things. Why is the human body *substantially* different than a corpse? Because of what it *makes present*."

"Ohhh," Sean said, with increasing relief. "My Sean-ness is the substance, not the atoms that make me present to the world."

"Well said!" I replied. "The substance of a thing is the heart of what it truly is in its entirety. As a human person, you are substantially a complex, body-soul unity that reflects the image of God—your entire 'Sean-ness', as you put it—which is so much more than just your physical cells. This difference between the real substance of a thing and the natural building blocks can help us describe the miracle of the sacraments. Faith in the sacraments is based on the Incarnation. Once you believe that God became flesh, you can see how grace works through nature. And it makes sense. As we often observe, greater realities are manifested to us through the natural world that we can perceive with our senses. The whole world becomes God's revelation of himself to us through the eyes of sacramental faith. You see the Lord's ferocity sculpted into the face of a lion or your own value to him in the splendor with which he clothes the birds. You see his mystery in the haunting depths of the ocean.

"Your Sean-ness, your greater reality, is something I can't look at under a microscope. Nevertheless, I can still have a real encounter with *you*. How?"

"By encountering the natural body that makes Sean present to the world," he said.

"Bingo," I said. "Substance is not the same thing as material building blocks. Substance is no more the physical particle than a home is a pile of wood and nails. The consecrated Host is substantially *him*, yes, while the building blocks *appear* to remain the same. In the Eucharist, this is Christ's Real Presence, body, blood, soul, and divinity. The change in substance is astounding! It's as though I am looking at the same musical score as before, yet somehow it's now an entirely different song. Personally, I find it more astounding than a visible miracle of molecular transformation. To me, the Eucharist is more amazing than when Jesus turned water into wine," I explained.

Sean responded, "Oh, I have no problem with the fact that the *Creator* is able to change physical particles if he wants to. They're his bricks in the first place. If he wanted to change molecules of bread into flesh in its physical appearance, then he could do that. He can do whatever he wants, he's God. Nothing's impossible for him. At the Cana wedding, he *did* turn water into wine in a way that was physically obvious. I have no problem with that. I have no problem with creation, Christmas, or Christ's Resurrection, either. He's God, and this is what he revealed and plainly displayed to his creation. My issue with the Eucharist is that a visible molecular transformation is simply not what we observe happening at the Mass, that's all."

"You're right," I affirmed. "In the Eucharist, the substance changes, while the physical particles appear to remain the same."

Sean asked, "Just curious, do we see a miracle like that anywhere else, where the physical particles appear one way, but *substantially* there's something different going on?"

I answered, "We see something similar in the dual-nature of Christ. He is 100 percent human, as his 'molecules' indicate. But even more astounding than material building blocks, he is 100 percent God, the Second Person of the Trinity. Substantially, he is God and man, fully both at the same time. But, by his physical appearance, one wouldn't have known he was God. With the exception of the Transfiguration miracle, he didn't typically walk around glowing, or anything like that."

Sean added, "I see the parallel. Simply looking at Jesus, a person wouldn't have known that he was God, but he *was*. Looking at the Eucharist, a person wouldn't know that it is the Body of Christ, but it *is*."

"You got it," I affirmed. "The Eucharist is a mystery. And it's an *amazing* miracle. It *should* blow our mind. I believe Jesus revealed enough for us to trust him about this, while we still don't understand exactly how it all *works*. To answer your original question directly, the idea that the molecules that comprise a mixture of bread change into flesh molecules is *not* what the Church teaches about the Eucharist. Instead, the Church teaches that the substance changes, while the material particles maintain the appearance of bread."

"Ohhh," said Sean. "But at RCIA, they talked about these miraculous proofs, in which the Host became a beating heart, and *did* undergo a change at the physical level that *was* visible."

"Yes," I agreed. "There are a number of reported occurrences of these types of miracles. I think God uses signs and wonders sometimes to give people enough evidence to take a leap of faith. He gave me a number of miracles to help me come to faith. But the Church doesn't teach that a molecular transformation is what's happening in the Eucharist. Rather, the Host *is* the Body of Christ substantially, while the part that is available to our natural senses still has the appearance of bread, at the same time. Regardless of their appearance, the physical particles have a new substance. The point isn't to solve this mystery, but to fall more deeply in love with it. The point is faith. The point is that the Lord himself seeks to saturate every aspect of your whole being. God loves you so much that he would make himself available to you in this special way. The point is love. With him, it's always love."

Sean nodded his head in serious thought. As I said earlier, my older brother said less about his faith than anyone else in the family. Whenever he did speak about God, what he said was important.

I added, "I really appreciate how seriously you're taking this matter and looking into it. People can err on the side of lazy indifference regarding important subjects that *ought* to be explored. It's good that you're asking these questions. That reminds me: people can also err on the side of trying to understand and explain *everything*, and thereby feel a false sense of control over every aspect of a mystery. This particular vice has people alleging to solve the mystery by turning it into an exact calculus. That error is just as dangerous, if not more, as ignoring these important topics. So, we don't want to ignore important mysteries, but we don't want to pretend that we've solved and mastered them, either. In the end, our proper posture toward the Eucharist is that of a baby sitting in the highchair, looking at Daddy with mouth open, ready to receive the food. It's not for the baby to comprehend the complex carbohydrates that constitute the green mush inside of a pea. It's for the baby to eat it."

Sean asked, "Catholics don't believe that a consecrated Host would appear as flesh particles beneath a microscope?"

"No," I affirmed. "The physical particles would usually still have the appearance of bread, even though it is, in fact, *not* bread, but really the Lord's Body given up for you."

"I believe in the Real Presence of Jesus in the Eucharist. Somehow, I feel like I already *knew* it was true. That ... what did you call it—hyper-realism misunderstanding, or something like that—that was my last question. I'm finishing RCIA and entering the Church. Thanks, *Brother Ian*."

I thought to myself, "I'm a Baptist minister. And I was just instrumental in leading somebody into the Catholic Church? I know a few Baptist deacons who would be none too thrilled about this."

Jesus said, "Blessed are those who have not seen, but yet believe." This statement describes my brother Sean. As he once said to me, "I didn't need to have a demon pulled off me in order to believe. To me, it's patently obvious to put my faith in Jesus." The Lord also said, "Behold one ... in whom there is no guile." This statement also describes Sean. He doesn't do sly or fake, he's real.

Looking off into the distance, Sean closed our conversation, "Libby's brother is going to embrace me at the Vigil. I know it. I *really* wish guys wouldn't touch."

Sean was thus the next convert into Catholicism. Libby was overjoyed to say the least, as were her parents. The first time I visited Sean after his entrance into the Catholic Church, his in-laws were visiting at the same time. As Sean had feared, his elated brother-in-law indeed reached out a caring hand, giving Sean the tender-yet-firm embrace of an affectionate, brotherly squeeze upon the shoulder. It was a glorious sight to behold. I am forever indebted to Sean's brother-in-law for this gift. And Sean's mother-in-law was outright beaming. She said to me, "I have been praying for God to lead Sean home into the Catholic Church ever since Libby first met him. God sure answered me! Better watch out—I'm praying for you next, Ian."

19

Crisis of a Closet Catholic

I prayed and reflected about the growing trend of conversions in the family. I thought long and hard about all the Catholic insights I already believed and had even been preaching. I remembered back to everything God showed me about the Church while I was in Ireland, before the spiritual winter. Inspired by my sister's request, I took a fresh look at *Rome Sweet Home*. Its impact on Shaylyn only enhanced my review of the material.

It was at this point in my research of Catholicism that I became bothered by a nagging observation: I had always been an outsider looking in. To date, my experience had been like that of viewing a stained-glass window from *outside* the building in order to comprehend it. From the outside, a person might look at this priceless work of art and wonder what the big deal is. You understand only when you look from inside the building and see the colorful glass narrative lit up by the light that shines through it. For a better perspective, I wanted to experience Catholicism from the *inside*.

To be clear, I had physically been inside Catholic churches before. And I had attended Uncle Tim's and Sean's weddings, both of which had been Catholic Masses. But I was still an outsider looking in, closed off and receiving nothing. My *heart* had never been to Mass before. I decided that it was time for me to attend a Catholic Mass—in a far-away town.

I called Grampa.

"Hello," he answered the phone.

"Hi Grampa, it's Ian."

"Hey Ian! What's going on?" asked Grampa.

I said, "You have been inviting me to Mass my entire life. Every summer and every Christmas, you invite me, and I tell you no every time. I'm sorry about that. If you'll still have me, I want to go to Mass with you next weekend. I can fly from Austin, Texas, to JFK or Newark airport."

"No need to say you're sorry. This is great! I would love to see you. And I would love to take you to Mass," replied a very happy Grampa. "I'll get the cribbage board ready."

Then I called Uncle Tim. "I read *Rome Sweet Home*. Dad doesn't know. I'm ready to try the Mass. I want to see what it's like," I explained. "I'll be joining Grampa next weekend at his parish in New Milford."

"Then I'm coming with you," said Tim. "I'll fly out to my dad's from Indiana, and I'll pick you up at the airport. Me, you, and Grampa—we'll all go to Mass together. I'm stoked!"

On the Friday of my flight, I woke up super excited. I felt right as rain, and couldn't wait to see my family in New Jersey. In order to arrive at the airport in Austin, Texas, two hours ahead of schedule, I had to leave at noon. At 11:00 that morning, I was simply vibrating with anticipation, like a puppy when you're about to throw the ball. I couldn't wait!

Then suddenly I keeled over in some of the most severe stomach pain and nausea I've ever experienced, as though something had punched me in the gut. My temperature spiked, I broke into a cold sweat, and I ran into the bathroom. Diarrhea and *profuse* sweating caused me to dehydrate rapidly, with my body temperature continuing to rise into the danger zone. I couldn't believe what was happening to me. The timing of it felt sinister.

I drove to the emergency room where they admitted me to the hospital immediately.

"Your temperature is over 102 degrees," said the nurse. "You're literally *cooking*. We have to get you onto a rehydration drip right away. We'll get your information later. Let's go."

There I was in a Texas hospital, on an IV, instead of on a plane to New Jersey. I called Uncle Tim from my cell phone to update him regarding the situation.

"You won't be picking me up at the airport today," I informed him. "I'm so sorry, Uncle Tim, but it looks like I won't be joining you and Grampa for Mass on Sunday morning."

Uncle Tim answered, "Yes, you will."

"I'm sick as a dog," I replied.

"You're about to get better," he asserted.

"Even if I did, it was a nontransferable, nonrefundable plane ticket."

"But I'm about to pray for you to be healed," he explained calmly.

"You don't understand!" I exclaimed. "I already tried that. It didn't work. God said *no*."

Uncle Tim replied, "No, *you* don't understand. The enemy is threatened by you attending the Mass and is trying to bully you out of it. He didn't count on me fighting back. Remember how you came out of agnosticism? God allowed something to happen to you, so that he could reveal his love to you. God has allowed this for the same reason—he wants to show you something.

"Ian, this is not a normal sickness. I believe that it is blatantly satanic, and the Church has *authority* over this. It's not that God didn't hear your prayer. Of course he did. I believe that what he wishes to impart to you is that, whenever *you* pray, you do so as part of a cut-off fragment, isolated from full communion with the united people of God. But whenever I pray as a Catholic, I pray in union with an army of the holy and heroic saints who have gone before. All those in heaven who cheer us on to finish the race strong are praying for you right now, along with me. When I pray as a Catholic, I stand in union with the Church militant on the earth, the Church suffering in purgatory, and the Church triumphant in the unseen world beyond. In the bond of peace with all of Christ's Church, in solidarity with the whole people of God, I pray in the name of Jesus that you be healed immediately, and that you get on a free plane tomorrow in time to join me and Grampa for Mass on Sunday morning!"

I thought, "Timmy sounds intense." Then I said to him, "It's worth a shot—amen."

"See you tomorrow," Uncle Tim said, "keep me posted about when the *free plane* lands."

As soon as we ended the call, my temperature dropped. And the stomach pain stopped.

"WHOA ..." I said to myself.

A couple minutes later, the doctor came in to check up on me. He took my temperature and said, "I don't believe it, 98.6 degrees."

With a bewildered look on his face, he asked me what happened—so I told him.

"Occasionally in this job I get to see a miracle. Make no mistake, that's what happened here today," said the doctor. "I am happy to say that you, my friend, are free to go! Stop at the receptionist's desk on your way out, and all the best."

I was grateful for the healing, but I doubted that I would get a free airline ticket. The September 11 tragedy was fresh in people's minds, and airlines weren't exactly breaking fare policies or giving away free boarding passes. But the doctor at the hospital confirmed that one miracle had already occurred.

I asked myself, "Could it be?"

With curiosity getting the best of me, I drove to the airport the following morning. After waiting in line at the airport's check-in desk, I handed my expired boarding pass from the previous day to the airline representative. She examined it then said, "I'm so sorry, but this ticket from yesterday is nontransferable and nonrefundable. We can't transfer this. We can't give you your money back, either. There's nothing we can do for you."

"I know. I tried to explain it to Uncle Tim," I replied, as though she knew who he was.

Then an oddly intense expression washed over her countenance. She stared intently at me for a moment. Then she looked around her, as though she wanted to confirm that nobody else was within earshot. At last, she leaned forward and spoke quietly.

"I don't know how to explain this," she said, "but I *know* that I am supposed to put you on the next flight out of here to New Jersey. Please do *not* tell anyone that I did this. I'm allowed, but some people wouldn't understand. Your flight boards in one hour." Then she handed me my free boarding pass.

"WHOA ..." I said to myself again.

I called Uncle Tim with my arrival time, and with the promise to tell him the whole story in person. When he picked me up in New Jersey, I exclaimed, "I was *healed*. I was healed immediately. My stomach got better, my temperature dropped. The physician called it a *miracle*. Then this lady at the Austin airport, after explaining that my ticket couldn't be refunded or transferred, gave me a new boarding pass—for free! She said she 'knew' that she was supposed to."

"Yeah, I know," he said, as though he was unruffled by the entire affair. "I've *been* Catholic for a while. I know the heavenly grace available by tapping into the Communion of the Saints. I know the power invoked at every Mass. You're about to see it tomorrow. Nephew, you've just taken your first step into a larger world."

Uncle Tim laid hands on me that night and prayed over me. Our prayer was followed by another epic hike along New Milford's train tracks, as we pondered together the majesty of the Living God.

Mass with Grampa and Uncle Tim was beyond description. During the Catholic liturgy, I kept thinking, "God is *in this*. It's undeniable." Seeing isn't believing; believing is seeing—and it definitely looks different from the inside. Kneeling at the altar between my grandfather and my godfather, I found myself back in the household of Saint Enda.

I prayed, "Thank you, Lord, for your intimate deliverance and love, thank you for your Son, and thank you for my family. Thank you especially for my Grampa and my GingGing, two pillars of faith who were once altar boys together right here in this parish—two fathers who prayed their lineage home. I kneel to you here as the beneficiary of their faithfulness, and I am most grateful."

Upon my return to Texas, I joined RCIA—in a far-away town.

Then I went through to the end, right? I courageously loved my sheep enough to come clean to them as they deserved, right? Wrong. Although that's how my story *ought* to go, it's not what happened. With the clarity of an Uncle Tim trip behind me, the enemy's counter-offensive was aggressive to say the least. When I faced the imminent consequence of losing everything, I became tortured and paralyzed by fear. And I dropped out of RCIA.

Then the pendulum swung in the opposite direction. I became overtly *hostile* against Catholicism, more so than ever before. "That makes no sense," you might be saying to yourself. "After what you were just shown?! Weren't you defending the Church and loading your sermons with beautiful Catholic doctrine?" As I said before, conversion is a holistic process that involves every aspect of the human person, not just rationality. Anybody who presumes the fallen human race to be made up of purely rational creatures need only read today's newspaper to observe otherwise.

I started putting down the Church from my pulpit, to the comforting sounds of "amen" from my congregation. During visits home,

I was especially awful toward Catholics whenever I was around my dad. I even mocked the Eucharist in front of Grampa during breakfast, and he had just returned from Mass. Nobody said anything, but the look on my Uncle Steve's face was one of horror and shock. My revolting behavior had a name: it's called "kicking against the goads" in the Bible.

At a family reunion, Libby's mother gave me my first rosary. It glowed in the dark, which was quite the personal touch. When I was a child, many of my favorite toys glowed in the dark, but to my knowledge, she hadn't known that. I responded by mocking the "prayer beads" and belittling her. As hurt as she felt, she would *not* retaliate. Upon refusing and *returning* her gift in a self-righteous tantrum, all she said was, "Okay." The meeker she was and the more she returned kindness for injury, the harder I kicked.

That same night we were all hanging out together on the porch when I stood up and went into a comedy routine bashing Catholics. My vicious jokes and comments are literally too offensive for me to repeat. Libby's mother could hear me from inside the house, and I knew it. Uncle Tim and Libby eventually left the porch.

I later learned what Uncle Tim and Libby said to each other when they were out of earshot. "Ian seemed so close there for a while," Libby said. "With all of these converts in your family, I had really hoped he would be the next. If the Catholic Church could get him, the Murphy's resident preacher, then it would speak to everybody in this family. I get it, he's got a lot on the line. But I had hoped. Looks like it's not going to happen. Ian is *obviously* determined to remain a Baptist."

"No," said Uncle Tim assuredly. "Ian is going to be the family's *next* convert into the Church."

20

From the Baptist Frontlines

Of all the fears that pressed upon me to avoid Catholicism, the most influential one was the fear of leaving my role as a head pastor. My ministry was booming. Aside from the financial remuneration of my job, I had never before experienced such momentum and impact in delivering the good news. Families continued coming to my church from miles away. Sunday morning services in the main sanctuary eventually reached standing-room-only status.

One of the primary reasons for growth was our thriving children's program. I learned quickly that, if you feed people dinner, they will come. We had the budget for it, so I hosted children's nights, with outdoor cookouts and activities that made Wednesdays feel like the weekly town festival. Many children came with their parents, but others, whose parents did not want to attend, we would pick up with a van.

I so enjoyed all of the creative things we did. Once I dressed up as Moses and walked the kids through all the miracles of the Exodus in a series of stations. I opened the event as Brother Ian and then my cell phone rang—it was Moses.

"Wait, you're on your way here?!" I said. Then I told the audience to hang on for a second, as I raced into the back for a fast change of outfit and a wig.

Then out walked *Moses*, in front of a large crowd of astonished children. "Hello everybody, I haven't done anything like this since the Transfiguration," I opened. For the parting of the sea, I packed baking soda into the base of a hollow staff that, upon touching a pool of vinegar, made the liquid sizzle and bubble to the children's delight. The whole evening was a smash hit.

Another time, the kids and I designed homemade jewelry for Mother's Day gifts using a craft kit that I had purchased at a hobby store. We made and successfully tested toy parachutes. We transformed the parsonage into a movie theatre and packed ourselves in to watch *Star Wars*. Yet another time, a group of us gathered a pile of the plainest-looking rocks we could find and put them into a rock-polisher. We reconvened later to see all of the gemstones that had been hiding beneath an ordinary, rough surface. It was an allegory, of course, for God's transformation of us.

I discovered that the specific activity we did was not the important thing. Rather, what made Wednesdays so special to the kids was that I was the *pastor*, and I was paying attention to *them*. That's all it took. The love is what made the night so grand.

The Sunday afternoon fish fry became for the adults what Wednesday evenings were for the children. Our youth group was also thriving. The kids visited the hospital and the nursing home. They wrote and performed their own hymns. Through their efforts, God rescued a home from drug trafficking.

The church was bustling with activity and vitality and *fun*. We were attracting new members, and even nonbelievers attended regularly. Numerous people reported feeling the rejuvenating energy of God doing something wonderful in their town, and said they felt excited to be a part of it.

But not everyone in the congregation was happy with the growth. One of the congregation's matriarchs approached me one day and complained, "I've been going to this church since I was a little girl, and I have always had my pew. I have seniority here! And everybody knows that it's my pew. But now with *your* preaching, new visitors *who don't know who I am* keep pouring in and taking *my seat*. Brother Ian, I'm a lady who prides herself on speaking her mind. And I don't mind telling you that I don't appreciate it."

A gentleman in the church expressed roughly the same sentiment. Then another. And then *another*.

Subsequently, one of the senior deacons approached me and said, "Brother Ian, there's a group among the deacons who just love what's happening here. They love your preaching, and they love you. They're gushing at every meeting about how the altar-calls are flooded with new Christians, the youth group is on fire, and the children's ministry looks like the way the kids flocked around the Lord himself." After a dramatic pause he added, "I am *not* part of that group."

He continued, "The group that's on *your side* is now talking about the construction of a new sanctuary, in order to fit all the newcomers. We have more people now than we ever did."

"Isn't that a good thing?" I asked, honestly confused.

"No!" he yelled. "It's NOT a good thing. I grew up going to church in this building. I married my wife in this building. Now they wanna tear it down."

"The church isn't the building," I explained, "it's the people. Maybe you've started serving the house of the Lord so much so that you've lost sight of a deacon's true calling: to serve the *Lord of the house*."

"And that's another thing, Brother Ian," he interjected abruptly. "I really don't care if that silver tongue of yours has something clever to say to me. What I *do* care about is that we used to be a nice church. But now, thanks to you, there are all these poor children in our company wearing their cheap, dirty clothes. And it's because you keep bringing in all these poor people and all their kids that they're talking about tearing down my building!"

I responded, "To tell me that I'm ministering to the children and to the poor is the single greatest compliment you could ever pay me as a Christian minister. *Thank you, Deacon.*"

He retorted, "Look here, I hope this is the last time I have to speak to you about this matter. You let those poor families know that they are not welcome here. I trust I've made myself understood. And I trust that you'll go to that other group of deacons and talk them out of this new-sanctuary proposal, before it goes to the ballot."

Tell poor families that they're *not welcome*? All I could do in response was stand there and blink a couple of times. Of course, I ignored the request of this deacon and continued with business as usual.

For the record, the attitude of these disgruntled individuals was not representative of the church family as a whole. Most of them gave me their full support. The hostile deacon, however, was a squeaky wheel. Although he was in the minority, he had a lot of influence in the community and was able to wreak havoc.

The following Wednesday, I drove the church van to pick up local kids for children's night, and accompanying me was the deacon who proposed the building of a larger sanctuary. He said, "While

I've got you alone, you should know that Satan is trying to attack all the great work God's been doing here, and he's doing it through some misled deacons. Some other people and I have been trying to protect you, but I suspect you've probably gotten wind of the problems by this point."

"Yes, sir, I have indeed gotten wind," I answered, as we both enjoyed the respite of a good laugh.

He continued, "We'll keep doing all we can. But people don't like change. There's a storm comin', as they say, and it'll get worse before it gets better. It's like the deacons have split into two factions ... I shouldn't have said that. I shouldn't worry you. The Lord's at work here. I don't want this stuff getting to you. You keep on doing what you're doing, and we'll take care of it."

My friend looked distraught. I comforted him, thanked him, and encouraged him, but he maintained the look of a man who's trying to protect his loved ones from bad news. I asked, "There's more, isn't there?"

"Did the Holy Spirit tell you?" he asked.

"Your face did," I said.

He took a deep breath and said, "The faction of deacons opposed to my new-sanctuary proposal have threatened that, if they lose the vote, then they're leaving the church in a group protest."

I thought to myself, "But the Bible insists that we remain unified in the bonds of peaceful fellowship, bearing with one another in love under one Lord, one faith, and one baptism. A group protest? It's what I get for trying to stay a Protestant—now I'm face-to-face with my own sheepfold falling into hostile fragmentation."

Later that night, I thought, "Like a purging forest fire, I'll simply let the dissenting group leave! All the troublemakers exiting at the same time? I should be so lucky. With them gone, we can begin construction of the new sanctuary, and this ministry shall continue to prosper."

My conscience yelled out from the peanut gallery, "Um, that doesn't sound right."

I responded, "I'm not talking to you right now. I feel better, and I need some sleep."

Later that week, I shared my thoughts with the deacon who proposed the new building. He replied, "I had the same idea at first,

Brother Ian. But turns out it's not that simple. You see, if this group leaves, it splits the church. Not only do they represent a sizable chunk of this congregation in and of themselves, but they include some very distinguished members who have a lot of clout around here. They'll bring a portion of the membership along with them, make no mistake about that. They also represent the lion's share of our financial resources. With them gone, my proposal is no longer viable.

"Lastly, if they leave, our current sanctuary would have more than enough room, eliminating the need to build. And I think that's their game in the end—keep the building. And with the building still here, then they'll just keep coming. Going around and around in circles, this problem will never reach resolution. And besides all of that, a bunch of people are starting to say that they have to concede to this threat, in order to keep our church family together. They say that even though what's happening isn't right, it would be a worse thing to split the church. I'm losing votes fast."

That Sunday morning, I was wearing my freshly dry-cleaned suit and finishing up shaving when I heard somebody unlock the front door and enter the house without knocking. While I was still shouting out to ask who was there, the man opened my bathroom door and walked in. It was the same deacon who had chastised me for bringing *poor kids* into his church. I stood there stunned, razor in hand, with my neck still half-covered with shaving cream. I blinked a couple times in ever-increasing bewilderment.

Eventually I said, "Excuse me?"

He began, "I had hoped we wouldn't have to talk about this again."

"I'm in the BATHROOM," I said, motioning to my razor. "Please respect my privacy; I will be with you in a moment, sir."

"No," he replied. "As I was saying, I had hoped we wouldn't have to talk again. But apparently, I didn't make myself clear."

"*I'm shaving*," I said in disbelief.

"I don't care," he said. "Now I've already got my brother deacon's new-sanctuary proposal pretty well voted down at this point. But the problem is that the church is crowded. Your preaching hasn't changed. You're still showing *welcome* to all these poverty types. I expect you'll change your preaching, and make very clear the true identity of this fellowship."

"Get out of my house," I said.

"That's just it—it's not your house. You like it? It can still be yours. It's the church's house. The church owns it. The church pays all the bills, too. And the church pays you a handsome salary. And we're happy to continue doing so! The learning curve of the first few months is rough, and I understand that. I'm happy for this to be water under the bridge. You're forgiven, and I admire your eagerness. I have hopes you and I will not only come to understand each other, but that we'll become the best of friends someday. I truly mean that. That was my dream for us when I first met you, and it still is. You and I could do amazing things together in this town."

After a long pause, he concluded, "I regret my rude intrusion, I surely do. But it was necessary. I walked into your bathroom this morning to remind you whose bathroom it is. I wish to make myself perfectly understood: if you do not change your preaching as I have directed, I will take away your house, your income, and your job. I can get more than 50 percent to vote to have you removed, and I'll do it. Good day, Brother Ian— that is, if you still wanna be *Brother Ian*."

Then he left. Talk about dramatic. His threats were nevertheless all too real. I sought the assistance of our Baptist *overseer*, the same term that means "bishop" in the Catholic Church. We called our overseer the Baptist general director of missions, and I anxiously hoped that his authority could put out the fire.

The general director and I had an outstanding meeting together at first. He encouraged me regarding the joyful reports that kept reaching his ears. The conversions and the growth at my church were among the happiest points of light across his region and an answer to his personal prayers. He said I was born to preach. Then he challenged me, too, regarding my obvious weight-gain—gluttony was a vice I had yet to be delivered from. He was an excellent mentor in every respect, and a beautiful missionary.

I then told him about the distressing events that had been happening.

"Ian," he said, "I want to be so clear here: you are doing exactly what Christ taught. It is your work as a Christian minister to reach out to the widows, the poor, and the little children. What that man said to you about the 'dirty poverty kids' is something I find hard to forgive, frankly. This is outrageous. This man is contradicting everything Jesus Christ taught and did. And he barged into your bathroom while you were in the middle of shaving, threatening to take away your job unless you made the poor people feel *unwelcome*? Goodness gracious! Never in my career have I heard such a thing."

I was initially consoled.

"But unfortunately," he continued, "there's nothing I can do for you. As Baptists, we hold to the autonomy of the local congregation. This awful deacon is allowed to do all of this, and I can't stop him. Mine is only a power of influence, and in the end, I cannot use it to violate the autonomy of the local congregation. I'm sorry to say, but it's up to this individual church what happens to this individual church. It's up to a majority vote in the final analysis."

"No, it's up to the Holy Spirit in the final analysis," I said. I was now disturbed. "What's happening is outright heretical—isn't that something which falls under your purview?"

"I understand your confusion, and I empathize with your predicament. I will keep you in close prayer. But there is really nothing I can do to help you," he repeated. "Of course I'll talk to him, but I know the man you're talking about, and I don't see it doing any good."

I said, "With all due respect, in a case like this one, I have a hard time making sense of your response."

He explained, "Ian, you seem to be asking me for something akin to 'apostolic authority' from the New Testament. Yes, when the New Testament churches encountered an issue like yours, they appealed to the authority of the apostles and those who succeeded them. In the original Christian churches, the authority of the apostolic witness superseded any congregational groupthink. Disciplinary measures reached out in love, hoping for a troublemaker's redemption. In a case like somebody hurting the children and persisting in violent actions, they could have the person removed—with the intent of caring for the whole flock and with the intent of provoking repentance in the wrongdoer. The motive was always love for everyone involved. The system worked. But we don't do that anymore. We do democratic voting."

My heart flinched at the revelation that our church was clearly *not* operating as a mirror of the original Christian congregations. As Scott Hahn would later write, "The Apostles were not disciplined by their congregations, nor did they take orders from their congregations.

Rather, it was they who presided in love over the Christian assemblies." I had always thought of my church as an authentic recovery of the original gospel witness amidst other branches of Christianity that had strayed too far from the source. As it turns out, I was the one who had strayed.

Now feeling even more disturbed, I questioned the director, "But I honestly thought that the Baptist denomination centered itself upon being the one that 'most closely resembles' the Church in its purest, original form—the one option, out of all the different denominations, that most closely resembles the Church during the time of the New Testament."

"We do," he said.

"But you just said that, as Baptists, we *don't* mirror the practices of the original Christian churches," I argued.

"But almost nobody does," he said.

I insisted, "It's not my intention to be argumentative. It's that, back when I was licensed as a Baptist minister, the ceremony revolved around how the Baptist denomination is the closest reflection of what Jesus wanted his Church to be. Sir, it is my sincere desire to bear witness to the way of Jesus. And you just told me that democratic voting does *not* bear witness to what Christ instituted."

"But almost all churches do democratic voting; it's simply what people do now," he explained.

I said, "The original Christian churches practiced apostolic authority in a case like mine where the exercise of discipline is definitively needed—is that right?"

"Well, that's true, Ian. But that's not the way we do things today," he said.

I asked him directly, "Well, is anyone following the New Testament on this? Does any present-day branch of Christianity still resemble the New Testament Church in this regard? Who *is* doing things the New Testament way?"

"I'm afraid the only folks who work that way anymore are the Roman Catholics," he answered with a disparaging snicker. "Yes, the only ones still practicing that are the *Catholics*."

At that moment, the man's entire demeanor changed. I understood the mental process going on within him because I recognized the same phenomenon within myself. As I had seen many times before, this Christ-like servant of God, with a gentle, humble, peace-filled spirit, suddenly resembled that of a hungry wolf on the hunt. As I noted earlier, there is another entity in addition to Jesus who elicits a singular rise out of people: his Bride.

The director proceeded to warn me about the dangerous idolatries of the Catholics. As I had done before myself, this man disparaged what he *thought* the Church was, not what it actually was. But there was no talking to him about it. With no substantiating facts offered, he simply dismissed my half of the ensuing dialogue as the deception of that crafty devil. At that point, I realized that the relief I was seeking was *not* going to come through him. In the end, this Baptist general director of missions had no idea how much he helped me convert to Catholicism.

21

The Comedy of a Broken Road

As God's perfect sense of timing would have it, my close friend Adam visited me shortly following my meeting with the Baptist general director of missions. Adam had become an adopted brother to me, and I was beyond grateful that he had driven to my parsonage for the weekend. With everything going on, it was good for me to see some family.

Adam was Catholic, but he joined me for all of the Sunday festivities at my church, from sermon to fish fry. Then the evening was ours.

"Ian," he said, "maybe my perspective as a Catholic can illuminate your current predicament."

I responded, "I'm all ears."

"I'll open by saying that you're a stunning homilist," he began. "There is undeniable power when the Word of God goes forth through you. Zeal, passionate love, and the fire of the Holy Spirit shine through this ministry. Many Catholics need that. I needed it today. I gave my heart back to Jesus this morning, and I want to thank you for being his instrument."

I was overjoyed at Adam's return to the Lord, and I felt moved and humbled by his encouragement, to the point of becoming speechless. I hope my face told him how much his words meant to me.

"But," he added, "today's service felt like the Ian show. Don't get me wrong—there was nothing you did to convey that impression. Instead, it comes from the structure of the Baptist liturgy. Maybe you don't like the word 'liturgy'. Maybe you don't know the word 'liturgy'. Maybe you don't think you have one. But you do. You have a specific order of stand-up and sit-down, with the preacher and his sermon at the center. The whole morning revolves around the preacher and his sermon."

I said, "I know exactly what you mean, please go on."

"You didn't draw focus to yourself," he explained. "You drew everybody's focus to God's love and our repentance. But the structure of the ceremony put you in the spotlight. Everything built up to the climax of the worship service: the preacher and his sermon. It didn't feel like it revolved around God. The altar wasn't at the center. I felt like I was attending a local town-hall meeting, where everything builds up to the president's keynote. You didn't even do Communion. You didn't do the Lord's Supper. Where was the Old Testament reading? The New Testament reading? The Psalm prayer? The Gospel reading? His Body broken for us—*do this in remembrance of me*—there was none of it. I left hungry for more. I still need to go to Mass."

In the fashion of Dr. Johnson, I listened carefully and nodded slowly. Then I responded, "I suspect everything you say is the truth. I've been back and forth for a while with this whole Catholic thing, and it cannot be a coincidence that you just reaffirmed a myriad of things that you didn't know I was going through."

"You're thinking of converting to the Catholic Church?" he said excitedly.

"I went to Mass," I admitted.

"What?" cried Adam.

"I joined RCIA," I admitted next.

"You what?!"

"Then I dropped out," I confessed.

"Oh my God!" he prayed.

"I suppose you could say that the Holy Spirit has used you to provide me with an *adamant* confirmation," I punned.

"Well this is great!" Adam exclaimed. "Start RCIA back up, and quit your job. Hey, you quit your job once before when God wanted you to. Simple. Not easy, but simple. I love solving problems—your wingman, at your service."

I answered, "That's the problem. Here I am fighting to protect my house, income, network, reputation, and job from this faction of protesting deacons. If I convert, I won't have to fight anymore. I just lose! I'll definitely lose everything. If I stay, I can fight to salvage at least *some* of my livelihood."

Adam got serious. He said, "You've got to trust God to take care of you, man. I have no right to judge you. I repented this morning of things that I'm ashamed to admit. There's no judgment here. As your brother in Christ and your family, I'm telling you that, as long as you remain part of a broken system, you will keep experiencing a lot of unnecessary suffering as a result. And life already has plenty of necessary sufferings as it is. You should become Catholic. That's the truth. No matter what things look like, it's the *truth* that will set you free. I want you to know the same peace I found today when I totally entrusted my life to the Lord."

For the rest of the night, I pondered everything my friend had said.

Several weeks later, during another visit with Adam, my church's recently hired youth minister joined us. She was a classmate of mine at the university, and in several shared classes I had witnessed first-hand how bright and gifted she was. With teaching for the Bible institute, being a fulltime graduate student, and serving as a fulltime head pastor, it became too much of a strain for me to continue as a youth minister, and I offered the role to this young woman. She was thrilled to accept it and lighten my load.

That particular evening she had come over to study Greek, and at one point Adam asked for a beer.

"You have alcohol here?!" she gasped.

I answered, "Yeah, I have some beer and wine in the fridge. You want some?"

"No!" she shouted.

Her strong reaction left me speechless. Adam, on the other hand, popped open his bottle in front of the youth minister and said mischievously, "Oh, do you have a problem with this beer?"

"Yes, I do," she said. "How can you drink alcohol? It's the devil's vomit!"

"Ahhh," said Adam after a few big gulps, "if that's the case, then I find it *surprisingly* refreshing."

I was about to play peace-maker and ask Adam to be respectful about scandalizing others, but then the youth minister began laughing, and I knew all was well. After Adam left, after the youth minister and I finished our study session, she asked me to get the bottle of wine.

"What?" I asked.

"Just get it," she said.

I brought her the wine and a glass. She ignored the glass, pulled the cork from the wine bottle, and could have beaten my friend in a chugging contest. Then she grabbed a pack of cigarettes from her purse and lit one up.

"Sorry," she said after her first smoky exhale, "I know you quit."

"I'm fine with that," I said. "What I'm *not* fine with is the way you chastised my friend earlier today for drinking a beer. As your boss, I feel inclined to point out some dangerous hypocrisy here. Biblically speaking, moderate drinking is permissible. But hypocrisy isn't. Jesus talked about that one quite a bit."

She responded, "I stand by chastising your friend for drinking alcohol, and I would do it again. I'm not wrong for drinking alcohol. He was."

"Huh?" I said.

She explained, "I'm sinning in secret. Adam was drinking in front of two other people in the daytime. That means he was damaging his Christian witness. It's wrong to damage your witness. In order to protect your Christian witness, you need to keep your sins a secret. You should even lie about it in public—to guard your witness."

"Let me get this straight," I said, "as Christians, we *should lie*? We ought to imitate the father of all liars, the devil, in order to bear witness to Jesus Christ—is that what you're claiming?"

"Yes," she said, as though it was common sense.

"And you're the one teaching the youth at my church? The Bible says not to lie, and so does the Lord!"

"That's your interpretation," she answered. "I have my interpretation, and according to the priesthood of each individual believer, it's up to me what the Bible means to me."

I kindly explained that if she passed this particular teaching on to the youth group, I would have to find a new youth minister. She respectfully promised to honor my wishes. She assured me that she had never taught this relativism before and never would.

This hypocritical teaching was unbecoming of this young woman. She is one of the most devoted servants of Christ I've ever met, which made my discomfort all the greater. I remembered Adam's words: "As long as you remain part of a broken system, you will keep experiencing a lot of unnecessary suffering as a result. You should become Catholic. That's the truth."

I pondered the times I had seen priests go out into a parish parking lot and light up a smoke. I had enjoyed seeing it, and for a while, I couldn't put my finger on *why*. It wasn't because I had been a smoker for years and it made me feel affirmed. I wanted to quit, and I imagined that maybe the smoking priests did too. And it wasn't because it affirmed me as a Protestant, either. In other words, I was *not* saying to myself, "Look at those Catholics sinning in public." After the exchange with the youth minister, I finally figured it out: I enjoyed seeing it because it was authentic. These priests were *real people* when they were around their flock. I longed for a shepherd like that. After the visits with my friend and that eye-opening night with the youth minister, I was again persuaded to complete the Rite of Christian Initiation of Adults and become Catholic.

Newly convinced that I should rejoin RCIA, anxiety gripped my heart. When I envisioned the likely consequences surrounding house, career, friends, reputation, income, Dad, and ministry, the anxiety worked on my spirit like a venom. Fear immobilized me. Thus, I landed on the following conclusion: I needed somebody to talk me out of Catholicism.

Maybe the people I had been reading in order to field my questions about the Church had been deceived. Perhaps Scott Hahn, Kimberly Hahn, Karl Keating, Pat Madrid, and Steve Ray were brilliant but misled nonetheless. Maybe the ancient and early Fathers were wrong about sacraments. Maybe God had dispensed a new revelation that *majority vote* and *individual interpretation* are his favored mechanisms for guiding the Church. With newfound purpose, I set out to find a brilliant mind who could tell me *that thing which I must have overlooked*—some previous oversight which could once-and-for-all resolve the inner turmoil and designate me a lifetime Baptist minister.

My first stop was Dr. Maurice Carver. Surely, the founder and president of a Baptist seminary would be able to talk me out of becoming Catholic. Always delighted to see me, he greeted me with the standard grandfatherly squeeze and shout of "*Murphy!*"

He asked, "To what do I owe the pleasure of the good pastor's company?"

"Besides I miss you, I do have a question," I said.

"What would you like to ask me about?"

I replied, "Dr. Carver, I want to ask you about the Catholic Church."

"I'm so glad that you came to me about this," he answered. "I'm already what you might call a *closet Catholic*. The Holy Spirit is now showing you the truth of the Church. Boy have you come a long way. I remember when you first showed up at my office door, wearing your black leather coat and just reeking of cigarette smoke and unstable dating relationships."

"You knew?" I said shyly.

"Of course I knew. I could smell it on your spirit and your jacket. You were a backslidden addict, stuck in the tar-baby of dysfunctional romance. Got your hands in and then couldn't get them unstuck again. Yes, covered in smoke and relationship-tar you came to me, *hee hee hee*," chuckled Dr. Carver. My mentor's laugh was one-of-a-kind. His *hee hee hee* was as jovial as Santa's *ho ho ho*, while at the same time sounding serious, raspy, and a little bit sneaky. What a joyful noise it was.

"Why didn't you say anything?" I questioned.

"Because the Holy Spirit told me not to," he explained. "The Lord said he had it covered. All I knew is that we had just prayed for another teacher, and then one knocked on my door. It's not my place to question the Lord's judgment. It's my place to acquiesce to it in gratitude. And now just look at you. A new man, indeed. And he's showing you his Church. Praise the Lord!" he exclaimed.

Feeling puzzled and troubled, I asked, "When it comes to the question of ecclesiology, do you believe that the Catholic Church has the fullness of truth?"

"Oh I know it has," he answered. "Come here, Ian. I want to show you something."

Then Dr. Carver led me into his personal office library. From the looks of his cluttered desk, he was obviously in the middle of writing a lengthy book about family counseling therapy.

"It's almost finished—but that's not what I brought you in here to show you today," he said.

I asked jokingly, "Do you have another antique Cadillac hiding in here, like that fine golden calf you have hiding under the tarp in your garage?"

"No, something far better," he said. Then he motioned to the television set across from his desk where the Eternal Word Television Network (EWTN) was already on. "We're right on time," he said with a sly smile. They were broadcasting a procession of the Blessed Sacrament.

My mentor became intensely solemn and said, "Ian, I want you to look at that procession. *Really look at it*; be *open* to the voice of the Holy Spirit who led you right here today for this moment."

After watching intently for a while, he said emphatically, "*God is present in this!* Look at it with eyes to see, and you can't deny it. Look at the sacredness they show to the Lord. Look at the reverence. *See* his *Real Presence* in this. Watching this is my refreshing break from the church where I'm an assistant pastor—my break from all the incompleteness and unnecessary mess my people are going through. How I wish I could be *there*," he said, motioning to the televised procession of the Eucharist, "adoring the Lord in union with the rest of the Church."

With his gaze fixed on the Host and his eyes tearing up, I saw an appreciation for the Eucharist and a longing for it that surpasses the orientation that many Catholics adopt toward the same miracle. It was as though the Sacrament was the most beautiful sight he had ever laid eyes on.

"But you haven't converted?" I questioned.

"That's true. It's a heavy reality I'm still working through at this point in my long life. I think about what it would do to my church, what it would do to the school, and what it would do to my family for me to enter RCIA at seventy-six years old. I have trouble surrendering to the Lord on this one. It feels like I would do more harm to my flock than good. My wife, Mabel, and my son, Donny, don't like that I watch Catholic Mass on the TV every day. I tell them they're lucky I don't go the whole way in," he said, still glued to the screen.

He concluded, "I imagine that you're going through many of those same fears for yourself. Don't let my struggle stop you. There are no words for how jealous I am that you will actually get to be there for yourself. You're still young. It's not too late for you. Forgive my hypocrisy, but you should enter the Catholic Church because it *is* Christ's Church. You go first, okay? And maybe I'll resolve to follow you in myself someday."

"You know I came here in hopes that you would talk me out of becoming Catholic," I said.

"God has a funny sense of humor, doesn't he?" he replied.

I thought to myself, "Well that didn't work."

Following thorough reflection, I discerned that I needed some-body *else* to talk me out of the Catholic Church. At that moment, the right person came to mind: Nate, one of the ministry team mem-bers from Pittsburgh. If anybody could talk me out of the Catholic Church, it was he. I had lost touch with him after moving to Texas, but I had never stopped missing him. I recalled all the fun we used to have together over wings and cards. I also remembered several in-depth conversations about the Catholic Church, *sola scriptura*, and the dynamic between faith and works. While president of Sam Brunsvold's student group, Nate was exposed to a variety of Chris-tian expressions; Catholics and Protestants had attended Sam's group together. And Nate knew theology. He would be the perfect man for the job.

I said a prayer, took a deep breath, dug up the old phone number, and hoped that it still worked.

"Ian!" shouted my old friend, sounding glad to hear my voice. "It's been years, man, so what's going on?"

"I'm embarrassed that it's been so long. As it frequently goes, but shouldn't, I don't call you up until I'm in pain and need," I confessed.

"Oh, no worries," Nate said, "I lost touch, too. It's called life. It's just so wonderful to hear your voice again. So tell me—what's the trouble? How can I help my old spades partner today?"

"Nate, I need you to talk me out of the Catholic Church," I said bluntly.

He replied, "Ian, I'm Catholic! I just converted last Easter Vigil. This is great."

"No, it's not," I said. "I'm a Baptist minister. I'm going to lose everything—you were supposed to talk me *out of it*."

An overjoyed Nate responded, "That's why the Holy Spirit led you to me. Our Lord wants you to become Catholic, too, for the *full-ness*. The fullness is awesome! I recently went through all the digging. I could assist in any doctrinal questions you have."

"I don't have any doctrinal questions. That's the problem. They're already answered, and I needed you to show me that thing I must have overlooked. I can't believe this. I've gotta go. Miss you, love you, bye," I said to end the call.

Nate was laughing so hard that it sounded like he couldn't catch his breath to speak. I think I heard a barely-discernible "bye" inserted among the jolliness, but I'm not sure. As I hung up the phone, I could still hear him laughing through the earpiece as it pushed down upon the hang-up button. I felt badly about hanging up on him, so I touched base again soon thereafter for an actual conversation. He was still laughing for joy.

After that first call, I thought to myself, "Well that didn't work." After even more thorough reflection than before, I discerned the following: I needed somebody *else* to talk me out of the Catholic Church.

I sincerely apologize if my outright stubbornness is frustrating to my readers. This book should have ended a long time ago. I can only laugh at myself and hope that my bumpy road is redeemed, maybe by making somebody out there feel understood. In hindsight, I see that the circles I was going in were more of an *ascending spiral*. I would keep coming back to the same point over and over again, but at higher elevations each pass. "Yeah, I've been here before," I thought, "but I have a better view of where I've been, by looking down upon the mountain which I've been circling—now from a higher vantage." At this point up the winding summit, I at least knew that I couldn't keep on doing this forever.

I prayed, "All right, Lord, we're going to do this one last time. I choose Dr. Paul Johnson as the person who can show me whatever I'm missing here and talk me out of Catholicism. I promise you that I will do *whatever Dr. Johnson says*, no matter what it is. This current struggle in my spirit is just as awful as my agnostic crisis of old. I need to put this matter of ecclesiology to rest for good, so I can move on with my life. Whatever Dr. Johnson says, I will interpret as your own voice speaking to me through him, and I will proceed accordingly and obediently."

If you were baking a loaf of "Ian's motivation bread" in this particular case, a few ingredients comprise the mixture. One of my motives in choosing Dr. Johnson was simply his witness. He showed me Jesus. Beyond the abundant feast of his mentorship, he was always the Holy Spirit's instrument in the classroom. Whenever he spoke, my spirit within me would leap for joy. I knew I was hearing the good, the true, and the beautiful. I knew that I was hearing the Word of God. Every time he taught, I knew I was hearing freeing and life-giving truth against deceptive and dangerous error.

Another motive for choosing Dr. Johnson was his wealth of knowledge. He was the smartest man I had ever met. Knowing Greek, he could read the New Testament free of translation issues that can result from rendering the text into the English language. And he had written his dissertation on the topic of wisdom. I knew that his own wisdom would be a priceless asset for my quest.

My primary motive, however, for selecting Dr. Johnson as my guide was that I knew he was a Baptist. He served on the faculty of a Baptist university that had no Catholics among their team of theology scholars. As a brilliant Baptist professor, surely *he* knew what I had been overlooking in my search for the true Church. In effect, by telling God that I would do whatever Dr. Johnson said, I was intentionally loading the dice in my favor. It wasn't pure obedience and acquiescence to Christ's Lordship at work. Rather, as insane as it is, I was attempting to pull the wool over God's eyes. I paid lip service to trust, while stacking the deck according to the outcome I desired. I had already presumed that Dr. Johnson would talk me out of Catholicism, then in the name of obedience and promise-keeping, I would subsequently be wrong to look into it again. The problem with this motivation was that God *always* wins at chess. Whenever you think you're luring him into a gambit, he checkmates you.

I went to Dr. Johnson's office hours, and knocked on his half-open door.

"Come on in, my brother," he said. "It's always great to see you. What's on your mind?"

I opened, "Dr. Johnson, I came here today to ask you about the Catholic Church."

"Why don't you shut the door," he said with intensity in his voice.

I pushed his door the entire way closed until it clicked.

"Please, sit down," he said with increasing earnestness.

I sat down, as a single bead of sweat rolled down my temple.

With a locked gaze, Dr. Johnson slowly leaned forward to break the deafening silence.

He said, "Ian, I'M CATHOLIC! I converted a few years ago. I've been attending Mass in a far-away town, while still maintaining Baptist membership locally. This school can't find out I'm Catholic. They don't have any Catholics among the theology faculty, if you've noticed."

"I know!" I exclaimed. "That's why I came to you—you were supposed to talk me *out of it.*"

"No," he replied. "The Holy Spirit led you to me, to hear the truth that you need to become Catholic too. You never should have dropped out of RCIA in the first place. That's the most bone-headed move you could have made. The Church is as she claims. She is the Bride of God's Christ in this world. In a world gone dark and chaotic, the Church communicates God's hope and mercy that are always available to save whoever wants to be saved. You need to start RCIA immediately, either picking up where you left off, or starting fresh. You need to tell your church, and you need to trust God to take care of you."

"*You're* keeping it a secret," I challenged him.

"But I still converted," he said. "As for my apparent hypocrisy about keeping it hidden from specific people at present, you're right. That's a conflict for me right now. And I feel the deepest sympathy for you regarding what you must be experiencing. I'm not sure what the university would do to me if they found out, but even the thought of risking my pension so close to retirement scares the hell out of me. Fear gets its hooks in deep, as you know. In addition, wisdom dictates that I reveal the appropriate things to the appropriate people in the appropriate time. Even if all fear was removed, the question remains if wisdom would have me wait for the right season to tell certain people. It's an honest question, and I need your prayers for me as I discern through it. In the meantime, it is clear that the next step for you is to re-enter RCIA and inform your church. As your mentor, your brother-in-Christ, and your friend, I'm telling you: Ian, *it's time.*"

I prayed, "Well that didn't work. Lord, *I get it.* Thank you for being as clever as you are patient with me, over and over again. I said I would interpret Dr. Johnson's guidance as yours and obediently do whatever you reveal. And that's exactly what I'm going to do."

"Dr. Johnson," I said.

"Yes?"

"I've made my decision. I'm enrolling again in RCIA to enter the Catholic Church this Easter," I proclaimed.

"Bravo!" he responded in celebration. "This is the smartest decision you could have made, and I'm proud of you. I don't need to tell you that the proverbial crap is about to hit the fan. God goes with you, and you have nothing to fear. I'm with you, too. If anything breaks badly here at the university, I'm in your corner. I will defend you from the inside. You set your mind on RCIA, and on finishing your coursework, thesis, and comprehensive exams. That's all that's on your plate. And it's plenty already—don't trouble yourself with anything else."

If I was going to go public, there was no need to commute to a far-away town. I attended Saint Luke Catholic Church in nearby Temple, Texas. At the very first Mass, the leader of RCIA approached me and invited me to enroll.

"Oh, you must have talked to my friend," I said.

"I don't know what you're talking about," he answered. "I just felt like I was supposed to invite you to join."

It was a welcome confirmation, so to speak. At the man's invitation, I enrolled that day. With that, I was back in RCIA and started attending Mass weekly at Saint Luke's. I informed my department chair, a couple members of my church, and a deacon. Within days, all hell broke loose.

22

All Hell Breaks Loose

I recall sitting in a diner my first week as a Baptist pastor and eating lunch with a deacon, when a loud pair of Texan cowboys seated nearby had a brief conversation that was impossible *not* to hear.

"How's things?" said the first man.

"Going," said the other.

"Yep," affirmed the first.

Then the second man said, "Got new neighbors. New family moved into the house next to mine. They're *Catholic.*"

The way he pronounced the word *Catholic* by itself comprised the entirety of their conversation. He spoke the word in a manner that conveyed disgrace, tragedy, and the insinuation that nothing else need be said. He may as well have announced that a family of *paroled convicts* had just moved in next door.

The first man responded by making a guttural noise. "Mmmm," he moaned in disgust. The sound reverberated through my chair as though it had been amped through a subwoofer. The deacon seated with me looked up at me and said, "This is Bible country. Some people don't take too kindly to Catholics in these parts."

A closet Catholic at the time, I defended the Church. I responded, "Your statement is incoherent. Catholics consider the Bible to be trustworthy, primary-source material that is inspired by the Holy Spirit. They read from both Testaments of Scripture at Mass. Deacon, you seem to be implying that Catholics don't belong in 'Bible country' when, in truth, they believe the Bible."

Deacon replied, "I can see we've got ourselves a caring and knowledgeable pastor. But it behooves me to tell you: that's some very dangerous talk around here."

I replied firmly, "I'm here to tell the truth."

"I'm just watching your back," he answered. "You keep talking like that, and you may not be here long."

After starting RCIA, and with that previous diner episode securely in my memory, I knew that I was in for it. When my parsonage phone rang, I thought to myself, "Here we go." The following week would indeed prove to be among the worst weeks of my life. But to my happy surprise, this initial phone call was among the best pastoral calls I've ever received.

The woman on the other end of the line opened, "Brother Ian, I'm not a member there, so I thank you for taking my call. I need your help, and you're like the pastor of this whole town."

"I'm so glad that you called me!" I affirmed. "God loves you, and I'm here for you—whatever the need."

"God bless you," she said. "First, I want you to know that you have nothing to do with why I don't attend your church. In fact, I consider going just for you sometimes. There's bad history there for me, from before you came on board. But I know Jesus. You know my daughter Annie—she goes to your church faithfully three times per week. She's in your youth group. You're the one who led her to Christ, and as a Christian mother, I have no words to express my thanks for what you've done for *me*. Annie's the reason I called. She fell back in with her old crowd a few days ago and got arrested. Judge was gonna put her in the juvenile delinquency center, but we talked, and she's doing community service instead. She's paintin' the fire hall over the next few weekends. She's there now with the other kids who accepted the judge's offer. That's where you come in. Brother Ian, Annie's scared you'll be embarrassed of her. She's ashamed. She won't talk to me about it, but I'm fairly certain that she's scared the Lord won't forgive her. Could you maybe drop by the fire hall this afternoon, as though by accident, and talk to her for me?"

I asked, "What was she arrested for?"

"Stealin'," she said.

"What did she try to steal?"

"A jar of Vlasic Stackers Bold and Spicy Sweet Heat dill pickles," answered Annie's mother. "My daughter got arrested by the police for stealin' pickles. Pickle thief—the things a mother deals with. I'm not a bad mother. I would have put some on the shopping list, if she had asked me."

"You're a wonderful mother! For example, what you're doing for your daughter right now is simply beautiful. *Pickles* ..." I said, trying with difficulty not to laugh. "You know, the hospitality ministry at the church typically gets a gift for any young person who comes to faith. Would it be acceptable if I showed up with a present for Annie?"

"I think I know what you have in mind, you precious, precious man. That would make her day!"

"I'm on my way."

After a quick stop at the grocery store, I arrived at the fire hall where a group of youngsters had already begun to put a fresh coat of paint on the old building. I walked up to Annie with a paper bag in hand. The poor kid couldn't look me in the eyes.

Annie asked, "My mom sent you, didn't she?"

"Yes she did, because she loves you," I answered.

"She told you?" asked Annie, looking at the ground.

"Yes, I know what happened," I answered truthfully. I knew firsthand that, if you're even a little tempted to try lying to a kid, don't bother.

"Judge said we could either paint the fire hall or go to juvy," she explained. "We picked *paint the fire hall*." Then, still looking at the ground, Annie asked, "Are you embarrassed of me?"

"On the contrary, I'm proud of you for taking responsibility for yourself," I said. "*Everybody* messes up. But *not* everybody accepts responsibility for their actions. I couldn't be more proud of you!" Then I told her about copying chapter four of my social studies textbook when I was tardy. "It's like when Aslan rips the dragon scales off of Eustace," I said, "like having a splinter removed from your foot. There's some pain, but it's good. Hey, the church has a gift for you."

Then I pulled out of the paper bag a jar of Vlasic Stackers Bold and Spicy Sweet Heat dill pickles. "These should keep you out of trouble," I said.

"My very own jar!" she exclaimed. "And I'm not sharing. Thanks, Brother Ian," she said, now able to look at me with eyes that were beginning to tear up.

She continued, "I remember when you preached about that Christian who stole pears and then just threw 'em to the pigs. He didn't want the pears. He did it for stealin's sake. That's not me. I did it for the sake of the pickles. Spicy dills are the most delicious things. When I saw them sittin' there on the shelf, with that stork on the sticker lookin' at me like that, I just wanted 'em so bad. So I took them for myself, without paying. I *stole*. It breaks the Ten Commandments, I know. But at least I did it for the pickles—not like that Augustine guy, before he got saved."

It was close to Thanksgiving, and there was a splendorous autumn chill in the southern air—always refreshing after a Texas summer. I told the kids, "I'm a repentant sinner who needs to take responsibility for *my* actions, so I'll put my lot in with you guys." Then I grabbed a paintbrush and joined the youth in their community service until evening. It was apparent that it meant a lot to them. For me, it was an unforgettable joy.

After I painted with them for a while, Annie asked, "Brother Ian, you promise you won't be mad?"

"I won't be mad; what's on your mind?"

"Since I got saved, I've been doin' some reading. Why aren't we Catholics? We should be Catholic. That's clear to me. Baptists trace their heritage back to the results of the Reformation. And they go back to Jesus, too, I mean they're real Christians, of course. But the Catholics trace back to Jesus and the apostolic authority of Peter—before the Church became disunited. Bible says we're not supposed to divide. That's a confusing presentation of the gospel to a world that's already real confused. Seriously, how can you be a Baptist? Why aren't *you* Catholic?"

"I am," I said. "I'm officially entering the Catholic Church this Easter."

"Good! You should!" she exclaimed joyfully. "I'm sure gonna miss you, Brother Ian."

"Nonsense, I can still visit," I replied.

"Are you my elder and that naïve?" she said. "I may be young, but I'm not stupid. They're gonna run you outta town! You're gonna feel all alone for a while. You're the person who introduced me to Jesus, so I want you to know this: when you're up there at the Vigil, you're not there alone. I'm entering RCIA as soon as I'm eighteen. At least one of your sheep is following you into the Church."

She wasn't the only one. I invited myself over to the home of the supportive deacon to tell him about my conversion personally.

I brought with me a letter of resignation. In it, I offered to stay on through Christmas of 2003. The church would have time to find an interim pastor to begin the new year fresh, and I would have the opportunity to say farewell to my beloved community. Across the Sundays of Advent, I could instill a few parting gems, express my profound gratitude, and encourage them with some ecumenical insights.

It was easier for me to let the deacon simply read my letter while I sat there. After he did so, I told him that I would be entering the Catholic Church at Easter. He started crying.

"These aren't bad tears, Brother Ian," he began. "Your news is incredibly affirming for me. You know that faction of protesting deacons trying to quash my building proposal and get you fired? Well, they got me thinking. They got me thinking about theology, especially the topics of Christian unity and authority. I've been reading, and I, too, am considering converting to the Catholic Church. You need to know: you are not alone! I still have a lot of questions and searching to do, but who knows—I might be right behind you soon. I'm what you might call a *closet Catholic* in some ways already."

One of the other deacon's wives paid me a personal visit a couple days later. Her husband was the same man who had treated me to lunch at the diner during my first week in town—and had warned me about the thread of anti-Catholicism that ran through the area.

"Brother Ian," said the deacon's wife, "I have a thought, but I'm scared to say it."

"Please go right ahead," I assured her.

She asked, "You know this group of deacons that's threatening to leave if they don't get their way, the ones talking about canning you as our pastor?"

"Yes, I'm fully aware of everything," I said.

"I think it's the devil's work. We don't battle against flesh and blood, but against real powers of evil. You're the best pastor we've ever had. I'm convinced the devil doesn't like you very much," she said.

"He's made that explicit," I said, "but why would you be afraid to say that? I'm encouraged by your words."

"The part that I'm scared to say to you is this: I think we need to call a priest. I'm serious. We need to call in a Catholic priest, in order to pray over you for protection. I *know* it," she explained.

"That's why I came alone. My husband doesn't like Catholics much. Usually, neither do I. There are times when I join in and make fun. But whenever something like this happens, I am forced to admit that there is a recognizable authority to the Catholic Church as the people of Christ. I'm a hypocrite, Brother Ian. I make fun of them, but whenever the real power of Satan in this world shows its face around me, guess right where I turn? I look straight to the Catholic Church, desperate for the authority the Lord gave the apostles. What are *we* gonna do? Vote about it? I'm serious. We need a Catholic priest right now. Call one."

I proceeded to inform her that I was in full agreement with her. In fact, I was entering the Catholic Church at Easter and had already handed in my resignation.

"What?" she blurted.

"Yes, that's right," I said.

"Well that definitely means you're not mad about my suggestion, so that's a relief," she said. "I want to thank you for everything. God's fed me through you so much already, and now you've given me *this* to chew on. I will think and pray on it. And I'll talk to my husband about what I've been thinking, I will. He's my husband, and he should know what I'm going through spiritually. I mean, if Brother Ian's going Catholic, then it's definitely something to look into at the very least. This was affirming for me. Thanks—thank you for everything."

The youth minister was also entirely understanding. As she put it, "Dr. Paul Johnson and you are my two main Christian mentors. Sometimes I wonder if Dr. Johnson is a Catholic. He uses Ray Brown as his primary textbook, and Brown's a Catholic scholar. Now you're entering the Church. I can no longer ignore Catholicism. Whatever happens, I will remain with you through all of this!" And that is exactly what she did.

Not everyone, however, was supportive. One man came pounding on my door, talking about how I had *gone crazy*. Then another, and then *another*.

A pastor's wife from a nearby church paid me a visit, literally waving her finger in my face—within an inch of my nose. She said, "You're crazy, and you're sick. You're crazy, and you're sick. You're crazy, and *you're sick!* You have a DISEASE!"

Then one of the leaders from the Baptist General Convention of Texas, who purported not to exercise authority within an autonomous congregation, called me up.

"You are *unfit* as a servant of God!" he insisted.

"I could have told you that," I said.

He went on, "You are unfit to preach the gospel. You should never proclaim the Word of God ever again for as long as you live. I beg you, before you destroy anybody else with your violent deception, to at least trust me that you are unfit to be a minister of God. Get out of that town, and don't you *ever* show your face there again! You've done enough harm already."

A classmate at the university called me next. "I heard you're becoming Catholic. I'm calling to say goodbye. My father says I'm never allowed to speak to you again. Goodbye."

A welcome break from the antagonism was a call from Annie's mother. "I knew it," she said. "You gave my daughter her own jar of pickles—that was truly inspired! Annie's eating them right now. She's even sharing them with her sisters, and that really means something.

"Anyway, my husband and I are requesting some Christian marriage counseling from you tonight, if you're available. We'll probably go late, because we need to cover a lot of ground. We're determined to let the Lord heal everything and redeem it! We're friends with another married couple who are having problems surrounding their kids, and we all want to get some good advice and pray together. Do you have a problem ministering to four grownups who are all older than you? Would that be strange for you?" she asked.

"I would be honored," I said.

She thanked me and continued, "Since we'll go late and need to talk uncensored, I'll make sure that all my kids are having sleep-overs at their friends' houses tonight. We'll still have our baby here but she's two, so she can't repeat anything she hears. I hope we can go as late as we need. I hope you're a night owl."

It was a beautiful night indeed—one of prayer, friendship, conversion, and reconciliation for four people who never set foot in my church while I was pastor. And their adorable baby fell asleep on my lap, which was lovely. We wrapped up at about 4:00 in the morning. Then I returned to the parsonage and collapsed into my bed.

Only a couple hours later, I was awakened by more angry knocks on my parsonage door. I was greeted by two angry deacons, accusing me of spending the night alone with a teenage girl.

"We saw you leave Annie's house at 4:00 this morning, so don't you deny it! You spent the night alone with her!" one of them yelled.

"This is ridiculous," I said, "Annie wasn't even there." I attempted to defend myself, still trying to peel my eyes open, "None of the family's kids were there, except for their two-year-old. I was in a private pastoral appointment with four adults. Besides the baby, I was the youngest person there. Annie's parents intentionally made sure that their kids were staying at friends' houses. Good grief—just ask them, okay?"

"No," the other deacon said. "We already *know* the truth. Besides, we saw you painting the fire hall with Annie, you pervert."

"Yes, at her mother's request. I joined *all* the kids who were there doing community service, outside, in broad daylight, along with several adult members of the firehouse, in support of the mercy shown by our local judge," I responded. "I thought the deacons wanted a pastor who reaches out to the troubled youth of this town and one who 'proactively forms community connections'—isn't *that* how you worded it? And I wasn't aware that painting fire halls was perverse."

It was no use. It wasn't even that I was *guilty until proven innocent.* I was just guilty, period.

And then there was my dad. Now that was a phone call to remember.

"IAN ... NOOOO!"

In the most dramatic fashion, my father bellowed in mourning rather than anger. To him, I was lost forever. To his mind, he wouldn't get to be with me in heaven because he had lost me to the Whore of Babylon, and I would spend eternity burning in the lake of fire prepared for the devil and his angels.

On and on he went. "Tim has deceived you! You are deceived! You couldn't be more wrong. You are now in league with the Anti-Christ, you *fool*, duped by Lucifer's masquerade. I have lost you forever. I have failed you, son. You are now lost, *forever.* Oh God, where did I go wrong? Not *you*, Ian—you *promised*—you promised me *never!* You will burn, for all of eternity, you *will burn.*"

"I love you, Dad," was all I could say.

Then I fell ill—very, very ill. I fell to the floor of my bedroom feverish and in wrenching pain. I started throwing up, and the vomit was mixed with blood. I called 911, and an ambulance rushed me to the hospital. After they hooked up the rehydration drip with anti-nausea medication, they ran some tests. The diagnosis: I had contracted a potentially deadly gastro-intestinal virus.

"You know the tiny villi that line the small intestine and aid in digestion?" explained the doctor. "You basically don't have any working anymore. That's what this particular bug does. It's rare in somebody so young—have you been under a lot of stress lately?"

"Yeah," I said.

The doctor continued, "If you hadn't called 911 when you did, you may have died from dehydration. But they got to you in time, and you're going to be okay. It'll be a long road to recovery. The virus is still in your system. Once it's gone, eating will be exceptionally difficult. You'll be on a strict diet, and full recovery will take about six months. You're lucky to be alive."

I was hospitalized for an entire week, then bed-ridden for a couple more weeks after that. Over the next six months I lost fifty pounds. Fast results aside, that is *not* a good way to lose weight.

During my first day in the hospital, the nurse announced happily that I had a visitor. It was one of the deacons from the church. I smiled and thanked him for coming and keeping me company. He smiled back, until the nurse left. Then his countenance turned to rage.

He yelled angrily, "Now that I've got you alone and you're down on your back, unable to fight back, I'm going to give you a piece of my mind!" Then he justified his condemning fury as being *the Lord's work.* He accused me of going crazy, deceiving people, breaking hearts, and becoming an agent of the devil. Being shouted at is never a pleasant experience, but the morphine I was taking added a surreal, nightmarish quality to the scene. I used the "call nurse" button for rescue.

I was visited by six other members of the church who more or less said the same thing. The Lord provided me with a much-needed respite from this series of hostile encounters when Annie's mom paid me a visit. She began by thanking me again for all the beautiful ministry I had done for her family. Then she updated me about the two deacons who had alleged that I spent the night alone with her daughter.

"I heard what they accused you of," she informed me, "and I am disgusted with them, plain disgusted. I defended you of course. I told them how Annie wasn't even home that night, and they got a piece of my mind while I was at it, too, for making up a lie like that. I tell you what, bunch of sick-minded hypocrisy—I'm sorry, Brother Ian. I'll work on that 'process of forgiveness' you talked about the other night. I'm in the early stages with this one. Anyway, their accusation is the last thing you need right now. So I wanted you to know: I cleared everything up with them, and that fire is officially put out."

"I appreciate you doing that for me," I said, "but you shouldn't have needed to in the first place. It's hard to believe that two deacons would make such wild assumptions and accusations. I'm having a hard time processing it."

"Now maybe you see why I don't go there anymore. By the way, if they kick you out of your parsonage, my home is yours," she assured me. "Here, Annie told me to give you this present from her. She used her whole allowance this week and paid for this with her own money."

It was a jar of Vlasic Stackers Bold and Spicy Sweet Heat dill pickles.

"She says, 'You're not alone,' and she's right."

On my last day in the hospital, the doctor informed me that a group of people, including a member of my family, was requesting that I be locked up in a psych ward through Christmas.

"I didn't know that Catholicism was now deemed a mental illness," I responded.

The doctor said, "It's not. Of course you're free to go. I just thought that you should be aware."

After hearing that, I simply couldn't bear the idea of being alone at the parsonage. As gracious as Annie's family was to offer me sanctuary, I didn't want to see any more grief brought upon them on my account. The parents of one of my best friends at the university had also offered me hospitality for as long as I needed, and I accepted their invitation. Then I informed a deacon that I would be in recovery for the next two weeks at the home of a friend. I told him that I expected to be well enough to preach one final time at the church—on the

Sunday closest to Christmas Day. Due to the illness, I hadn't yet had an opportunity to tell the entire congregation about my decision to become Catholic. This last sermon would be my opportunity to inform them, express my gratitude, and say farewell.

After a couple more weeks of bed rest, I was still in a lot of pain but back on my feet again. With Christmas only a few days away, I phoned a deacon to confirm that I would preach my last Sunday.

"I'm sorry, Brother Ian," he said. "The deacons held a vote. The decision was that you are unfit to preach, and you are not welcome in the church ever again. We ask that you make no contact with any members of the church. The vote was unanimous."

It broke my heart. I knew my deacon friend was one of those votes, and it killed me. "Maybe his motive was to protect me from harm," I thought, in an attempt to comfort myself. The attempt failed, as I couldn't get over the fact that the same group of people who once cried for joy at my ordination had unanimously labeled me *unfit* as a minister. I wasn't even allowed to say goodbye. And I suspect that most of the church never found out that I became Catholic.

With a friend's help, I used the holiday to move my belongings out of the church parsonage and into storage. As we loaded the moving van, two deacons stood guard on the property in order to prevent any conversations with parishioners. I moved into a dorm on my school's campus and consoled myself with the prospect that I could focus on my master's degree, now only three semesters away from completion.

Shortly after the start of the spring semester, I was called into a private meeting with a high-ranking college administrator. His fine-looking office was filled with beautiful art and comfortable furniture. I felt initially excited to hear whatever he had to tell me.

He opened our meeting saying, "Ian, I understand that you are enrolled in RCIA and that you are becoming Catholic this Easter—is this correct?"

"Yes, sir, that's right," I answered.

He responded in a super-friendly tone of voice, "In that case, I think it would be appropriate for you to transfer immediately to Franciscan University of Steubenville in Ohio, in order to complete your degree. Don't you think you would be happier there? Is that okay with you?"

"No, it's not," I said. "They're a great school from my under-standing. But I'm getting my degree *here*, under an amazing faculty! I'm proud of this school. And I'm deep into the program—I'll grad-uate in May 2005."

He responded bluntly, "This is a Baptist university that gradu-ates a lot of professional Baptist ministers and missionaries, and its board of donors has certain expectations about our public image. The school's top-ranking graduate student in theology is becoming Catholic—that sends a message that doesn't reflect our mission. I'm asking you to leave."

"I'm not leaving," I insisted, in disbelief at what was happening, "I'm already well into drafting my lengthy thesis. I'm holding a 4.0 grade point average, for crying out loud! It's illegal to discriminate based on religion. You cannot kick me out of school for becoming Catholic!"

"No, we can't," he said. "You're right—we cannot kick you out of school for becoming Catholic. But there could be a problem with your thesis."

"*Excuse me?*" I questioned. "My thesis proposal was officially approved by the theology faculty last semester."

"I am 'unapproving' it," he said.

"You can't do this," I said.

"I just did," he replied. "I have hereby officially unapproved your thesis proposal, as is within my authority to do. You are now writing a thesis that does *not* have approval. You are free to remain here and complete the program, and you are free to complete your thesis. But in light of the fact that your paper is no longer approved, you do the work at your own risk. After reading the finished paper, the faculty will *then* decide if it meets with the school's specifications, in order to determine at that point in time whether or not you will graduate. Please understand that, GPA aside, an approved thesis is a require-ment for your degree. That is all."

Later that day, Dr. Johnson treated me to an early dinner at a fancy, exclusive, and very *private* restaurant in order to discuss the way for-ward. While we waited for our meals, he imparted to me some import-ant words of wisdom.

"Be *extremely* careful here," he said. "Prudence is your best ally right now and integrity your best defense. Guard your heart from any thoughts of hatred or vengeance—these are not of God. We do not battle flesh and blood. Love your enemies. Whenever life looks like 'you're damned if you do and you're damned if you don't' our sovereign God has a plan, and he is faithful. *Trust him.* Our Lord always has some unseen third way, not yet revealed. Let him do his job. And you do yours. Complete the coursework; write the thesis."

"Knowing that I might not graduate?" I asked.

"Yes," he asserted. "Don't write the thesis *to graduate.* Work for the sake of the scholarship itself. Enjoy the purified motivation of your studies, and live by faith. Practice your trust in God this way. As I said in our last meeting, the crap is hitting the fan. I guarantee you that I will do everything in my power from the inside to get your paper reapproved. But I *can't* guarantee that my efforts will succeed. I cannot guarantee that you will graduate. God's plans for your work may transcend a degree title altogether. I don't pretend to comprehend his ways and thoughts, which are far higher than my own. You may not graduate. That is true. Finish your classes and write the thesis anyway. God has a plan. Trust God, before you get to see what his plan is."

"Thank you. This is hard. It's *really hard.* But I'll do it," I responded.

Dr. Johnson then added, "You should also know that the faculty in the department of theology had a meeting about you. Some deacons from your church contacted the school. In the name of *warning the school*, they have accused you of mental illness and thus introduced the notion that you are a danger to the other students."

"Catholicism is *not* a mental illness," I said.

"These are fearful times," he responded. "I'm so sorry for what you're going through. Stay sober and sharp. Stay on your guard and prayerful. Wear wisdom and gentleness as if they're your jacket. Be careful that, in every public interaction, you indicate wellbeing and temperance. *You are being watched.* Right now, I believe it's unsafe for you to so much as express anger or anxiety publically."

I vented, "So let me get this right—in graduate school, with my graduation being threatened by blatant discrimination and my thesis deadline and comprehensive exams lingering over my head, I can't feel stressed out? I spent a week hospitalized and was kicked out of town—but no anger, and no anxiety allowed? To me, a person who exhibits no emotion while his life is hell is the person who appears to be crazy."

He replied, "I understand. You're right. And this is manifestly absurd and unjust. I know how unfair this is. Nonetheless, leave room for God's magnificent redemption. The worse it is, the better it is—look at the Cross. Prudence dictates that you avoid the appearance of all evil right now. You're allowed to feel angry and anxious. Simply don't express it in public. My heart and my prayers are with you through this. And God is with you! Fear not, son."

His words were freeing and consoling, and the steak was particularly delicious albeit painful to my weakened stomach. I went back to an empty college dorm room that night. My world had been a picture of liveliness. Now, I was despised, accused, labeled, threatened, sick, scrutinized beneath a microscope of suspicion, and abandoned. The *presence of absence* in my room was palpable. I prayed, "The Lord gives, and the Lord takes away. Blessed be the name of the Lord."

Taking one day at a time had become my mantra, and I fell asleep asking for the grace to make it through the next day. I woke up the next morning to find a piece of threatening hate-mail sitting on my pillow. Sealed in a red envelope, the message had been penned anonymously. Yes, someone had broken into the dorm and entered my room while I slept to leave the angry letter. At that point, all I could do was say, "God, please help."

23

The Scalpel of the Great Physician

No matter how bad life got, God was always closer than I could have realized. As "The Footprints in the Sand" story goes, it is during those times when we feel abandoned by God that he is carrying us.

During the week I was hospitalized, something significant happened that initiated the Great Physician's spiritual healing process. Specifically, on my last day in the hospital, one of the angry deacons apologized to me. He was one of the deacons who had come to my front door accusing me of being a pervert. He was also among those who had chastised me during the early days of my illness. But on his second visit to see me in the hospital, at the end of my week there, he began weeping openly—then he told me how sorry he was. This man blessed me with his repentance.

"I accused you falsely," he confessed with his voice cracking. "I didn't listen to you when you told me the truth about that night. Then I came here a couple days ago, and I yelled at you while you were sick. The things I said were wrong. Can you ever forgive me?"

"I love you, and it's already gone," I replied, when he grabbed me for a manly, Baptist hug.

The deacon continued, "After Annie's mom spoke with me, I went to the parsonage. Brother Ian, there were pools of vomit mixed with blood. You were *really sick*. I want you to know, it's all cleaned up. I understand if you need to be with family right now, but the parsonage remains yours until the end of the year, if you need it. I also took it upon myself to have your whole wardrobe professionally dry cleaned for you—it's my penance. You're the best thing that has ever happened to this town, and you go with my blessing. You are truly a man of God."

I've mentally filed this moment along with the Nuns' Walk of Northern Ireland, my first meeting of each infant niece and nephew, and the other most beautiful things I've ever seen. Father Sean Kealy at Duquesne University would later tell me this: more than the sweat of the workers and more than the blood of the martyrs, the most precious thing to God is the teardrop of one repentant sinner. I believe that.

My conversion was indeed difficult for my Baptist congregation to comprehend. As a person who himself had formerly bashed Catholics publically, I understood their perspective and what they were experiencing. The grace of God's loving kindness washed over me. To this day, I feel nothing but love and gratitude for them, and for all of my Protestant brothers and sisters in Christ. They were the people whom God used to introduce me to his Son, and there is only gratitude.

Writing a thesis, taking graduate courses, and preparing for comprehensive exams, all while wondering whether I would be permitted to graduate, was harder than I would like to admit. I prefer to think of myself as a man of purified motives, who would happily immerse myself in graduate-level work for the sake of the education itself and the edification of my spirit. In reality, I found out how important the actual recognition can be. There's validity to the importance of earthly credentialing, certainly. At the same time, it was an uncomfortable look at my true priorities. In truth, I have a mixture of motivations for most endeavors. And in the case of my master's degree, I had been deriving a large proportion of personal drive from the goal of obtaining the *title*. The removal of this motive was definitely purifying.

As difficult as it was, I followed Dr. Johnson's guidance and maintained top marks in my coursework. On faith, I prepped for my comps and continued to press forward drafting my "unapproved" thesis.

Following the hospitalization, Dr. Carver had encouraged me to take a leave of absence from my teaching at the Bible institute in order to reduce my anxiety levels. I followed his advice, too. He hated to lose me, but my health was more important to him than my service. He was happy that I agreed to his recommendation. Of course, the Lord immediately sent him a new teacher—a brilliant man with a doctorate of divinity degree and a sacramental mindset. My classes at the institute would be in the best of hands.

Meanwhile, I enjoyed my RCIA classes immensely. The priest who taught the course was spectacular. I remember how well he fielded my questions. For instance, one time I asked him in class, "Father, I see that the Catholic Church seems to assign varying degrees of severity to different sins, with some rendered *venial* while others are deemed *grave*, even *deadly*. But doesn't the Bible teach us that *all* sin is equally grave in the eyes of God, and that all people fall short of his glory?"

He responded, "Thank you for that excellent question! I'm so glad you're asking about these important matters. And I'm glad that you see this class as a place where you are free to ask the tough questions. I don't want anybody entering the Church if their conscience is against it—that will only come back to haunt you later, and the Church wouldn't have you betray your conscience."

"Thank you, Father," I said, comforted by his words.

He continued, "To answer your inquiry: the question is flawed. It's flawed by an *either-or* outlook. According to the way in which you formed your question, *either* all sin is equally grave to God *or* sins have differing degrees of severity. In truth, this matter is another one of those *Catholic both-ands*. Yes, all sin is equally grave to God. I would agree whole-heartedly with that statement. And yes, some sin is venial while other sin is deadly, at the same time. What appears to be a contradiction disappears altogether as soon as you examine the whole picture. Modernism tends to reduce morality to quarantined moments of time, evaluating right and wrong by placing a single, isolated instant on trial. But people don't exist in isolated moments. Instead, we live across a trajectory of life that has a momentum to it, either growing or declining across time—sometimes growing in some areas while declining in others."

"Please go on," I said, as my brain's dimmer switch slowly increased illumination.

"For the *full* picture, we grow and decline along the path of life," he explained. "Jesus shows us this reality in the beatitudes. He doesn't merely say, 'Was that isolated action merciful, or not?' Rather, he says that those who *show* mercy *will be shown* mercy. Notice he's talking about a timeline here, the timeline, or trajectory, or *overall path* of one's life. Yes, we always live in the present moment. We're bound to the timeline in the present. But, what we do in the present moment is influenced by whatever we've *been doing*. And what we do in the present moment will influence our habits, tendencies, and character in the *future*. In the Bible, Jesus shows us a look at the whole trajectory of salvation. So that's what the Catholic Church looks at. Does this observation make sense so far?"

"Yes!" I answered, as the light became even brighter.

"Now to your specific question," continued the priest, "a venial sin and a grave sin are actually the *same* sin, just at different points along the person's trajectory, that's all. For example, consider a man who cheats on his wife. The adultery started earlier in the man's heart, probably with deliberate fantasy. Then, there was the real contact with another person, then an emotional bond, and ultimately a physical affair. Back when the man first told the other woman that she was pretty, the overall sin was still in its infancy—in its venial stage. It would have been easier to confess and repent at that point in time, and far less damaging to the marriage. But at the grave point of a full-blown sexual affair, the adultery had become deadly. In reality, the whole sin was a long-term snowball that gained momentum over time. That entire sin-trajectory is grave to God. At the same time, the sin held a different level of severity early on in the life of the time-bound human subject. To sum up, varying degrees of severity on the timeline are a reality, so the Church acknowledges and talks about that. And the whole sin-trajectory is grievous to God, so we acknowledge and talk about that reality, too. It's another *both-and*, rather than an *either-or* situation."

"Wow," I replied, "what a superb response! My question was not only answered; the question itself has altogether disappeared. You're really good at this."

"Thanks," he said. "Do you have a sponsor?"

"What's a sponsor?" I asked. "Do I need one?"

"See me after class," Father said, smiling. At the close of the night, he offered to be my sponsor. I was moved by his offer to say the least, but having known for myself the weight of being a head pastor, I couldn't bring myself to add another task to his already-full plate.

Instead, I went searching for another willing sponsor. In particular, I attended the Catholic Student Organization (CSO) meeting at my university that Wednesday evening. To my understanding, every Catholic student enrolled at the college was a member. With perfect attendance that evening, there were seven of us there, plus a Catholic professor from outside the department of theology.

One of the students greeted me, "Hi. We're small, but mighty. We hope you'll join us. It would increase our membership by over 10 percent in one night."

"I'll join," I said. "Who's your president?"

Another young woman then waved at me by wiggling her fingers. I believe she was a graduate student in the English program.

"Will you sponsor me through RCIA?" I asked her.

"I would love to!" she exclaimed. "But just so you know, I already have a boyfriend."

"That's best, because I probably would have asked you out. Now the process can stay pure and true," I answered.

The bit of flirtation aside, the moment made for the greatest ice-breaker of all time, with everybody laughing profusely at the exchange. Pure and true our relationship remained, and she was the best sponsor a person could have. I once sat in on a parish talk she gave about the topic of virtue ethics. I still teach that very subject to this day, thanks to her inspiration. And her boyfriend became an encouragement to me as well. Although he was a Protestant, he was seeking. And he was honored and excited at his girlfriend's role in my journey.

The Lord continued to flood healing into my soul. I got a call from the youth minister at the Baptist church, and she had an update for me.

"Ian, you've got to hear this," she said. "The Baptist general director of missions was upset by what had happened to you at the hands of several members of the Baptist General Convention of Texas. He also wanted to understand better what had occurred. He conducted a personal investigation, by interviewing a number of church members and deacons in order to surmise exactly what had taken place. He concluded his investigation deciding entirely on your behalf! In fact, he preached at the church last Sunday.

"In his sermon, he rebuked the people who hurt you. He rebuked the faction of deacons who had threatened to split the church. He said that you're a man of God, and among the most fit preachers he had ever met. He said that the church was still immature, but he had great hope that they would be ready—sometime soon—for another powerful move of the Holy Spirit to sweep through the town. I looked across the sanctuary, and every head was nodding in agreement. Even the deacons who had caused problems were nodding. Two of them were crying."

I can't begin to describe the healing she administered to my heart with this update.

She continued, "Now you're still *not* supposed to visit, and you're still *not* allowed to preach there. But they say it's 'because sensitivities are too charged' at the moment. A lot of people feel guilty, and the convention wants those people to be assured of God's unconditional forgiveness. The leadership feels like seeing you would open up wounds of self-condemnation, or something like that. Some people who were never part of the problem feel guilty for no reason, so I've been comforting them for you. I'm sorry you can't say goodbye in person, but there's real repentance. Now they're better off than ever because of everything that happened. They are in solid, good hands with an excellent interim pastor. Ian, they're going to be okay, and you need to know that. God really made a difference through you! They love you, and they miss you dearly. And they know you love them."

Hearing this news felt like getting a late Christmas present from the Lord himself.

Another healing moment occurred on Ash Wednesday. But this moment has a back story. During my first semester at the university, I asked the head of the Theology Department if I could give a talk at the campus chapel service. I recall how the large-hearted man gave me a chuckle and an affirming pat on my shoulder, and then explained to me how it *worked*.

"I admire your ambition for big venues," he said, with genuine care in his voice, "and our chapel has a faithful audience each Wednesday of around a thousand people. It has indeed become a venue of renown. We have the governor of the state of Texas lined up this school year, for example.

"Speaking for the chapel service is usually reserved for the university administrators and other dignitaries who are connected to the school. Visiting speakers come in by invitation. When it comes to the matter of persons *requesting* to speak, the waiting list is quite long indeed."

Dr. Johnson echoed the same sentiment when he proudly handed me an audio copy of the outstanding chapel talk he had delivered after waiting *years* for the opportunity. "I already had years of full-time service to the department under my belt," he said, "and I had already been named the head of New Testament studies—and I *still* had to wait a couple *more* years before they gave me the podium at the campus chapel. As a student, you shouldn't get your hopes up."

As providence would have it, the university dedicated one chapel service each school year to the Catholic Student Organization in accordance with the university's anti-discrimination policy. Every Ash Wednesday, the CSO was permitted to select a speaker of its own choosing, absent any intervention from the administration. The members of the CSO's leadership team chose me. They had no idea that I had eyed that platform before. They came to me bursting with excitement.

"Okay, here's the deal," said a notably enthusiastic undergrad. "So, we get any speaker we want, one day per year. We want you! We may be tiny, but we got the best. The school's straight-A grad student in theology converted to us. You're the biggest thing that's ever happened to the CSO, and we're *not* gonna waste it. Will you do the Ash Wednesday service for us, *please*?!" she begged.

"Nothing would give me greater pleasure," I said. The girl jumped up and down. I prayed silently, "God, what are you up to?"

Through this timely loophole, I suddenly found myself standing in front of almost a thousand people, behind a podium that I never thought I would see from the back. In the front row of the audience sat seven Catholic students with sooty Ash Wednesday crosses on their foreheads. They were all clapping, cheering, and woo-hooing, as a disarming rumble of laughter rippled through the crowd.

However, as I was about to begin, a prominent Baptist leader, also seated in the front row, came to his feet. It was the same individual who had asked me to leave and had "unapproved" my thesis. When he stood up, silence spread throughout the audience. Then the man simply walked out. I noticed that his wife remained behind, still seated to hear the talk.

After a prayer, I opened the lecture, "As we can see, there's a bit of controversy surrounding my speaking here today, and it's a representative instance of some widespread and longstanding tensions between Catholics and Baptists."

This *stating the obvious* seemed to restore the disarmed atmosphere. Funny how people calm down as soon as somebody says, "Hey, we all see this elephant sitting here in the room, and it's okay to talk about it." I could now proceed with eased nerves.

I continued, "The focus is typically placed upon the differences between Catholics and Baptists. I'm not here to talk about those differences today. I'm not saying they're not important. No, those differences are in fact real, and they are very important to us. But I believe that these important differences between us have received, to date, the disproportionate bulk of our emphasis. We also have important similarities, too, so I would like to open with those.

"Both Catholics and Protestants believe in the Trinity: Father, Son, and Holy Spirit—Three Persons who are mysteriously at the same time one God. Both Catholics and Protestants believe that Jesus Christ, the Second Person of the Trinitarian Godhead, was completely human and completely divine mysteriously at the same time, and is himself the ultimate revealing of God to the creation. He is also God's good news to all of us. Both Catholics and Protestants believe that Jesus is the one who saves us. Both believe that we indeed need the Redeemer, Jesus, to wash away the sin that separates us from our loving Creator. We both believe in heaven and hell. We both believe in Christmas and Easter. We both believe that Christians are the temple of the Holy Spirit. We both believe that prayer really works, that the Bible is the inspired and trustworthy Word of God, and that Christians should go to church."

At this point, the tension in the room appeared to vanish entirely.

I added, "Here's another similarity between Catholics and Protestants: both groups contain numerous members in name only, who are not living out a saving relationship with Jesus Christ. As long as that's the case, I believe we should focus on that."

A dramatic hush fell over the attentive crowd. I thus proceeded to introduce the significance of Ash Wednesday and Lent, with a little history and theology to flesh out the season of *dying to one's self in order to find life in Christ*. There was that theme again—dying to live. I provided an altar-call in which five nonbelievers came forward from the crowd and gave their hearts to Jesus for the first time. I offered a rededication opportunity for backslidden Christians to recommit, and hundreds of hands were raised across the room. Finally, I invited the priest who joined me that day to stand up, ready to administer ashes to anybody who wished to receive them.

The university's Baptist campus minister was the first to get in line. When people saw her receive ashes on her forehead, hundreds of others lined up. I stood there in awe of God's handiwork as hundreds of Baptists lined up to wear ashes that day in union with the whole Church.

A stranger approached me afterward to introduce himself.

"Ian," he said, "I hope this doesn't sound strange to you, but I was forty minutes away from here when the Holy Spirit spoke to my spirit. He said, 'Drive to the chapel service today, I have somebody I want you to meet.' It was crystal clear in my heart. I had no idea what was taking place here today. I simply obeyed. Now I know—I was led here today to meet you. I'm a Catholic. I work for Bishop Gregory Aymond at the chancery in Austin, Texas. How would you like a job working at the chancery under Bishop Aymond and myself, as a campus minister giving talks to Texas A&M University and the University of Texas?"

I told him that I would be very interested, thanked him, and gave him my phone number.

Two days later, I met with Bishop Aymond face-to-face. He said, "Ian, within forty-eight hours word has already reached my ears, more than once, about the powerful move of the Holy Spirit that happened at your talk. The Holy Spirit sent a shockwave, and its ripple effects are out there. I would officially like to offer you a position. I'm also offering you housing—if you're willing to commute to and from your classes, you are invited to live at the parsonage in Austin with some of our seminarians."

And with that, I was back in a parsonage, with some particularly wonderful roommates, and back on the public speaking circuit.

Shortly following the move into my new residence, I was between classes when I ran into the wife of the Baptist leader who had previously given me some trouble.

"I'm so glad to have run into you today," she began. "I know about everything my husband said to you. I want you to know that, upon seeing the Lord work through you at that chapel service and watching five students come to Christ, I went home and had a word with him. When I told him what happened, he became truly sorry. He's going to make everything right."

And so he did. It was another beautiful instance of repentance when the man saw me in the school hallway and approached me, seeking to reconcile.

"Boy was I wrong," he began. "I looked at your thesis so far, too, and its scholarship is extraordinary. I've already cleared everything up with the theology faculty. Your paper is officially approved, and I'll be proud to see you walk in the 2005 commencement. Can you forgive me? I'm a sinner. And I can be an idiot sometimes," he said humbly.

"Me, too," I said. "You already had my forgiveness, sir, and thank you so much!" All I could think about in that moment were the words of Dr. Johnson: "Leave room for God's magnificent redemption. The worse it is, the better it is—look at the Cross."

After that landmark moment, yet another previously hostile administrator met with me. He said, "Your chapel talk brought me nothing short of a conversion experience. I honestly used to believe that Catholics weren't true Christians. Forgive me. I couldn't have been more mistaken. Catholics are true Christians, and for me, that realization is a *conversion*. I hate that we're losing you. I hope the Catholics appreciate what they're getting." Baptist hugs are something uniquely special in Christianity. Thankfully, converting to Catholicism from out of the Baptist tradition is a matter of addition, not subtraction. I brought the hugs with me.

Celebrating over steak with Dr. Johnson, and showering him with thanks for his mentorship and saving wisdom, I let out an exhale of tremendous relief from my soul. Between bites of perfectly red ribeyes, Dr. Johnson raised his glass and said, "I would like to propose a toast: to the faithfulness of God."

"Amen," I cheered.

He added, "Now don't let this new job at the chancery distract you from your homework. Your degree comes first. If I so much as *smell* a decline in the quality of your work, we'll have a chat," he said grinning ear-to-ear.

"Yes, sir!" I agreed. It was a grand celebration.

Dr. Johnson once said to us in class that life will have good times and bad—adding that the good times are *better*. I found his statement

of the obvious to be humorous and refreshing. He got me thinking about how life has both good times and bad. As the Bible says,
"Through many tribulations we must enter the kingdom of God"
(Acts 14:22). I really wish it didn't have to get so awful. But on this
side of Eden, suffering is the fertilizer of life. If you want a healthy,
fruit-bearing plant, then you have to cover it in a bunch of crap. As I
said earlier, we were all born into the miserable lie of playing God for
ourselves, and we continually need to have our own way of thinking
turned on its head. Our sufferings play an illuminating and redemptive role in this life-giving process.

Leaving the Baptist church brought on some intensive hardships
and persecution in my life. Yet I had also witnessed the healing power
of God at the same time. God led his people into the Promised Land
through both good and bad, and he set them apart "by trials, by signs,
by wonders, and by war, by a mighty hand and an outstretched arm,
and by great terrors" (Deut 4:34). And what was the reason for all of
this? "To you it was shown, that you might know that the LORD is
God; there is no other besides him" (Deut 4:35).

I had gone through some intense experiences, both good and bad.
In all these things, I came to know that the Lord is God, there is no
other. I had been ripped from my comfort zones, but I also had experienced how the Lord is a Great Physician. "For he wounds, but he
binds up; he smites, but his hands heal" (Job 5:18).

24

All Heaven Breaks Forth

The new ministry position at the Catholic Diocese of Austin was wonderful. Whenever I wasn't playing Sam Brunsvold at local universities, I helped the chancellor compile and edit a pastoral manual—a project that personally introduced me to all the vicars and their corresponding roles. Through this experience, I received a firsthand look at the inner workings of the Church—what a blessing for somebody in RCIA.

It was also great to be back in Austin, because I got to visit with my sister Sarah's family and Dr. Carver more frequently. The Catholic parsonage provided the perfect atmosphere for me to complete the remainder of my thesis. The university even scored me another talk in front of a thousand students, at its annual tent revival. The remaining time in the theology program became some of the happiest months of my life.

Nevertheless, there was one spiritual concern that still required God's healing grace before I could officially enter the Church at the 2004 Easter Vigil. Namely, I still couldn't bring myself to believe in the Communion of the Saints. That is, I couldn't ask for prayers from angels or saints in heaven. I had no theological issue with the practice. After all, I had no problem with asking for prayers from Christ's followers on *this* side of eternity. I simply couldn't bring myself to ask for prayer from someone on the *other* side.

I had been raised with an emotional allergy to the very idea of the intercession of the saints. Growing up, my dad taught me that asking the saints to pray for us was idolatry. By every possible means he instilled deep within my heart that *prayers to the dead are evil*. Years later the aversion to the practice still lingered.

God went to work on this issue with style.

Before landing the new job at the diocesan office, my savings had depleted rapidly. At one point, it was going to take a financial miracle for me to remain in school. My brother Sean came to my rescue. He prayed, "God, if you give me any surplus of money, it will all go straight to Ian." The day after he said this prayer, Sean received a check in surplus of a thousand dollars.

Libby called me up with the good news. She said, "We put together a care package that includes the money. You should ask your personal guardian angel to have this package hand-delivered to you, so that the enemy can't interfere. You've dealt with enough of his interference lately."

"Okay," I said, in a patronizing tone of voice that communicated evident disbelief.

"I'm serious, Ian. The Communion of Saints includes God's host. Saint Michael was God's instrument for defeating Satan and the other angels who rebelled. This is real. You already know that fallen angels are real. Why struggle with the notion of the angels who are on God's side? *You have a guardian angel*," she insisted, "ask for his help."

"I can't," I said.

"Why not?"

"I just can't. I've mentally filed it along with stuff that's *bad*," I explained.

She replied, "Then I'm lending you my angel. I've asked him to *hand-deliver* this money to you."

The next day, a man was wandering about outside the college residences. He looked lost. Then he walked up to me holding a box. "I don't suppose you're Ian Murphy?" he asked.

"That's me," I said.

"Here," he replied, handing me the package that Sean and Libby had overnighted.

After I signed for the delivery, he started walking away from me. "Wait!" I stopped him.

"Yes?" he said.

"Who told you who I was?" I questioned.

"Nobody," he said, beginning to look confused.

I asked him, "Then how did you know it was me?"

"I ... *I don't know*. Somehow, I knew. I looked at you, and I knew. Come to think of it, there are hundreds of people around here.

Wait a minute, I have no clue how this happened!" he exclaimed in bewilderment.

Confounded at the experience, I called Libby. "It was hand-delivered!"

"I know," she said.

"No, I mean miraculously, impossibly HAND-DELIVERED!" I yelled in amazement.

"I know," she repeated. "Welcome to a larger world. Now may I have my angel back, please?"

I thought to myself, "*You mean this is real?*"

Even with that, I couldn't bring myself to talk to anyone from *the other side.*

In another experience, while my life was still a living hell, I was deep in prayer when a human voice spoke to my spirit. It wasn't like the Holy Spirit. It was definitely good. It was a person, and the voice sounded clear as a bell in my heart.

"Ian, this is Teresa of Ávila," the voice said.

I wondered, "Am I going crazy right now?"

"No, you're not," she answered. "This experience is real. You have been under painful attack by the enemy. Deceived people have accused you falsely, and they doubt your testimony. I have been through this trial. I understand how it feels and what you are going through. Heaven is not blind to your suffering. I know that the spiritual attack is real, and I want you to be comforted in the knowledge that somebody knows and understands. You will doubt this experience, so I am providing you with a sign. So that you know it's really me talking to you right now, your birthday is my feast day."

With no internet access available, I frantically went hunting for a Catholic liturgical calendar. I was in the home of a Catholic friend when this happened, who had a liturgical calendar shoved atop a row of books in the house library.

As I flipped through the months leading up to October, I said to myself, "No ... it can't be. It just *can't be*! It's too unbelievable. I've seen some amazing things in my day, but not this. I live in the really real world, where dead Spanish women don't talk to you from beyond the grave. God, do you *enjoy* taking my skepticism and turning it on its head? Do you delight in taking my understanding of the universe and obliterating it?"

Clinging to the tip of the iceberg that I could see, my flesh hoped to be wrong—while my spirit hoped to be amazed. When at last I flipped the calendar to the month of my birth, I was amazed to find that, sure enough, my birthday, October 15, is the feast day of Saint Teresa of Ávila. Stunned beyond belief, my knees buckled and I dropped to the floor. *"You mean this is real?"* I again thought to myself.

Even with that, I couldn't bring myself to talk to anyone from the other side—not even a Hail Mary, as beloved as the Blessed Mother already was to me.

Libby talked to her angel, and that was evidently real. Then a Doctor of the Church from the Church Triumphant had communicated with me, with an accompanying sign. But I still couldn't be the one to contact them.

I reflected, "Of all the issues which a convert could get hung up on, I struggle with *this?* No issues with Mary or the Eucharist. But *prayer requests* have me befuddled—that should be the easy one! I won't ask somebody from the Church Triumphant to pray for me. But I can ask my friends to pray for me, no problem there. I prayed 'go away in the name of Jesus' directly to a demon, and I saw how very real that was. So I'll apparently address a *demon*, but I can't bring myself to address one of *God's angels?* That's irrational. Why am I like this? I don't know."

A friend from campus ministry days was a particular help to me regarding this issue. He reminded me of what Sam had taught us, that faith is never something we just *know about*—it's something we live.

I was now face-to-face with the domain of my free will. What would it mean if I went through the motions of the Easter Vigil, while my heart remained unwilling to trust the Church's authoritative teaching? To my conscience, the lukewarm option was no longer available. Either I would freely choose to act with trust in Church teaching, or I would remain a Baptist. I could not in good conscience enter the Church for a show of intellectual assent, while freely choosing to live as though I was the authority. God indeed searches the deep places. As dramatic as my public journey had been at points across my life, the interior life is where the real drama of conversion takes place.

After intensive prayer, I realized that Saint Teresa's personal consolation had not only comforted me, but also given me sufficient resolve to make a willful commitment and enter the Church in good conscience. I told the Lord that I would indeed trust his authority and engage the Communion of the Saints for myself, and I asked that he would provide the occasion.

The 2004 Easter Vigil was unforgettable. People reported that I was glowing as I stood there with my sponsor's hand firmly on my shoulder and made my commitment public. To receive the Eucharist in all of its fullness was the greatest miracle yet. I didn't know how hungry I was until I partook. No visible lights appeared, no audible bells chimed. Again, the interior life is where the real drama happens. I was now a member of the household of Saint Enda, and I could sense the love, relief, and celebration of countless multitudes watching. I finally understood what Uncle Tim was talking about. I now stood in union with an army of the holy and heroic as a heavenly powerhouse of grace flooded my soul. How had I ever gotten along without it? All hell breaking loose around you is nothing compared to all heaven breaking forth within you. I was *home*.

Catholic infancy was for me an experience of wide-eyed wonder at the world around me. As I mentioned earlier, believing in sacraments is an entire worldview. I now saw the household from the inside, with the stained glass windows illuminated. I experienced how divine grace builds up human nature. I saw how greater invisible realities were truly made present throughout God's visible creation. I saw God's royal ferocity sculpted into the face of the lion, his infinite mystery in the haunting depths of the oceans, and ten sermons in an oak tree. I was adventuring now in that invisible place where beatitude, integrity, and solidity of virtuous character is what matters—infinitely more than any visible recognition ever could. I had accessed the greater unseen reality, the rest of the iceberg, where we live trusting God rather than by what we can currently see. I was on the adventure of the interior life, where one's personal relationship with God deepens in untold ways, bearing visible fruit that brings glory to his name. In all things, I beheld God's handiwork with a new sense of awe and worship, and I wondered where I was to go next for the perpetuation of this newfound growth.

Back during my struggle with the Communion of the Saints, I had prayed for the Lord to provide an occasion for me to reach out in trust and fully tap into the whole community of God. Their love was already felt, and I had already deferred to the authority of the Church on the matter. But I hadn't yet opened myself completely to their help. Not long after the Vigil, God arranged the occasion.

With schoolwork going well and graduation secure, life eventually brought me to a crossroad. The question of where God would next lead me soon took center stage. My position at the chancery was a temporary contract. In addition, I had no living arrangements or work lined up after May 2005. Dr. Carver wanted me back at the institute, but he was still not in a financial position to provide salaries to his faculty. Bishop Aymond wanted me to become a priest, but I liked girls too much. It was Dr. Johnson's conviction that I should pursue a Ph.D. in theology, but I couldn't afford it. My own personal discernment aligned with Dr. Johnson's suggestion that I advance to the Ph.D. level—but only a full scholarship could open that avenue.

The only university I knew of which offered a full scholarship for Ph.D. candidates in theology was Duquesne, where Sam Brunsvold had been enrolled. I applied even though Duquesne's application made clear that, unfortunately, they could only award three such scholarships each year.

Sitting outside the parsonage in my prayer chair one night, I looked heavenward at the starry sky. "Okay, Lord, it's time," I prayed. "I'm already persuaded in my rational mind to trust your authority, over and above my own understanding. But even the demons *believe*—and *tremble*. Intellectual assent by itself merely renders me all the more accountable for how I actually live. As Sam said, in the end love is something that you *do*. It is time for me to embrace more deeply what is mine by grace as a Catholic. I put my trust in you in this present moment, and in the authority that you left on the earth for me as a gift."

Then I took a deep breath, and continued praying, "Sam Brunsvold, I believe that you are a saint among the great cloud of witnesses who surround me now and cheer me on to finish the race strong. *I miss you*. When you were stolen from me, I didn't stop needing you. I need you now. I ask that you pray for me. Pray to our Lord Jesus that, if it's God's will, Duquesne University will grant me one of their three full scholarships so that I can enroll in the doctorate program for the 2005–2006 school year. *Phew*—there, I did it. Amen."

Dr. Johnson had written one of my recommendation letters, and he was anxious to confirm that they had received it. This precious man had overnighted his letter, insured it, and certified it. At Dr. Johnson's request, I called the Theology Department at Duquesne to find out if they had received his letter. The chairman of the department at the time was Dr. (and Fr.) Michael Slusser. He was at his desk when I called, and he answered his phone.

"Hello?" he said.

I replied, "Hello, is this Father Slusser?"

"It is. With whom am I speaking?"

"This is Ian Murphy."

"Oh Ian, I'm so glad you called me. I received every piece of your application minus your cover letter. That's all we need. I want to set an accurate expectation for you so that you can plan accordingly. While your application glows in the dark, so do numerous others. I'm confident you should have no worries about getting accepted into the program. However, as for the three assistantships, there is no telling who will be selected.

"We have a record number of applications for the 2005–2006 school year for the Ph.D. program. They are some of the best we've ever received—we are humbled by this honor. Applications for the scholarship include a couple distinguished alumni from our Master of Arts program, a man who left medical school for theology, and a guy who received his M.A. degree with honors from Yale University. You're in the running. However, the competition is fierce. Everyone so far is deserving. Not being selected for the scholarship is a real possibility, and I am informing everybody accordingly."

I tried to mask my disappointment and responded, "I am only loved by your candor. Thank you for setting an accurate expectation; I wouldn't have it any other way." That much was the truth.

"Thank *you*, Ian," he said. "Before we hang up, I would like to ask: How did you hear about our program?"

I answered, "I was friends with an alumnus of yours."

"Who?" he questioned.

"His name was Sam Brunsvold. He was—"

"*You knew Sam?*"

"Yes," I said, "I attended his Friday-night group during my time at CMU. He was my mentor and a good friend. He had named me his intern, shortly before he was murdered."

"Ian," said Father Slusser, "I want you to mention this fact in your cover letter, okay? To have Sam's legacy back in our program would mean the world to the faculty here. I want the committee to know, because your personal connection to Sam is a blessing to this whole department!"

Then Father Slusser said something that sent chills up my spine. He addressed Sam directly, "Sam Brunsvold, if you're up there sending us good Ph.D. candidates, well, God bless you!"

Following two stretched weeks of waiting by the mailbox, a letter from Duquesne finally arrived. I had been accepted into the program, and I had been selected to receive one of their three full scholarships. "*This IS real!*" I shouted with delight. Dr. Johnson was my first stop. He leaped out of his chair cheering.

The help I received from Sam Brunsvold marks the moment that fully resolved my apprehensions about asking for prayer from saints and angels. Since then, I've solicited their prayers daily. Now it's getting me to shut up that's the problem. It wasn't so much that God was trying to teach me a lesson or pound the truth into my thick skull. Rather, God is a loving Father, and I had been missing out. He wanted his baby to experience all the love and support of his whole family.

I had previously looked with a disparaging eye at the Communion of the Saints, as though Protestant Christians had the 'pure Bible' while Catholics had the 'Bible *and friends*'. Then God led me to a profound truth: that his family is like an earthly family. It's not *detracted from* by the addition of another soul. It's *added to*, and one's heart gets bigger with more and more love upon the arrival of each new relationship. To sum up, God's final resolution to my struggle with engaging the Communion of the Saints came through Sam at roughly the one-year anniversary of my Catholic confirmation. This observation raises an interesting truth about entering the Church— it's not the end of the story. It's the beginning.

25

The Life of the Cross

As a friend once said to me, "The fullness is awesome." I couldn't have said it better. Life as a Catholic is the adventure of a lifetime. It has been characterized by wonder and awe, the transforming power of sacramental grace, ongoing conversion in the interior life, and the meaningfulness of human suffering. For me, Catholicism has meant joy not as an absence of sorrow, but as a presence amid sorrow—the Lord's presence. And it has meant peace not as an absence of turmoil, but as a presence amid turmoil. It has meant a Love that grieves with me when I grieve and laughs with me when I laugh.

Catholicism has meant a diminishing amount of panic over the *weeds* of this world. God is aware of the weeds, and that by itself is sufficient for me now because the Lord promised to deal with them. In the meantime, as the weeds grow side-by-side with the wheat for a short while longer, I don't have to worry about them. Instead, I turn inward to the figurative weeds and wheat that exist side-by-side within myself and allow the Lord to go to work on them.

In other words, Catholicism has meant looking away from the temporary power of the kingdom of this world and instead turning toward the reign of God advancing in human hearts—the human heart being the throne he's really after. It also means the freedom *of* authority. No longer lost in a labyrinth of doctrinal contradictions, I am free to grow in my friendship with Jesus.

Catholicism has also meant unprecedented challenge in the spiritual life—the healthiest sort of challenge. The Baptists I knew seemed to emphasize four deadly sins: drinking, smoking, swearing, and premarital sex. My busy schedule as a pastor didn't afford me any time to drink or date. I had already quit smoking by the delivering grace of God. I found that every single swear word has some safe equivalent, and I prefer my brother Jesse's approach of yelling "Burger King!" anyway. I felt the Baptist framework had rendered me a pretty holy guy. Then Catholicism showed me otherwise.

The Church speaks of seven deadly sins, including gluttony, sloth, and greed—commissions *and* omissions. And with pride on the list, I was in trouble. According to Catholicism, sin is not merely a *breaking of rules*. Rather, sin means a *fractured relationship* with God and man, and any failure to love is sin. It isn't merely a *rule* that is broken with sin. It is a *heart* that is broken—ultimately, the heart of God.

The saints have taught me that when one becomes dreadfully overwhelmed, one can simply reflect upon and accept the love of God that is always bigger than the sin. As a Catholic, I have become aware to an ever-increasing degree of my *radical dependency* upon the divine mercy of God, and that it is always available.

Life is hard, and each day indeed has enough trouble of its own, as Jesus put it. But at least once per week I get to *check out* of this world in order to participate in the activity of heaven! At each Mass, I come into momentary participation with the Son's faithfulness and love, ever-present to the Father, and praise him in the Spirit along with the people and the angels who are united around the world and beyond.

I now have the help of the sacraments, each one conducting God's love and life into me in its own special way. Christ's yoke has indeed been easier than the burden of taking control into my own hands. The sovereign God humbled himself to yoke himself to *me*, so that we could be together. Yoked to the One who is sovereign above all others and loves me madly, I need not fear that any bully—human or spiritual—will ever have the upper hand.

I enjoyed the opportunity to visit Libby's mom shortly after the Easter Vigil when I entered the Church. The last time I had seen her, I had returned that glow-in-the-dark rosary she had given me and insulted her. Her response was simply to get me a new rosary and a confirmation candle, as well. The new rosary was made out of marble from the Connemara region of County Galway, Ireland. "You're ready, now," she said, reflecting the love of Christ himself.

My sister Sarah entered the Church next. Then my cousin Nicole became Catholic from out of atheism. Some years later, when I was visiting my brother Jesse, he told his Baptist wife that he was joining RCIA to enter the Church. It was the bravest thing I've ever seen.

My 2005 return to Pittsburgh, Pennsylvania, in order to start the program at Duquesne was a bittersweet move—bitter in the Texas goodbyes, but sweet in the reunion with Nate and other friends from CMU. I was also not too far from my dad, and I paid him a visit during my first year of doctoral coursework. Not surprisingly, he met me with an arsenal of anti-Catholic arguments. It seemed he had been rehearsing the presentation. He concluded his diatribe saying, "The Lord's Supper is purely representational."

"Dad?"

"Yes," he answered.

"Remember that day inside the urban-ministry van," I asked, "when you officially asked Jesus to come into your heart and thereby confirmed your faith in Christ at the age of adult consent?"

"I can name the date," he said proudly.

I asked, "Was Jesus present in that?"

"Of course he was," Dad said.

"Just as a representation, right? He wasn't literally *there*," I responded.

Dad affirmed emphatically, "No—he was literally there."

"When you married Mom, was Jesus there?"

"Of course!"

"Just representationally, right? He wasn't literally there," I suggested.

Dad insisted, "That's wrong. He was literally present with us."

"Could you see him?"

"No, but he was there. The Lord was really present! Ian, what are these Catholics teaching you?" said Dad with concern. "I raised you better than this."

I asked, "Wherever two or more are gathered, the Lord is truly present in the midst of them—was God's presence at your wedding like that?"

"No, it was special," Dad explained. "Marriage is a special event, and a unique reflection of being joined to Jesus in the future, at the Wedding Feast of the Lamb in heaven. Ian, you know this."

"So you're claiming that Jesus was truly present at your marriage, but not in the same way that he had made himself present to the congregation at last week's regular church service—his presence at the wedding was special and unique. Is that right?" I asked.

Dad replied, "I'm not just claiming it, I am insisting on it. That is the truth!"

I asked next, "Was Christ really present at your baptism?"

"Yes!" Dad said, seeming increasingly irritated by the exchange.

"But private prayer merely represents a conversation with God," I proposed. "When a person is alone praying and confessing sins to God, two or more people are *not* gathered, so private prayer must therefore only *represent* a dialogue with God."

"Absolutely not," responded my father. "Prayer *is* an actual conversation, with God actually on the other side of the conversation. He listens, he speaks, and he forgives."

I said, "But in private prayer, two or more people aren't gathered."

"The Bible affirms the indwelling Spirit of God. It also affirms that God is present where two or more are gathered. He can be present in special, unique ways in each context. He's God! We don't have to understand exactly how his presence among us happens. We trust the Lord as our best friend," he explained.

I then asked, "Was Christ truly there at your baptism in exactly the same way as he was back when you first gave him your heart?"

"No, baptism was special and unique," Dad proclaimed, "like my marriage. Ian, you cannot limit the ways in which God Almighty chooses to make himself present to his people."

"Exactly. In fact, you just affirmed the Real Presence of Christ at your confirmation, at your baptism, at your marriage, and in confession. It would seem that you have no problem with the Real Presence of Christ in any of the sacraments—*except* the Eucharist. When it comes to the Lord's Supper, you suddenly insist that it's *purely representational*. Why is that one so hard? You yourself insist that one cannot limit the ways in which the Almighty can make himself truly present to his people."

"Ahhh, I walked right into your trap," said Dad, shaking his head. "How did I *not* see that one coming?"

I said, "Dad, I'm a real Christian. I am not lost, and the Church is not *Babylon's Whore*. Can you at least consider the possibility that, in the fulfillment of Passover, God's Christ instituted yet another miraculous avenue of his presence? When God entered the world, the dirty world didn't taint God. In the dramatic reversal of the Incarnation, the clean thing rendered the dirty thing to be clean again. As

Athanasius said, 'Flesh did not diminish the glory of the Word; far be the thought. On the contrary, it was glorified by Him.'

"Can you let go the misplaced sense of trust in your own way of thinking that characterizes pride, and *allow flesh and blood to make you clean*? It was indeed an offense to the people of Jesus' day. But can *you* allow the reversal? Can you consider that God has yet again made himself truly available to whoever wants him, in a unique and special way—one which we can't fully understand?"

"I hear you now. You have given me *much* to think about," he said.

Not long thereafter, my dad had a heart attack. He died—but was revived in the ambulance.

I visited him again the following Thanksgiving. It was an indescribable blessing. While the turkey was cooking, we sat together at his kitchen table over cups of coffee.

I looked up at him, amazed to see him alive. "Dad?"

"Yes?" he answered.

"What happens when you die?" I asked.

My father leaned back, and he sat there for a while. He lifted his mug and took another sip of coffee. Then he put his mug back down on the table. Eventually, he spoke. "Are you sure you want to hear this?" he questioned.

I asserted, "Yes, I do."

He began, "After the EMTs pronounced me dead, I was still completely aware of myself."

"You were at the edge of this life?" I asked.

"No," he responded, "I wasn't *close to* the edge—I had crossed *over* it. I crossed over to the other side. What happened to me ... it wasn't what I was taught as a Protestant. I didn't see the face of my Lord. Rather, I went to a place of *reckoning*. It wasn't a painful place. I was totally self-aware, and the stage was set for me to reflect about my past. It was as though I was seated at a table on a dark stage, for me to put my life out on the table and be cleansed. There was no physical pain. There was a longing, though—for physicality, and for the company of my loved ones.

"Before long, I was given an offer. I could stay there and continue reflecting, where there would be no physical pain, but the spiritual longing would persist. Or, I could return. I would be in pain, but

I would feel the love and company of my family directly. When I chose to come back, I heard the techs say, 'We got him back! Oh my God, we got him back.' It's interesting that I have no conscious memory of my time in the ICU. But I remember everything from during the short time I was dead. I wish I could report to you that I saw the face of my Lord right away, as I had always thought would happen. But that's not how it went down."

When I told Uncle Tim everything Dad had described to me, my uncle's response was priceless. Tim said, "All I know is, I want to get holy *fast*. I don't care if purgatory isn't physically painful. I don't want to sit alone in the dark and put my memories out on the table for reflection and cleansing. I prefer to go straight home; thank you very much, Mike."

My dad's description matched in detail a description of purgatory I had read from one of the saints. Of all the other people whom God could have blessed with eyewitness evidence of purgatory, he picked my father. Somehow, that's perfect. I love the way God works. My dad proceeded to spend his borrowed time doing his reckoning on the earth. He went around making amends and asking forgiveness from people he had wronged across his life. He quit smoking, and he devoured spiritual books in his free time.

Two months later, Dad visited me in Pittsburgh.

He said, "Ian, I've been reading the Catholic books by Mike Aquilina that you gave to me, and that man is on fire with the Holy Spirit. I also started watching reruns of Bishop Fulton Sheen on cable, and so is he. All five of my children entered the Church, and I didn't raise any stupid kids. I cannot believe these words are coming out of my mouth, but I would like to set an appointment with you soon—to talk about becoming Catholic."

It was the last time that I would see my father alive. He had another heart attack only a few days later and finally went home. I consider him the tenth convert to Catholicism in my family.

Flashing forward, I would like my readers to know that God indeed had plans to purify my dating habits. Specifically, he would one day lead me to a dry spell devoid of all romantic experiences and even interests. During a period of celibacy that would last for six painful and confusing years, God would prepare me for my wife. During that barren time, the Lord would connect me more deeply to Saint Augustine, whose own record of disastrous relationships was indeed worse than my own. If God could make that guy a saint, there was hope for me. Yes, God was going to prepare me for the sheer beauty of self-donation that characterizes true love. He was going to prepare me for my remnant of Eden, Rachel, who would become his priceless gift to me in the sacrament of marriage. Rachel and I were married on November 28, 2014. Rachel is God's love language to me—his greatest "I love you, Ian," aside from Christ himself.

Again, becoming Catholic is the start of the story, not the finish. I would one day come to host three seasons of my own radio show, give a lecture at a national Catholic conference, and enjoy a couple cable-TV appearances. I would also come to teach an honors course filled with non-Christians and backslidden Christians in which every student experienced some conversion-level encounter with Jesus Christ before the end of the semester. But those are all stories for another time.

If you are a Catholic Christian reading this now, I thank you for sharing my life with me. I could never adequately express my appreciation for all you have given me. I remain hungry for what cradle Catholics in particular give to me. There is something instilled in a person who grows up saturated by graces that had been missing from my own life for too long.

I'm reminded of my Grampa, who was a lifelong faithful Catholic. He said to me after my conversion, "Ian, I have buried two wives and two sons, and it is truly well with my soul. How? Because I take a humble posture toward God. My trust in the Almighty is total." I saw that same solidity of character in my GingGing and in my two Catholic high-school teachers—the ones who first turned my eyes toward Rome. Cradle Catholics: I need what you give me. I need that quiet strength, and I thank you for showing it to me.

I say humbly that converts have something you need, as well; we are different organs in the same body. Of course we are all converts. But converts into the Church—specifically ones out of agnosticism or atheism—offer something unique. In a sense, they grow *forward* in the faith. Often such converts meet *people*, before they meet paintings or statues. Like the disciples themselves, they first get to know the Lord in his humanity. They walk with the human Jesus initially; then the more they see, the more they wonder who he is.

In contrast, cradle Catholics are often introduced to the ancient and early Church Fathers, and the original eyewitnesses, through the imagery of iconography. People who grow up in the Church initially meet saints who wear colorful robes and halos, as depicted in so many beautiful works of art. These inspired artistic images are indeed beautiful, and they communicate life-saving realities. But sometimes, when Christians first meet these people through depictions of honor and grandeur, it can unfortunately generate a dangerous sense of *distance*. Such images can feel far away from one's own experience to the point of seeming unrelatable. This impression may even work to etherealize the faith in such a manner that one's heart becomes disconnected from the raw reality of it all. There's a resulting struggle to make it concrete.

In other words, some who grow up in the Church may feel like they grow *backward* in the faith. They initially encounter some untouchable image of glowing holiness, and then they slowly begin rewinding the clock back to learn about a human being who wrestled with God—just as they do.

As a convert out of agnosticism, I grew *forward* in the faith. I originally met those exceptional people who knew the original friends of Jesus long before I learned that they were Fathers of the Church. I met a man who doubted Christ and persecuted his followers until he was knocked down and blinded before I heard him called Saint Paul. In the *Confessions*, I met a proud and pleasure-loving young man who turned to God for mercy and then later found out that he became a bishop and a saint of the Catholic Church.

I believe that my perspective and that of other converts can rekindle or awaken the faith for Christians who feel distanced from the gospel. I invite you to get to know the saints again for the first time—and discover how *not alone* you really are. I invite you to realize the power invoked at the Mass, and know that the Holy Spirit is as active in the world today as he ever was. I encourage you not to feel panicked by the weeds in this world. God has allowed them to grow for a short while longer, side-by-side with the crops. He is aware of it, and has everything covered. In the meantime, you get to keep growing in Christ. Know the transforming power of sacramental grace, and realize what you have—and how *loved* you are by our Lord.

If you are a Protestant Christian reading this now, I cannot thank you enough. You are my brothers and sisters in Christ, and there is only gratitude. It can be difficult to hear one's own foundations challenged, and it takes great courage to expose yourself to that. I admire you, and continue to need so much *from* you. Thank you for listening to how God led my life. Stay close to Jesus. He does not disappoint.

If you are a nonbeliever reading this right now, my heart goes out to you most of all—as my burden has always been for other doubting Thomases like myself. I have come to believe with all of my heart that you have a Creator who loves you, more than you could ever know, that your soul was paid for by the blood of the Lamb, and that God is *pursuing* you for a personal friendship. Keep asking the questions. Keep seeking. Keep digging. Try prayer, even if it sounds like mine once did: "God, if you even exist at all, I could use some help right now." He'll hear that.

As you know, the world we share has gotten smaller. We live in a world of *pluralism*, with numerous ideologies, life-philosophies, religions, and worldviews out there all claiming to be correct. As soon as you take a stand, somebody is there to critique it. In such a quagmire, it can become an attractive offer to adopt a hands-off approach to the whole matter altogether and take no stance—make no commitment, adopt no opinion. The problem is, that position is already a stance, already a commitment, and already an opinion. Please don't give into this deceptively attractive offer. It's just sloth masquerading as light. There *are* things we can know about the mystery. There have been things revealed from beyond.

Think about it: what would be the *best* way for us to find out about the great mystery—the mystery of what we're doing here on planet earth, with this self-aware existence and the capacity to love, surrounded by marvels such as beauty, honor, and wonder that indicate there is indeed something *more*? Would the best way be for people to try to figure it out? Or would the best way be for that mystery to come here and show itself to us? If that mystery truly showed up and revealed itself to us, would it look like we expect? Or would it surpass all of our limited expectations, flip our shortsighted understanding upside-down, and blow our minds, as Jesus does?

Please, keep searching. Envision yourself as that baby in utero, looking for God in the womb. Consider that, while God made himself available to be found in our world, he is not confined within it—he transcends it, surrounds it, and surrounds you, with more planned for you than you could possibly imagine. And whenever you stretch out your own curious little feet against the farthest reaches of human imagination, take a quiet moment. Really listen, *hear*, and sense if *Someone* is pushing back. Imagine Jesus approaching you alone and asking you his question personally, "Who do *you* say that I am?" Imagine him addressing this invitation to you: "Come to me, all who labor and are heavy laden, and I will give you rest. Take my yoke upon you, and learn from me; for I am gentle and lowly in heart, and you will find rest for your souls. For my yoke is easy, and my burden is light" (Mt 11:28–30).

ACKNOWLEDGMENTS

Many people have played a vital role in my story. To protect some of their identities I have changed some of the names in this book.

I firmly believe that God's favorite means of communicating with me is through other people—so I *thank you*, Sam, Grant, Tony, and Scott.

Thank you to my whole family, and special thanks to Uncle Tim for being the best godfather ever, and to Mom for instilling in me the truth that Jesus Christ is the beginning and the end of all things—and ought to be everything in the middle, too.

Thank you, Gregory, for being my godson; and thank you Serena, for being my goddaughter. This testimonial is the most important gift I could ever give to you.

Thank you, Margie. Your email asking me about faith got me to write this book. The entire book could have opened with *Dear Margie*, and closed with *Love, Ian.*

Thank you to the Catholics who supported me before I entered the Church: especially Libby, Peg, Adam, Nate, Maggie, and two teachers from Mount Pleasant Area Junior and Senior High School.

Thank you, Rachel. And thank you, Jesus.

SOURCES

Augustine, *Confessions*. Translated by F. J. Sheed. Edited by Michael P. Foley. Indianapolis: Hackett Publishing Company, 2006.

Hahn, Scott. *Reasons to Believe: How to Understand, Explain, and Defend the Catholic Faith*. New York: Image, 2007.

Hahn, Scott and Kimberly. *Rome Sweet Home: Our Journey to Catholicism*. San Francisco: Ignatius Press, 1993.

Jacks, Bob and Betty, and Ron Wormser, Sr. *Your Home A Lighthouse: Hosting an Evangelistic Bible Study*. Colorado Springs: NavPress, 1987.

Maxwell, Arthur. *The Bible Story*. Hagerstown: Review and Herald Publishing Association, 1953.

McDowell, Josh, Sean McDowell PhD, et al. *Evidence That Demands a Verdict: Life-Changing Truth for a Skeptical World*. Nashville: Thomas Nelson, 2017.